A
COLORADO
READER

Edited by Carl Ubbelohde

Revised Edition

PRUETT PUBLISHING COMPANY • BOULDER, COLORADO 80302

ISBN: 0-87108-028-1

Revised Edition, 1964

Sixth Printing, 1978

Pruett Publishing Company
3235 Prairie Avenue
Boulder, Colorado 80301

Printed in the United States of America

PREFACE

This collection of essays was completed only with the generous and friendly help of many people, and it is a pleasant task to publicly acknowledge my indebtedness to them. Mr. Don Watson, Professor George P. Hammond, Mrs. Rufus Rockwell Wilson, Mr. Robert L. Perkin, Mr. Jack Foster, Professor Robert G. Dunbar, Mr. Forbes Parkhill, the Denver Westerners, the Denver Post, and Mr. Robert West Howard have extended generous assistance. Professor Karl Hulley and Mrs. Agnes Wright Spring have been most helpful in clearing obstacles along the way. The librarians of the State Historical Society of Wisconsin and Norlin Library, University of Colorado, aided me in many ways. Miss Lucille Fry was especially helpful. My colleagues Robert G. Athearn and Lee Scamehorn provided gracious assistance. Peter Mitchell and Duane Smith aided in the labors in many ways. My wife, Mary, helped in all stages of preparing the collection. I am most grateful for the assistance of all these people.

TABLE OF CONTENTS

1. WHAT IS "THE WEST"? by Walter Prescott Webb . . . 9

2. CORONADO'S SEVEN CITIES by George P. Hammond . 20

3. JOURNEY THROUGH LOUISIANA by Zebulon Montgomery
   Pike 40

4. THE MOUNTAIN MEN by Rufus Rockwell Wilson . . . 59

5. THOMAS FITZPATRICK--INDIAN AGENT by LeRoy
   R. Hafen 74

6. THE GOLD RUSH by James F. Willard 84

7. LIFE IN THE GOLD TOWNS by Colin B. Goodykoontz . 100

8. LEGAL BEGINNINGS AND A MINERS' CODE by Thomas
   Maitland Marshall 112

9. A COUNCIL ON WAR AND PEACE 116

10. SAND CREEK by Robert L. Perkin 126

11. THE DENVER AND RIO GRANDE RAILROAD by Robert
    G. Athearn 143

12. UNION COLONY'S FIRST YEAR 158

13. LURING THE HEALTH-SEEKER by F.J.Bancroft. . . 167

14. THE FIRST FIGHT FOR STATEHOOD by Elmer Ellis . 174

15. ADDRESS TO THE PEOPLE OF COLORADO 182

16. JOHN W. ILIFF--CATTLEMAN by Agnes Wright
    Spring 194

17. THE SILVER MINES OF LEADVILLE by Stephen
F. Smart 208

18. WATER CONFLICTS AND CONTROLS by Robert G.
Dunbar 219

19. THE MEEKER MASSACRE by Forbes Parkhill . . . 231

20. THE UNCOMPAHGRE UTE "GOES WEST" by Walker
D. Wyman 248

21. TROUBLE IN CRIPPLE CREEK by Stewart H. Holbrook . 254

22. GOVERNOR WAITE AND HIS SILVER PANACEA
by Leon W. Fuller 266

23. HARD ROCK DRILLING CONTESTS IN COLORADO
by Victor I. Noxon and Forest Crossen 274

24. THE PROGRESSIVE PARTY IN 1914 280

25. THE TUNGSTEN BOOM by Percy Stanley Fritz . . . 292

26. THE DUST BOWL 302

27. THE AIR TRANSPORT INDUSTRY IN COLORADO
by Lee Scamehorn 308

28. CORRECTING NATURE'S ERROR by Oliver Knight . . 322

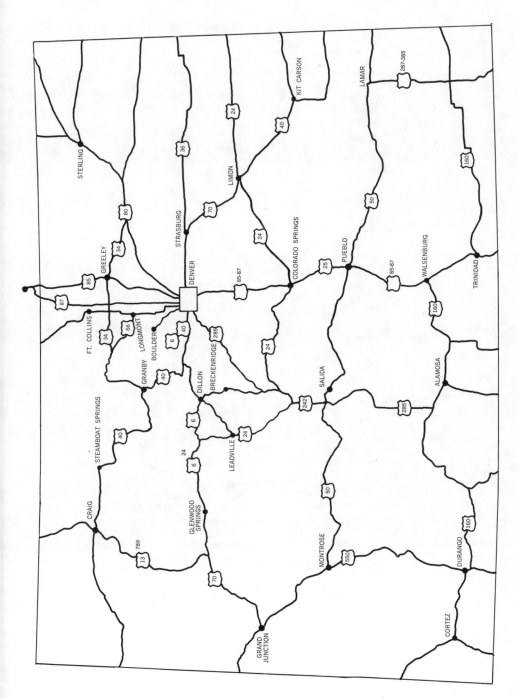

7

ONE: WHAT IS "THE WEST"?

by Walter Prescott Webb

The story of any state of the Union is only a chapter in the history of the region. Colorado's history, in many ways, is a miniature reflection of the history of the whole American West. To underscore this fact, the introductory essay presented here is a suggestive and helpful statement by the late Professor Walter Prescott Webb, a scholar who was wise in the history of the West and the ways of men. *

*   *   *

WHAT IS "THE WEST"?

What is the West?

Who but an editor would ask such a question? Who but a genius could answer it? Until the genius comes along, ordinary mortals will look at the West in uncomprehending awe and undertake to say what it is and what it means. Each sees something different and comes up with his own answer, but the answer never quite satisfies him for he can not put in prose or in poetry or on canvas what the West makes him <u>feel</u>. All the arts combined cannot convey the full feeling that the West engenders.

The most definite and understandable thing about the West is this: It is a territory that can be marked off on a map, traveled to, and seen. Everybody who knows anything knows when he gets there. This territory begins in the second tier of states west of the Big River.

------

*from Walter Prescott Webb, "What Is 'The West'?" in *This is The West*, edited by Robert West Howard, The New American Library, A Signet Book, copyright 1957 by The Westerners, Chicago Corral, pages 9 to 17. Used with the special permission of Mr. Robert West Howard.

A cord drawn from the southern tip of Texas to the fartherest boundary of central North Dakota marks its eastern limits. It stands
almost in the tropics, and extends almost to the northern limits of
the temperate zone. Its feet are warm, but its head is often cold.

From the eastern line the West extends to the Pacific Ocean,
hemmed in by Canada on the north and Mexico on the south. It com-
prises half the area of the United States, all or part of seventeen
states, and has a complete monopoly on the only boundary separating
this country from Mexico, the only neighbor with a different language,
tradition and civilization. Its length will approximate 1500 miles, its
width a thousand; an airline road around its border would be five
thousand miles in length, one-fifth the distance around the world.
This is the West, as distinguished from the other two regions, the
North and the South.

Like Caesar's Gaul, the West is divided into three parts, three
strips, laid one beside the other on a north-south axis: the Great
Plains on the east, the Rocky Mountain chains in the center, the Pacific
Slope on the west, three contrasting features encountered by any traveler moving by any route from east to west. Though these gigantic
natural features give variety and part of the character to the country,
combined they do not explain it. One can never understand the West —
all of it — in terms of the rolling plains, the craggy mountains, or
the slopes to the sea, for none of these is common to the entire region. They divide rather than bind the West to an inevitable destiny.

The overriding influence, the force that shapes more things in
the West than all else, is the Desert. That is its true unifying force.
It permeates the plains, climbs to all but the highest peaks of the
mountains, dwells continuously in the basins and valleys, and plunges
down the Pacific slopes to argue with the sea.

It is the guest that came to dinner, never to go away. It has
stripped the mountains of their verdure, making them rocky; it has
dried up the inland seas, leaving Death Valley completely dry and
Lake Bonneville a briny fragment magnified by the name of Great Salt
Lake. The Desert has been the great designer of the American West,
painting the landscape with gorgeous colors, chiseling the grotesque
mesas and pinnacles, building the plains with the stripped-off soil

10

laid down by perishing rivers. The Desert shortened the grass on its borders before destroying it in the interior. It never permitted trees on the plains it built, and where it found them it beat them down to sage and shrub, reducing the leaves to thorns and the sap to grease and oil. Those it could not destroy, it shriveled, and those it could not shrivel, it petrified.

The Desert designed the animals as it shaped the land and made a grotesque joke of vegetation. It compelled them to conform to its colors, put horns on toads, made snakes that travel sideways to keep from sinking in the sands, grasshoppers that fly five miles to find a sprig of grass. One thing it required of all: that they be parsimonious with water. The rabbits require little if any, the antelope do without for long periods, rodents and plants, like the Joshua tree, manufacture their own. The horned toad requires none and can live long without food. The little prairie dog is one of the Desert's jokes. He is a mis-named squirrel, because the Americans who named him could not believe that a squirrel would live in a dug-out. As for water, the prairie dog will not touch the stuff.

What is the West? asks the editor. It is many things, amazing, complicated and confusing. Suppose we ask instead: What is at the heart of the West? Where the center from which all other force and power radiate? The answer is simple if we will only see it. The heart of the West is a desert, unqualified, unaltered, absolute. Draw a line from the eastern boundary of the West to the Pacific, stand on its mid-point, and if you are not in the Desert you are near it, in a land with many of its characteristics.

One reason we do not understand the West is that we will not face a fact. We do not want the Desert to be there. We will not go to the heart of it to make a beginning, to get our vantage point. We prefer to loiter on its edges, approaching it from the outside rather than going to the inside, and planting our mental feet in the center where the power of it is to be found. Let us take our stand there, in the place of its greatest intensity, and measure its radius and its circumference and influence. There it lies around us, palpitating in the sun, its sands shimmering in the distance, its mirages playing tricks with our vision, its mountains etched against the sky, a crosscut saw with missing teeth; by night it is a deceitful benediction,

11

its breeze a sorceress, its heavens full of stars bigger than marbles or so small as to make the Milky Way an unbroken powdery scarf of gossamer light. By day it throbs and writhes in the sun — a live thing devoted to the destruction of all other life. By night it is a mystery.

> O wilderness of drifting sand, O lonely caravan!
> The desert heart is set apart, unknown to any man.

Its radius is variable, its circumference uncertain, for the Desert expands and contracts as its enemy, rain, retreats or advances in eternal conflict. Always at the margins there is dampness, at the borders moisture, at the limits wetness. But at the center there is little of these. When the Desert pokes a hot finger into the border regions, the people speak of drought; when it pulls the finger back, having touched rain, they like to think that their country is "getting more seasonable." At the heart of the Desert there is no drought, only an occasional mitigation of the dryness. Drought comes only where there is rain.

It is the Desert, the dry mantle spread over all but the margins of the American West, that contributes most to its unique character. It binds the plains, the mountains, and the slopes together, puts them in the same bed, under the same blanket.

The effect of the desert is expressed by the poet and song writer better than by the historian. Bob Nolan's song, "Cool Water" has caught the spirit of the thirst of the American West.

COOL WATER

All day I've faced a barren waste without the taste of water — cool
    water.
Old Dan and I with throats burnt dry and souls that cry for water —
    cool, clear water.
Keep a-movin', Dan, don't you listen to him, Dan,
He's a devil, not a man, and he spreads the burning sand with water.
Dan, can you see that big green tree where the water's running free,

And it's waiting there for me and you.
The shadows sway and seem to say, "Tonight we pray for water —
    cool water."
And 'way up there He'll hear our pray'r and show us where there's
    water — cool, clear water.
Keep a-movin', Dan, etc.

Dan and his rider suffered in the extreme what everyone in the West suffers in some degree, and all share with horse and man the longing "to rest where there's no quest for water."

Under its desert influence the West exhibits many strange things. It is a place where nature tried her hand at the unusual, at making a show place. It has a spectacular quality which lures thousands to it yearly. They go there to see things they cannot see elsewhere in the nation, or the world. It is the only part of the country where the rivers run into both seas, the Atlantic by way of the Mexican Gulf and the Pacific directly. It is the region of the greatest extremes. It has the highest altitude, 14,495 feet at Mt. McKinley, and the lowest, 280 feet below sea level in southern California. It has no navigable streams, and only three big river systems. Many of its rivers, Lost River in Idaho and the Humboldt in Nevada, have no mouths in the ordinary sense, but simply disappear in the earth. It has the only volcano; its one body of water worthy of being called a lake has no outlet; and is so salty that the human can not sink. There is nothing to compare with its Grand Canyon, Painted Desert, Petrified Forest, and Yellowstone geysers. Its forests, scattered among its mountain tops, furnish the largest and oldest living things on earth, the Sequoias, which were saplings two thousand years before Christ appeared on earth. In the West dwell four-fifths of the surviving American Indians, four-fifths of the American Japanese, and three-fifths of the Chinese. Along its southern border live practically all the American people who speak the Spanish language. It is in some respects the most American of the three regions; in other respects it is the most cosmopolitan, having the largest contingent of world civilizations as represented by the Indians, Japanese and Chinese.

It has registered the highest temperature in Arizona and the lowest in North Dakota, the highest annual rainfall in the Olympic

13

Mountains and the least at Phoenix, Arizona. To go West is indeed like going to the circus, where all the extraordinary things are on display. It is the highest, the lowest; the hottest, the coldest; the wettest, the driest.

Once we are willing to grant the Desert its sovereignty over the West, we are prepared to understand much of the life that goes on there, its history. A desert is a place acquisitive people put off taking until the last. To put it another way, the desert puts off the taker to the last, compelling him to occupy the more hospitable places first. The West remained a vacancy down to the time of the Civil War, and after. It was not left vacant because of its position, but because it hurled back the invaders. The Spaniards attacked it in the sixteenth century and were thrown back many times before they abandoned it in the eighteenth. One of their wisest officers, sent to inspect it, recommended that it be given back to nature and the Indians, who had it all along. The Americans began their attack early in the nineteenth century and recognized it for what it was and is. Lewis and Clark crossed it in 1803-06, Zebulon Pike penetrated it in 1807, and Stephen H. Long in 1819-20. They all described it as a desert, and Major Long made a map in which he laid down a white blotch and wrote in the middle of it in block letters THE GREAT AMERICAN DESERT. Jefferson Davis, when Secretary of War, was so convinced that the West was a desert that he imported two shiploads of camels to solve the transportation problem. Daniel Webster was so convinced that he refused to exclude slavery in the territories, saying that God and Nature had already decided that there could be no slavery in that arid land. "I would not," said he, "take pains uselessly to reaffirm an ordinance of nature, nor re-enact the will of God."

Behind the forerunners, the explorers and statesmen, came the land-hungry American pioneers. Their drive west was more like a response to instinct than to intelligence. They came with a great deal of pioneering experience but none with the sort of country they were approaching; they had never lived in a land without trees, where the spirit of the desert reigned.

They hit the first tier of the West, the plains, and were hurled back to re-form and try again. Then they did a remarkable thing, they jumped almost two thousand miles to Oregon, to California, and to Santa Fe. They beat out the three trails that had been marked by Lewis and Clark, Pike, and Long. The Oregon Trail led them to water and trees; the California Trail led them to gold; the Santa Fe Trail to the Spanish settlements in the upper Rio Grande Valley. They made history, but they did not take the West. It lay almost unscathed between them and their homeland, gorgeous, spectacular and formidable, and at its heart lay the Great American Desert, palpitating, expanding, contracting, at the whim of the seasons. Over the plains and through the mountains roamed the most nomadic and ferocious tribes of Indians known on the American continent. A concerted attack was now made on the heart of the West from its eastern and western borders, but for twenty years, 1850 to 1870, there was little progress.

By 1875 the army had rounded up the Indians, conquering them at last, but the pioneers had not occupied the land vacated. A few hunters roamed the plains to exterminate the buffalo herds; a few miners panned gold and dug silver in the mountains, but there were few permanent settlers. There had not yet appeared an American institution adequate for the job.

What is the West? To most people it is cattle on a thousand hills and bowlegged cowboys eating at chuck wagons, singing ballads, riding horses all day long, sleeping under the stars, and having a good time generally. But ranching is not an American institution; it did not come with the pioneers from the East. It came from the South, and with its coming the West was under attack from three directions. Ranching is a Spanish and Mexican institution, borrowed — horse, saddle, bit, spur and lariat — from Mexican neighbors who knew arid lands. The first longhorns were borrowed or stolen. The Americans in Texas learned the cowboy skills, and in Texas the cattle multiplied, but it was not until after the Civil War that they swarmed north, accompanied by cowboys and horses. By 1875 this Spanish institution of open range ranching had covered practically the entire West, covered it sparsely but with some success. Aside from the Mormons in Utah and a few other islands of settlement, the cattlemen were the first permanent occupants of the vacant spaces.

Their tenure was brief because the American pioneers — the

15

farmers — had learned something about living in the new country. They had invented a barbed wire with which to fence a treeless land, learned the principles of dry-farming which made agriculture less hazardous, and how to use the scanty waters for irrigation. Thus equipped, the farmers' invasion of the West was renewed and has continued to the present time. In reality, theirs has been a war on the Desert. They plow up the grass in the wet years but the desert winds race in and take the soil away in the dry ones. They fight for water everywhere, take it from the rivers until they are dry, from beneath the surface until there is no more, and when all sources fail, as they do, they invite the President to make a tour of inspection of the ruin and go on government relief. They have occupied the Desert but they have not conquered it.

What historically has the West been? It has been the greatest challenge offered to the European nations in their attempt to take the present territory of the United States. It defied the Spaniards for two centuries. It held the Americans off until they had taken all else, hurled them back time after time, and never admitted them until they had changed many institutions and practices. The West demanded a new set of institutions and a new mode of pioneering of a people who thought they knew all about it. The necessity for this change of institutions was recognized by the first American who understood the West. In 1878 Major John Wesley Powell wrote:

> The physical conditions which exist in that land,
> and which inexorably control the operations of men,
> are such that the industries of the West are neces-
> sarily unlike those of the East, and their institutions
> must be adapted to their industrial wants. It is thus
> that a new phase of Aryan civilization is being devel-
> oped in the western half of America.

The greatest social revolution that occurred in the history of American pioneering took place on the near edge of the West, and had to take place before the land could be occupied.

The West is one thing to the people who dwell there; it is another to people who live elsewhere. It thrills its occupants because it challenges them, makes them struggle and fight. People

16

respond to a challenge, they love a fight. Even though they come out of it scarred up, they remember it with pleasure. The fact that they met the challenge, and survived, makes them come out thinking well of themselves, ready for the next round. They love the memory of their ancestors who crossed the country or stopped in it. They make grim and sardonic jokes of their own hardships, remembered and experienced. In their adjustment they made so many changes in their ways that they sometimes seem strange and even bizarre to those who do not know their reasons. They are unconventional because they could not make conventions work, found success only by defying them. They altered everything, would try anything, and were satisfied with nothing. They puzzled their neighbors, one another, and themselves.

John J. Ingalls tried to tell what the West did to normal people. Though he was speaking of Kansas, what he said applied to more than Kansas.

> For a generation Kansas has been the testing-
> ground for every experiment in morals, politics, and
> social life. Nothing has been venerable or revered
> morely because it exists or has endured . . . every
> incoherent and fantastic dream of social improvement
> and reform, every economic delusion . . . every polit-
> ical fallacy nurtured by misfortune, poverty, and fail-
> ure, rejected elsewhere, has here found tolerance and
> advocacy . . . . There has been neither peace, tran-
> quillity, nor repose. The farmer can never foretell
> his harvest, nor the merchant his gains, nor the poli-
> tician his supremacy. Something startling has always
> happened, or has been constantly anticipated.

What is the West? There it is: the place where something startling has always happened. Where it is ever anticipated.

What is the West to the outsider, him who dwells beyond its greening borders? It is mainly an imagination. Its extremes and its wonders — grand as they are — never come quite up to what the outsider expected. Only the distances and the magnitude of the plains and the mountains exceed expectations. But he goes there in

17

vacation and drives from place to place in search of what he is looking for.

What he is looking for, aside from the natural wonders, he does
not find. Indians, for example, and horses, cows, and cowboys. He
sees mostly miniatures in show windows, buys them to send home to
prove that he has been in the West. These tourists are today one of
the best money crops, an indestructible annual resource.

But those who go are as nothing to those who remain away, and
visit the West vicariously. They people it with imagination. The cowboy is their darling, better dressed and more heroic than any cowboy
ever was. He rides ten thousand screens all over the world, albeit
more concerned with his heroines and villains than with his cattle. He
becomes a peace officer because everybody else is afraid to, and he
kills more villains than ever swung from ropes in the West or got off
the train at high noon. He has a few horse races with the Indians
where there might otherwise be awkward pauses, and he is almost
sure to pull the gambler off that old stagecoach, do a kindness to a
small boy, makes himself generally agreeable to all except evil men.
He saves more gold and girls than the U.S. Treasury and the Salvation Army combined. He has been known to fire thirty-seven shots
from one six-shooter without reloading. He does the most incredible
things, the same things over and over, and the world loves him.

He never existed. He is a myth. The West that he has created
never existed either. It is a myth too. But maybe the West created
him and the myth. There seems to be a kinship between the myth and
the mirage, something where there is nothing, one the product of the
human mind playing over the Desert, the other the product of human
vision trying to perceive what is on it, and both turning up with what
was never there.

People love myths and preserve them in their affection. But real
people — realists among people — do not love the Desert. They live
by it, around its borders, as close to its fire as they can, but they do
not face it. They look the other way, towards greener country or at
the high clouds, and let themselves think like small children that now
the Desert has gone away. And that too is myth, for the Desert
abides. It is the heart of the West. It makes it what is is, keeps it

from being what some would have it be.

Those who live in it or around its borders, as all Westerners do, should not avoid facing the Desert, whose near presence gives them their chief problems, makes them Westerners.

If those who live within its reach were a primitive people, they would probably seek out the strongest force in nature operating on them. If in doing this they discovered that the Desert was the supreme physical force, then as true nature worshippers they would devise rites and ceremonies designed to placate it, become supplicants. In such rituals, whatever the religion, the supplicant faces that which he implores. The Mohammedan faces Mecca five times a day in prayer; the Christian looks upward to heaven for his God; the primitive sun worshipper towards the burning orb in the sky. And so, if Western people who dwell around the margins of the Great American Desert were nature worshippers who had found the most powerful force affecting them, they would surely look inward, towards the Desert, forming a huge concentric circle around that barren waste which is the glowing heart of the American West.

Western people are not nature worshippers; they are not going to bow down even to such a powerful force. But in their attempt to deal with the problems it creates, they should not deny the Desert. They should face it more than they do. They should never forget that though it is neither god nor devil, it is their nearest and most dis-agreeable neighbor — more a devil than a man — and that it has no intention of going away.

TWO: CORONADO'S SEVEN CITIES

by George P. Hammond

The first penetration of white men into the American Southwest came from the south, particularly characterized by the ill-fated Coronado expedition of 1540-1542. Although no member of that expedition probably ever touched the soil of Colorado, the episode forms a major chapter in the history of the Spanish borderlands and, considering the riches of gold and silver safely hidden in the Colorado mountains, ends on an ironic, if not tragic note. *

* * *

CORONADO'S SEVEN CITIES

One day in the summer of 1536, more than four hundred years ago, four strange figures appeared in Mexico City. Three of the men were Spaniards, the fourth was a negro slave. Gaunt, bearded, barefooted, they looked like — and were — men from another world. As they made their way slowly through the heat-baked mud streets, passers-by stopped to stare at them, dogs barked at their heels, and street urchins hooted at them.

These four ragged men, dressed in skins and tattered strips of cloth, were Cabeza de Vaca and his three companions, Dorantes, Castillo Maldonado, and the negro Estevan . . . .

The wanderers made a strange sight in a city accustomed to strange sights — a city strange in itself. For this was the Mexico of early Spanish conquest, and it was less than a score of years since Hernando Cortés had sunk his fleet of eleven ships in the Gulf of Mexico and had entered the old Aztec city, capital of a large and

------

*from George P. Hammond, *Coronado's Seven Cities*, United States Coronado Exposition Commission, Albuquerque, 1940, pages 1 to 76 *passim*. Used with special permission of the author.

wealthy civilization. This city had been built in the very midst of a lake for defense against enemies. But Cortés and his men could not be stopped, and in less than two years they had defeated Montezuma, the Aztec king, and his people and set up a Spanish city on the exact spot of the old Aztec temple. Here the Spaniards planted the Christian cross and Spanish flag . . . .

In Europe at this time the Reformation was in full bloom; England's Henry VIII, embroiled in marital troubles and ecclesiastic politics, had lately beheaded his second wife, Anne Boleyn; Spain was beginning its third war with France's handsome Francis I. Sir Francis Drake, famed English explorer, was yet unborn, the piratical Hawkins a mere child, and nearly a hundred years were to pass before the English founded their first American colony on Virginia's muddy James river . . . . Spain was in undisputed possession of the New World.

But if the appearance of the four wayfarers who entered Mexico City that summer day was odd, their story was a hundred times more so. The people of Mexico were amazed as they listened to the leader, Castilian-born Cabeza de Vaca, relate as bizarre a tale as had ever been told.

The four, said he, had been members of an ill-starred Spanish expedition, under Panfilo de Narvaez, which had set out eight years before to explore Florida. Losing contact with their ships, the Spaniards were soon swallowed up in the everglades and harried by Indians. When starvation faced them, they ate their own horses. Reaching Florida's west coast at last, the desperate and famished soldiers determined an attempt at escape by sea . . . . The men felled trees for the purpose of making boat frames and covered these with hides of the devoured horses; they fashioned ropes from manes and tails. Then the Spaniards hoisted sails of shirts and hides and put to sea in their flimsy "horsehide" boats.

Disaster followed disaster, however, for storms came up and separated the tiny crafts. Some were wrecked, and the men drowned. Some of the boats were carried out to the open sea and never heard from again. Cabeza de Vaca and a small number of companions survived. They were washed ashore during a gale, landing on an island near the present site of Galveston, Texas.

. . . They would have died if friendly Indians had not found and taken care of them, building great fires to warm them until they reached the Indian villages.

When winter came, the troubles of the Spanish refugees multiplied. The diet of the Indians was so poor that both Indians and white men suffered and became ill. By spring about half the Indians of the village had died, and only fifteen of the Spaniards were left.

The Indians blamed the white men for their misfortune, and for a time threatened to kill them. Soon Cabeza de Vaca took his men to the seacoast, where they found strawberries and other things to eat. They became well and strong again, and the Indians were so impressed by this that they thought Cabeza de Vaca might cure them. As he wrote later, "they wished to make doctors of us, without examination or asking to see our diplomas."

Cabeza de Vaca had seen the Indian medicine men make mysterious signs over those suffering from illness, so he imitated them and became a medicine man also. He said prayers over the sick and made the sign of the cross, and the sick Indians got well; at least, they said so . . . .

From information gleaned from . . . natives, four of the survivors hit upon an idea to escape from this bestial existence, and struck out westward across the unknown country, hoping to reach Mexico . . . . A year later Spanish slave-hunters found the four, naked, haggard, and barely distinguishable from Indians, on the west coast of Mexico. Moving from one tribe to another, and enduring almost unbelievable hardships, the four had made their way across what are now Texas, New Mexico, and Arizona to become the first white men to cross the continent . . . .

Although the Spaniards of Mexico City were captivated by their countrymen's strange experiences, their ears were pricked, not by what the travelers had seen and endured, but by what they had heard. Some of the Indians they had met in their cross-continent trek . . . had told them of a land to the north abounding in gold and silver, with

22

great cities whose houses were many stories high, whose streets were lined with silversmiths' shops, and whose doors were inlaid with turquoise.

'Round and 'round Mexico City's shops, churches, and gaming halls the exciting tales of the fabulous land flew — and grew; and Mexico's eager populace immediately concluded that Cabeza de Vaca's stories proved the legend of old that somewhere in the West were seven golden cities, enormously wealthy, inhabited by an unknown race of people. Here, then, within reach, were riches beyond the wildest dreams of man.

To New Spain's competent, well-loved Spanish viceroy, Don Antonio de Mendoza, Cabeza de Vaca's stories were good news indeed. Both Mexico and Peru, it was true, had yielded great riches, but here was still another Mexico, or another Peru . . . .

And there was another consideration that weighed heavily on Viceroy Mendoza and the king. Spain had only recently become the champion of Catholicism in Europe. After the discovery of America she was determined to spread the Christian doctrine to all the heathen . . . . Here indeed was an opportunity which the diligent Mendoza could not pass up — not without being remiss in his duty to Mother Church and without being faithless to his king and master.

But the astute viceroy, before equipping a large-scale expedition to search for the Seven Cities, determined to send out a small exploring party to verify their existence, and looked around for a leader. The Spanish wanderers, satisfied with their pioneering hardships, declined the job, and Cabeza de Vaca hurried off to Spain to regale King Charles and his court with his experiences.

. . . finally Marcos de Niza, a Franciscan friar who had just come from Peru and Central America, both recently conquered, was picked to lead the exploring party. With the negro slave, Estevan, whom the viceroy had bought from a member of Cabeza de Vaca's party, and some Mexican Indians, he set off for the mysterious north country in the spring of 1539.

The search for the Seven Cities had begun.

23

* * *

Less than a year later Fray Marcos was back in Mexico City with reports that not only corroborated, but far outstripped in grandeur, those heard by Cabeza de Vaca. He had actually seen one of the Seven Cities.

"The city," wrote the friar, "is larger than the city of Mexico . . . . The doorways to the best houses have many decorations of turquoises, of which there is a great abundance . . . ." They told me that "Cibola is a big city in which there are many people, streets, and plazas, that in some sections of the city there are some very large houses ten stories high . . . . They say that the houses are of stone and lime . . . that the portals and fronts of the chief houses are of turquoise."

But what his excited listeners apparently failed to grasp — and likely cared little about — was the fact that although the friar had seen the town, he had not seen its riches. He had only heard about them from the Indians in the north.

Upon reaching the uninhabited lands on the journey northward, related Fray Marcos, he had sent Estevan ahead with a few Indians to scout the way and pacify the natives, because Estevan had a gift for dealing with strange Indians. They agreed that if the negro found signs of a rich country, he was to send back a messenger with a wooden cross the size of a man's hand; if the news was still more promising, he would send a cross twice that size; and if the country ahead was richer than Mexico, the cross was to be even larger.

Imagine Fray Marcos's amazement a few days later to receive a messenger bearing a cross as big as a man. As the friar followed the negro slowly through the mountainous valleys of northern Mexico and into the burning deserts of southwestern Arizona, his Indian guides making the way cheerful by playing flutes and beating drums, he received equally large crosses every few days, but saw nothing to justify them. From natives along the way he learned that to the north was a rich kingdom called Cibola, comprising seven cities, and he pressed on, certain that these were the ones which had been described by Cabeza de Vaca.

24

Meanwhile Estevan, accompanied by a small number of Mexican Indians as his personal bodyguard, had developed delusions of grandeur and was heading for trouble . . . . He strutted, issued orders, and behaved altogether in a manner distinctly distasteful to his native hosts, which reached a climax at Cibola. A faculty for attracting pretty Indian women didn't add to his popularity. Bedecking himself in bright robes, tufts of parrot plumage, and with bells and gaudy bracelets on his arms and legs, he became a sort of walking musical rainbow. With him the negro carried a "magic" gourd, filled with pebbles and decorated with a red feather and a white one, which he sent ahead to notify the villages of his coming.

The gourd and Estevan's general magnificence awed the natives and earned him courteous receptions and many gifts of skins, turquoise, and other presents from chiefs along the way, until he reached Hawikuh, a Zuñi pueblo in western New Mexico . . . .

Smarter than their southern brethren, the Zuñi Indians were neither impressed with Estevan's gaudy splendor nor awed by his gourd. "It was nonsense for him," reasoned the tribal wise man, "to say that the people in the land whence he came were white, when he was black, and that he had been sent by them." Estevan was promptly disposed of with a few well-placed arrows and his Indian companions sent scurrying southward to tell Fray Marcos of the disaster . . . .

Dismayed and alarmed by Estevan's death, Fray Marcos nevertheless pushed on till he neared Hawikuh. Fearing to approach the town because of the hostility of the natives, he obtained a bird's-eye view of it from a hill. Perhaps the sun shining on the houses made them glitter like gold and silver; perhaps the heat waves rising from the desert in a glorious mirage magnified the size of the town. At any rate, it is certain that the friar got an incredibly distorted impression of Hawikuh, an idea that was enhanced by the marvelous stories he had heard along the way . . . .

But his brief look was enough. Satisfied that this was one of the Seven Cities, Fray Marcos turned around and headed back for Mexico. . . .

Mexico City was electrified by Fray Marcos's news, and as the friar's accounts spread through the country the thrill of a combined

25

treasure-hunt and Christian crusade gripped the entire populace.
Around again the tales of the Seven Cities flew; and again they grew:
"The town that the friar had seen was bigger than two Sevilles . . . .
The house walls were of solid gold . . . . The women wore strings
of gold beads . . . ." All New Spain was set by the ears. Here was
another — a new — Mexico.

Viceroy Mendoza was convinced, and promptly launched preparations for a large military expedition to Cibola . . . .

Lured by riches and glory, men from all walks of life — soldiers of fortune, noblemen, settlers — flocked to join the venture.
Fired with the thought of new converts to the Faith, Mexico's churches
worked unceasingly to promote the expedition. Men sold their estates,
personal belongings, anything they could lay hands on — to get money
to go to Cibola . . . .

To head the expedition to Cibola, Viceroy Mendoza . . . chose
his young friend, 30-year-old Francisco Vazquez de Coronado, who
was given the title of captain-general. Born in Salamanca, Spain, of
prosperous, aristocratic parents . . . Francisco Vazquez had come
to the New World with Mendoza in 1535 to seek his fortune. There
the viceroy's friendship, a fortunate marriage, and his own capabil-
ities brought him into prominence . . . .

After serving the viceroy ably in several missions, Coronado
had been elected to Mexico City's town council . . . . And in 1538
. . . Mendoza had appointed Francisco Vazquez governor of New
Galicia, a wild, sparsely-settled frontier province on Mexico's west
coast . . . .

New Galicia, because of its location, was made the organizing
ground and starting point for the Cibola expedition. Tirelessly and
enthusiastically Coronado and his aides labored to whip the venture
into shape, and Viceroy Mendoza spared no expense to insure its
success. From Mexico City came quantities of supplies; from the
royal arsenal in Spain, galleons brought arms and ammunition; from
the viceroy's stock farms came prize horses. Money was advanced
to quiet insistent creditors of improvident soldiers, and provision
was made to support families of departing bread-winners. It was one

26

of the largest enterprises ever attempted by the Spaniards in the New World . . . .

By mid-February, 1540, the expedition was ready to start, and Viceroy Mendoza and many another Spanish notable arrived in Compostela, New Galicia's principal seat of government, to hold a grand review and inspection of the army.

*　*　*

It was on Saturday, February 21, that final preparations were being made for the official review. The little valley in which Compostela lay, surrounded by high and jagged mountains, was dotted that night with the campfires of the soldiers and their retainers . . . . Men everywhere were cleaning and shining their weapons and armor, crossbows, big muzzle-loading muskets, and little cannons. They knew that every man, every horse, and every bit of armor and baggage must pass the viceroy's inspection.

After a solemn high mass on Sunday, February 22 . . . the review and inspection of the expeditionary force began. The viceroy and his official party took their stand at a prominent place, and the army began to march past . . . . Well might Viceroy Mendoza have rejoiced at the pageant that passed before him that Sabbath day. This was no bouregois army of the masses, no melting pot of varying social strata, of mixed creeds and standards. Here was represented the flower of Spanish aristocracy. Almost without exception these cavaliers were gentlemen of high birth . . . proud, arrogant scions of Castile . . . . All told, there were approximately three hundred of them in the review; two hundred and thirty were mounted, each with a number of extra horses; the remaining sixty-two were formed into infantry companies . . . .

Pedro de Castañeda, member and chronicler of the expedition, termed this army of eager conquistadors "the most brilliant company ever assembled in the Indies to go in search of new lands." But while these cavaliers who were to set out for the Seven Cities ranked together on a high social plane, there the uniformity ended. In garb and weapons Coronado's force differed very greatly. Some of the soldiers wore coats of mail, a few had iron helmets and other odd

27

pieces of European armor, while others were garbed in a nondescript assortment of native American war-dress — helmets of buckskin, buckskin jackets, and other primitive protective apparel.

As befitted his rank, General Coronado wore magnificent gilded armor and a plumed helmet . . . .

An auxiliary force of more than eight hundred Mexican Indian allies, armed with anything they could manage, brought the total military strength of the expedition to well over 1,100 men, and in addition there were the menials — personal servants, negro bearers, lackeys, grooms, herders. Nearly six hundred saddle- and pack-horses, some mules, and thousands of cattle, sheep, and swine, transported on the hoof for food, comprised the army's live stock . . . .

The parade over, the army gathered to hear Viceroy Mendoza deliver what Castañeda described as "a very eloquent short speech." Earnestly the viceroy reminded the soldiers of the allegiance they owed their general; in glowing terms he pictured the benefits, spiritual as well as financial, that might result for all from the enterprise.

Now the muster roll. With characteristic Spanish passion for detail and in compliance with a royal decree, a complete record was made of every man, each piece of equipment, every horse . . . .

As a final rite the prospective conquistadores took an oath of allegiance to the crown . . . .

The formalities were over; the army was ready to march.

*   *   *

On the morning of February 23, 1540, amid the clank of armor, high-spirited shouts, and the bleats and squeals of herded stock, the long march to Cibola began, over the same road that Fray Marcos had traveled a year before . . . .

Slow and laborious was the army's progress. Straying cattle, heavily-laden pack animals, and the thousand-and-one other delays that beset a traveling army retarded the march and tried the patience of cavaliers anxious to reach the Promised Land . . . .

April first found the expedition in Culiacan, northernmost Spanish settlement, on the Culiacan river, thirty-odd miles from the coast. In more than a month the army had traveled the discouragingly short distance of 350 miles . . . .

By this time Francisco Vazquez had reached the conclusion that the army's progress was much too slow, and he decided to lead a faster-moving advance party ahead of the main caravan . . . .

* * *

After two weeks in Culiacan, on April 22, Coronado set out with about seventy-five horsemen, twenty-five foot soldiers, some Indian allies, and animals for food driven on the hoof. The main army . . . remained at Culiacan with orders to follow the general a fortnight later . . . .

Continuing on their way . . . Coronado's party paralleled generally the coast, though veering off farther inland from time to time. Innumerable rivers, some carrying large amounts of water in the rainy season, flowed from the mountain slopes into the Gulf of California, and the army must of necessity cross all of them on its way to the north. So, crossing from river valley to river valley, the expedition followed the old Indian trails . . . .

The route now led by way of Pericos, over rolling hills and sharp dales covered with a dense growth of the thick shrubs and trees that characterize the region. In the vicinity of Pericos, an ancient native settlement, the country opens out into broad flat plains, much of it extremely fertile and supporting a tremendous growth of native vegetation . . . .

For several hundred miles north of Pericos, the old trail to the north country varied but little, passing through Mocorito, Sinaloa, and Fuerte, all situated in rich valleys that have always supported a considerable population. North of Fuerte, the lay of the land changed, becoming more rolling and less densely covered with vegetation, but from the Mayo to the Yaqui rivers the route lay again through beautiful valleys, especially through that of the Rio de los Cedros, and then along the east bank of the Yaqui to Soyopa . . . .

Coronado's party, avoiding the difficult ridges behind Soyopa, struck more toward the northwest, along Rebeico canyon to the vicinity of Matape, and thence across to Ures in the Sonora valley . . . .

. . . the Spaniards passed through a settlement visited by Cabeza de Vaca and his companions four years earlier and which they had named Corazones, Hearts, because the inhabitants had given them hearts of animals and birds to eat.

The Indians in the country, remembering the peaceful and harmless Cabeza de Vaca, were friendly enough. But the land was anything but promising, although there were provisions here. The natives, clothed in deerskins, were Job-poor, and lived in humble huts framed with poles and covered with mats . . . .

Up the Sonora river struggled the expedition . . . and then, thirty miles south of the present Arizona state line, through a wide open pass to the northward-flowing San Pedro, and down this stream to a place called Chichilti-Calli, near the present Fort Grant, in southeastern Arizona . . . .

At Chichilti-Calli the weary and discouraged Spaniards halted for two days to rest themselves and their poorly fed and exhausted horses. It had been a trying journey from Culiacan, and the expedition now faced a serious food shortage . . . .

Alarmed by the shortage of supplies, the expedition struck into the Apache region of Arizona's White Mountains, an uninhabited 100-mile stretch. The journey grew more perilous and progress slower . . . .

The carefully conserved food supply finally gave out altogether. Horses and Indian bearers dropped by the wayside to gasp out dying breaths . . . . Over the Gila river and up through eastern Arizona toiled the exhausted and starving band. They now found fresh grass and many nut trees, which alleviated their hunger a little but did not provide substantial nourishment.

30

Two weeks after leaving Chichilti-Calli the army camped on the banks of a red, swiftly flowing stream which they appropriately named Colorado river (now Little Colorado). Eastward the famished pioneers pushed on and camped the next night in the Zuñi river valley, near the Arizona-New Mexico line. Several Zuñi Indians were seen that day, who, on sighting the Spaniards, scurried off to spread the alarm. That night some Indians approached . . . but the nocturnal visitors fled when the Spaniards girded for battle.

The next day, on July 7, 1540, the army reached its goal — Hawikuh, the first of that group of towns which Fray Marcos had seen from a distance and described so glowingly as Seven Golden cities. The Spaniards were both amazed and enraged to see no golden walls, no silversmith shops, no turquoise-studded doors. Instead, their startled eyes gazed on what Castañeda described as "a small, rocky pueblo, all crumpled up."

Poor Fray Marcos.

"The curses that some hurled at him," said Castañeda, "were such that God forbid they may befall him." . . . .

What the Zuñis thought of the Spaniards is mere conjecture. They had never seen white men, had never heard the sound of guns. Nor had they ever laid eyes on a horse . . . .

Whatever their thoughts, it was soon evident that the Hawikuh Indians had ideas of their own. Ten or twelve miles before reaching Cibola, a few of them came out to meet Coronado's advance party. They were well treated by the Spaniards, who desired to learn something about their country, especially where the rich cities were. Through an interpreter, Coronado informed the Indians of his desire to be friends with them, gave them presents, and urged them to accept peace, but they were terrified and soon rushed for their weapons . . . .

Angry Spaniards pleaded with Coronado to attack, but he, anxious for peace, hesitated. Desperately in need of food, however, and all peace efforts having failed, Coronado gave the signal to his men to attack after the friars had signified ecclesiastic approval.

31

The soldiers soon scattered the Indians, who fled to the strong walls of Cibola for protection . . . .

Though the Zuñis were awed and frightened by the horses and firearms, they waged a stubborn battle . . . .

. . . Outnumbered more than two to one and weakened by hunger and the long march, the Spaniards were hard pressed for a time, and the outcome of the battle doubtful.

Arrows and stones, however, were no match for guns and Spanish military tactics. The Zuñis abandoned the pueblo and took to their heels. Into the buildings poured the famished Spaniards to find plenty of maize, beans, fowl, and their first square meal in months — that which "we prized more than gold or silver," said one . . . .

*   *   *

Established at last in their new quarters in the famed Seven Cities, Coronado and his men settled down to eat, nurse their battle bruises, and ponder the uncertainties of life. They had reached the end of the rainbow and had found, instead of the expected pot of gold, bitter disappointment . . . .

*   *   *

Meanwhile . . . the main army, having left Culiacan with 600 pack animals, were plodding at snail's-pace through the plains and mountains of northern Mexico, over the trails Coronado's men had blazed. Carrying their heavy weapons, weary and footsore, the adventurers trudged alongside their provision-laden horses, day after day and week after week.

In the Sonora valley near modern Ures the army settled down to await orders from Coronado. There in the distant north the Spaniards built houses and established a town . . . .

*   *   *

Up in Cibola meanwhile things were happening. /Coronado/ . . .
set out to visit the other villages of the province, most of whose inhabitants had fled to Thunder Mountain fifteen miles away. Anxious to be
at peace with the Cibolans, Coronado, in a conference with the tribal
leaders, urged them to bring their people down to their homes in the
valley, but without avail.

The Cibola Indians, doubtless in the hopes of getting rid of their
unwelcome white visitors, told Coronado of the province to the northwest called Tusayan. And in mid-July Chief Ensign Don Pedro de Tovar,
with twenty soldiers . . . trekked across the deserts seventy-five miles
to explore the Hopi settlements of northeastern Arizona . . . .

From the Hopis, Tovar learned of a great river to the west, and
returned to Cibola with this news.

Late in August, Coronado dispatched the army master, Don
Garcia López de Cardenas, with twelve men to find the river . . . .
Up through Arizona's Painted Desert the explorers plodded and in
about three weeks they stood awe-stricken on the brink of the Grand
Canyon, at its eastern end, gazing down at the Colorado River far
below . . . .

A few days after the Cardenas party had started on their journey
into Arizona, Coronado had visitors — Indians from a pueblo to the
east called Cicuye, located near the present town of Pecos, thirty
miles southeast of Santa Fe . . . .

. . . The Indians brought presents of skins to Coronado, who
reciprocated with gifts of glassware, pearls, and jingle bells . . . .

The hides . . . puzzled the Spaniards not a little, and when an
Indian drew pictures on a skin of the animals from which the hides
had come, the white men were still more puzzled.

"They seemed to be cattle," said Castañeda, although "this
could not be determined from the skins, because the hair of the skins
was so woolly and tangled." What the visitors were trying to picture
was the American buffalo.

Captivated by the descriptions of these strange animals and eager to learn more of the country to the east, Coronado sent Captain Hernando de Alvarado and twenty men with the returning Cicuye natives to explore the region . . . .

Five days after leaving Hawikuh, Alvarado's party arrived at the great rock of Acoma — "so high," said a Spaniard, "that it would require a good musket to land a ball on the top." . . . .

From Acoma the Spaniards went northeast, crossed the Puerco river, and on September 7 reached the broad, fertile Rio Grande valley and the province of Tiguex, at the Albuquerque-Bernalillo area . . . .

So impressed was Captain Alvarado with the Rio Grande valley and its pueblos that he immediately dispatched messengers to Coronado and advised him to bring the army there for the winter.

Alvarado's party spent several days in the Tiguex province, reporting eighty pueblos in the valley, and then struck out northeast to Cicuye . . . .

At Cicuye the Spaniards met an Indian from the country to the east. This character was to influence greatly the fortunes of Coronado and his expedition. He was promptly dubbed "the Turk," because, said the Spaniards, "he looked like one" — a good enough reason.

Guided by the Turk, Alvarado and his men continued in an easterly direction, crossed the Sangre de Cristo mountains, and followed the Canadian river into the Texas Panhandle plains. There they got their first amazed glimpse of the buffalo . . . .

. . . As the Turk conducted his sight-seeing tour through the buffalo country, he entertained its members with fanciful tales of a land to the east called Quivira whose riches defied comparison, where gold and silver were as common as prairie dust.

Buffalo no longer held the interest of the Spaniards, and they started back immediately to tell Coronado the wonderful news. The chase for the phantom gold was about to begin again.

*   *   *

While Alvarado and his men were toiling over the buffalo plains, the main army under Don Tristan de Arellano had arrived at Cibola from Corazones, after a comparatively uneventful journey . . . . .

. . . At Cibola, where Francisco Vazquez had lodgings ready for them, the army was again reunited, except for those who were still out exploring.

As soon as Coronado received Alvarado's favorable report of the Rio Grande Valley, he at once sent Army Master Cardenas and a force to the province of Tiguex to prepare winter quarters for the army. Five days later Francisco Vazquez, having learned of still another province, called Tutahaco, himself was on his way eastward with about thirty men. A few days later he was reunited with Cardenas and Alvarado and their followers, and the Turk, at Alcanfor, in the Albuquerque-Bernalillo area. This pueblo became the army's headquarters for two years. Meantime the large force which had arrived at Cibola from Corazones was to proceed directly to Tiguex after resting for twenty days.

Cardenas had found the Tiguex Indians of Alcanfor and neighboring pueblos docile, and made it known to them that the army would need suitable quarters there. Reluctantly, it seems, the natives gave up their pueblo and moved in with friends and relatives in nearby villages . . . .

In this province of Tiguex, Coronado listened eagerly to the Turk's flights of fancy. Glibly and graphically the Indian described the wonders of the fabulous land to the east, a land called Quivira. There was a river there, he boasted, which was two leagues wide, in which there were fish as big as horses, and hundreds of large canoes with more than twenty rowers on a side. The canoes carried sails, and the chiefs lolled under awnings in the stern, and on the prows there were great golden eagles. The high lord of the land took his afternoon nap under a great tree on which hung little golden bells which lulled his eminence to sleep as they tinkled in the breeze. And the everyday dishes of even the poorest natives there were made of wrought plate, and the jugs and bowls were of gold.

Eureka! It was the Promised Land! . . . .

. . . when the ice moved out of the Rio Grande and the last
tardy patches of snow disappeared from the mesa, preparations for
the journey to that fabulous land were begun.

On April 23, 1541, the entire army evacuated Alcanfor and,
with the baggage, pack-animals, and with the Turk as guide, moved
slowly out of the valley northeast toward Quivira . . . . Leaving
Cicuye . . . the caravan trekked eastward and nine days later reached
the buffalo plains. There it encountered nomadic tribes of Querecho
Indians, who greeted the white men with characteristic native stolidity,
exhibiting no surprise whatever at what must have seemed at first a
fantastic optical illusion . . . .

From the Querechos the Spaniards obtained information — all
vague — about settlements farther east, and of a large river with
many canoes on it.

Forty-odd days after leaving Cicuye the expedition was wandering aimlessly on the limitless plains — Spaniards and guides alike
confused and bewildered. Patience and food supplies were almost exhausted, and the army faced a crisis. Only meat was plentiful, for
the Spaniards killed hundreds of buffaloes from the herds that roamed
the prairie . . . .

Alarmed by the shortage of provisions and the slim prospects
of obtaining any on the plains, Coronado was moved to call a conference of his captains. It was decided that the general, with thirty
horsemen and a few foot soldiers, should proceed in search of Quivira;
the remainder of the army was to return to the Rio Grande valley . . . .

Doubts about the Turk's veracity had beset Coronado since leaving Tiguex, — a suspicion shared by many in the army, for they had
heard some very disturbing stories about him. Although he was held
under lock and key and unable to communicate with any one, he had
told his guard exactly how many soldiers had been killed during the
fighting in the valley. Moreover, one day the guard had seen him
talking to the devil in a pitcher of water, an incident which in itself
was enough to frighten any common soldier!

These actions of the Turk had already aroused uneasy feelings. In addition, the gifted yarn-spinner's directions for reaching Quivira had been contradicted by the Querechos and by the Teyas, a tribe met later. Ysopete, another plains Indian with the army who had been picked up in the pueblo country, had declared boldly from the start that not only was the Turk lying about Quivira's riches, but that he was leading the expedition astray. The Turk's reputation as a soothsayer now hit rock bottom. He was in disgrace.

Plans completed, Coronado's small force, guided by Ysopete, struck out northeast; the Turk, ignominiously in irons, trailed along. Meanwhile the army . . . set out wearily for its old quarters on the Rio Grande.

Forty-odd days later, Coronado and his men reached Quivira, near Wichita, Kansas, historians believe — and another dream was shattered, another legend exploded.

"The guides," wrote Coronado, "had pictured it as having stone houses many stories high. Not only are there none of stone, but on the contrary they are of straw. And although when I set out for the province I was told that I could not see it all in two months, there are not more than twenty-five towns, with straw houses, in it."

The nearest thing to gold that the Spaniards found in Quivira was a copper plate which a chieftain proudly wore suspended from his neck.

The Turk, at last, had to explain, and finally he confessed that the whole fantastic Quivira story was a plot hatched by the Pueblo Indians to lure the white men from the pueblo country. The Turk's instructions were to lose the Spaniards on the plains, where, when their provisions gave out they would perish . . . .

Justice, swift and sure, descended on the Turk. He was promptly garrotted.

Coronado and his men lingered nearly a month in Quivira, and then, because of the approach of the rainy season, turned their weary footsteps toward the Rio Grande . . . .

* * *

In mid-fall, 1541, Coronado was back in Tiguex with the bitter news of Quivira . . . .

The Coronado expedition's second winter in New Mexico was not so severe as its first, but most of the men were without adequate clothing; and food was none too plentiful. Discontent festered in the army, many of whose members had gotten their fill of pioneering hardships. They had found no fabulous treasures, no large cities with turquoise-studded doors, no gold and silver. The lolling chieftains with their tinkling bells, the wealth of Quivira — all were a gigantic myth, a will-o-the-wisp which they had sought in vain. Fond thoughts of home and of the comforts of Spanish civilization began to fill the conquistadóres' minds, and agitation to abandon the expedition and return to New Spain spread through the camp . . . .

Early in the spring of 1542 the army broke camp on the Rio Grande and headed for Mexico, retracing dejectedly the route which two years before it had followed northward with such high hopes . . . .

In midsummer the disillusioned, tattered, weary cavaliers reached New Spain . . . . At Culiacan they rested for several days. Some of them dropped off at various points along the way; the rest went on again.

Coronado finally reached Mexico City accompanied by about a hundred men. There he reported to Viceroy Don Antonio de Mendoza, who had been faithful to the last to the army he had sent into the unknown lands of the north. The viceroy was not pleased, but he could not blame Coronado for not finding cities like Mexico when there were no such cities . . . .

Coronado's contemporaries in New Spain believed the venture a failure, and were not hesitant in denouncing it as such. As a matter of fact, with the return of the expedition died the Spaniard's hopes of fabulous riches, of another Mexico or another Peru . . . . The dreams of Seven Golden Cities in the north had been shattered.

It is true that Coronado's men found no visible treasures. But they accomplished things of much greater importance, the significance of which was left to later generations to recognize. The vast natural wealth of the large portion of the United States which they had explored could not be visualized by men who dreamed of golden cities, but it is evident that even they had some dim idea of the potentialities of the new land.

Listen to a philosophic last word from Pedro de Castañeda:

"I have always noticed, and it is a fact, that often when we have something valuable in our possession and handle it freely, we do not esteem or appreciate it in all its worth, as we would if we could realize how much we would miss it if we were to lose it. Thus we gradually belittle its value, but once we have lost it and we miss its benefits we feel it in our hearts and are forever moody thinking of ways to retrieve it. This, it seems to me, happened to all or most of those who went on that expedition which in the year of our Savior Jesus Christ, 1540, Francisco Vazquez Coronado led in search of the Seven Cities of Cibola."

THREE: JOURNEY THROUGH LOUISIANA

by Zebulon Montgomery Pike

*Despite Coronado's failure to find the Seven Cities of Cibola,
Spanish interest in her northern frontiers did not completely die, and
early in the seventeenth century she conquered the Pueblo lands
again. After its founding in 1609, Santa Fe served as an outpost for
New Spain's borderlands, checking the challenge that France in time
exerted as she attempted to push the outer limits of her province of
Louisiana westward. Then, in a series of European-made agreements,
France first ceded Louisiana to Spain (1762); France recovered the
province (1800) and, finally, France sold Louisiana to the new United
States in 1803. Three years later, Lieutenant Zebulon Montgomery
Pike was sent westward with a group of twenty-three men to gather
scientific information and to seek out the headwaters of the Arkansas
and Red rivers. The following selection is from Pike's own account
of his journey, from the great bend of the Arkansas River, in present
Kansas, where his party divided into two groups, until his capture
by the Spanish in the San Luis Valley of Colorado. After the events
related here, Pike and his men were interrogated at Santa Fe and
Chihuahua and then were escorted to the border dividing the United
States and New Spain, and there released.**

*   *   *

PIKE'S JOURNEY THROUGH LOUISIANA

. . . Tuesday, 28th October. — All was in motion as soon
as possible, my party crossing the river to the north side, and
Lieutenant Wilkinson launching his canoes of skins and wood. We
breakfasted together, and then filed off. I suffered my party to
march, and remained myself to see Lieutenant Wilkinson sail . . . .

------

*from Zebulon Montgomery Pike, *Exploratory Travels Through the Western Terri-
tories of North America: Comprising a Voyage from St. Louis, on the Mississippi,
to the Source of that River, and a Journey Through the Interior of Louisiana, and
the North-Eastern Provinces of New Spain. Performed in the years 1805, 1806,
1807, by Order of the Government of the United States,* London, 1811.

We parted with "God bless you," from both parties; they appeared to sail very well . . . . Arrived where our men had encamped about dusk . . . .

Wednesday, 29th October. — March after breakfast, and during the first hour passed two fires, where twenty-one Indians had recently encamped . . . . Killed a buffalo. Halted, made a fire, and feasted on the choicest pieces of meat. About noon discovered two horses feeding with a herd of buffaloes; we attempted to surround them, but they soon outstript our fleetest coursers; one appeared to be an elegant animal. These were the first wild horses we had seen . . . . The snow fell two inches deep, and then it cleared up . . . .

Saturday, 1st November. — Marched early . . . . Encamped in the evening on an island. Upon using my glass to observe the adjacent country, I observed on the prairie a herd of horses. Dr. /John H./ Robinson and Baroney /A.F. Vasquez/ accompanied me to go and examine them; when within about a quarter of a mile, they discovered us, and immediately approached, making the earth tremble under them; they brought to my recollection a charge of cavalry. They stopped and gave us an opportunity to view them. Amongst them there were some very beautiful bays, blacks, and greys, and indeed of all colors. We fired at a black horse with an idea of creasing him, but did not succeed; they flourished round and returned again to view us . . . .

Sunday, 2d November. — In the morning for the purpose of trying the experiment, we equipped six of our fleetest coursers with riders, and ropes to noose the wild horses, if in our power to come amongst the herd. They stood until we approached within forty yards, neighing and whinnying, when the chase began, which we continued two miles without success. Two of our horses ran with them, but we could not take them. Returned to camp. I have since laughed at our folly for endeavouring to take the wild horses in that manner, which is scarcely ever attempted even with the fleetest animals and most expert ropers . . . .

Wednesday, 5th November. — Marched at our usual hour . . . . we foolishly concluded to halt the remainder of the day and kill some

41

cows and calves, which lay on the opposite side of the river. I took post on a hill, and sent some horsemen over, when a scene took place which gave a lively representation of an engagement. The herd of buffaloes being divided into separate bands, covered the prairie with dust, and first charged on the one side, then to the other, as the pursuit of the horsemen impelled them; the report and smoke from the guns added to the pleasure of the scene, which in part compensated for our detention.

Thursday, 6th November. — Marched early . . . . I will not attempt to describe the droves of animals we now saw on our route, suffice it to say, that the face of the prairie was covered with them on both sides of the river; their numbers exceeded imagination . . . .

Saturday, 8th November. — Our horses being very much jaded, and our situation very eligible, we halted all day. Jerked meat, mended our mockinsons, &c.

Sunday, 9th November. — . . . We this day found the face of the country considerably changed, being hilly, with springs. Passed numerous herds of buffaloes and some horses . . . .

Tuesday, 11th November. — . . . Finding the impossibility of performing the tour in the time proposed. I determined to spare no pains to accomplish every object I had in contemplation, even should it oblige me to spend another winter in the desert . . . .

Wednesday, 12th November. — Was obliged to leave two horses which entirely gave out . . . .

Thursday, 13th November. — We marched at the usual hour. The river banks began to be entirely covered with woods on both sides, but no other species than cotton wood . . . .

Saturday, 15th November. — . . . At two o'clock in the afternoon, I thought I could distinguish a mountain to our right, which appeared like a small blue cloud; viewed it with the spy glass, and was still more confirmed in my conjecture, yet only communicated it to Dr. Robinson, who was in front with me, but in half an hour it appeared in full view before us. When our small party arrived on the hill, they with one accord gave three cheers to the Mexican mountains. Their appearance can easily be imagined by those who have crossed the Alleghany, but their sides were white as if covered with snow, or a white stone. These proved to be a spur of the grand western chain of mountains, which divide the waters of the Pacific from those of the Atlantic . . . . They appeared to present a boundary between the province of Louisiana and North Mexico, and would be a defined and natural limit . . . .

Sunday, 16th November. — . . . The Arkansaw appeared at this place to be much more navigable than below where we had first struck it, and for any impediment I have yet discovered in the river, I would not hesitate to embark in February at its mouth, and ascend to the Mexican mountains, with crafts properly constructed . . . .

Monday, 17th November. — Marched at our usual hour: pushed on with an idea of arriving at the mountains, but found at night no visible difference in their appearance from what we had observed yesterday . . . .

Tuesday, 18th November. — As we discovered fresh signs of the savages, we concluded it best to stop and kill some meat, for fear we should get into a country where we could not obtain game. Sent out the hunters . . . . In the evening found the hunters had killed without mercy, having slain seventeen buffaloes and wounded at least twenty more.

Wednesday, 19th November. — . . . I found it expedient to remain and dry the meat, for our horses were getting very weak . . . . Had a general feast of marrow bones; one hundred and thirty-six of them furnishing the repast . . . .

Friday, 21st November. — Marched at our usual hour . . . discovered the tracks of two men . . . . This caused us to move with caution but at the same time increased our anxiety to discover them . . . .

Saturday, 22d November. — Marched early, and with rather more caution than usual. After having proceeded about five miles . . . Baroney cried out "Voila un sauvage," when we observed a number of Indians running from the woods toward us. We advanced towards them,

43

and on turning my head to the left, I observed several running on the hill, as it were to surround us . . . . This caused a momentary halt, but perceiving those in front reaching out their hands, and without arms, we again advanced. They met us with open arms, crowding round to touch and embrace us. They appeared so anxious, that I dismounted from my horse, and in a moment a fellow had mounted him and driven off. I then observed the Doctor and Baroney in the same predicament. The Indians were embracing the soldiers. After some time tranquillity was so far restored, they having returned our horses all safe, as to enable us to learn they were a war party from the Grand Pawnees, who had been in search of the Ietans /Comanches/, but not finding them, were now on their return . . . .

We made for the woods and unloaded our horses, when the two leaders endeavored to arrange the party; it was with great difficulty they got them tranquil, and not until there had been a bow or two bent on the occasion . . . we found them to be sixty warriors, half with fire arms, and half with bows, arrows, and lances. Our party was in all sixteen. In a short time they were arranged in a ring, and I took my seat between the two leaders: our colours were placed opposite each other; the utensils for smoking &c. being prepared on a small seat before us. Thus far all was well. I then ordered half a carrot of tobacco, one dozen knives, sixty fire steels, and sixty flints to be presented to them. They demanded corn, ammunition, blankets, kettles, &c., all of which they were refused . . . . The pipes yet lay unmoved, as if they were undetermined whether to treat us as friends or as enemies; but after some time we were presented with a kettle of water, drank, smoked, and ate together . . . . The Indians now took their presents and commenced distributing them, but some malcontents threw them away, as if out of contempt. We began to load our horses, when they encircled us and commenced stealing every thing they could. Finding it was difficult to preserve my pistols, I mounted my horse, when I found myself frequently surrounded, during which some were endeavouring to steal the pistols. The Doctor was equally engaged in another quarter, and all the soldiers at their several posts, taking things from them. One having stolen my tomahawk, I informed the Chief, but he paid no respect . . . except to reply, that "they were pitiful." Finding this, we determined to protect ourselves as far as was in our power, and the affair began to wear a serious aspect. I ordered my men to take their arms, and separate themselves

44

from the savages; at the same time declaring to them I would kill
the first man who touched our baggage, on which they commenced
filing off immediately. We marched about the same time, and found
after they had left us, that they had contrived to steal one sword, a
tomahawk, a broad ax, five canteens, and sundry other small articles.
When I reflected on the subject I felt sincerely mortified, that the
smallness of my number obliged me thus to submit to the insults of
lawless banditti, it being the first time a savage had ever taken anything from me with the least appearance of force . . . .

Sunday, 23d November. — . . . As the river appeared to be
dividing itself into several small branches, and of course must be
near its extreme source, I concluded to put my party in a defensible
situation, and ascend the north fork to the high point /Pike's Peak7 of
the Blue Mountain, which we conceived would be one day's march, in
order to be enabled, from its summit, to lay down the various
branches of the river, and the positions of the country . . . .

Monday, 24th November. — Early in the morning cut down
fourteen logs, and put up a breast-work, five feet high on three sides,
and the other was thrown on the river. After giving the necessary
orders for the government of my men, during my absence, in case
of our not returning, we marched at one o'clock with an idea of arriving at the foot of the mountain, but found ourselves obliged to take up
our lodging this night under a single cedar, which we found in the
prairie, without water, and extremely cold. Our party, besides myself, consisted of Dr. Robinson, and privates Miller and Brown . . . .

Tuesday, 25th November. — Marched early, with an expectation of ascending the mountain, but was only able to encamp at its
base, after passing over many small hills covered with cedars and
pitch pines . . . .

Wednesday, 26th November. — Expecting to return to our
camp that evening, we left all our blankets and provision at the foot
of the mountain . . . . We commenced ascending; found the way very
difficult, being obliged to climb up rocks sometimes almost perpendicular; and after marching all day we encamped in a cave without
blankets, victuals, or water . . . .

45

Thursday, 27th November. — Arose hungry, thirsty, and extremely sore, from the uneveness of the rocks on which we had lain all night, but were amply compensated for our toil by the sublimity of the prospects below. The unbounded prairie was overhung with clouds, which appeared like the ocean in a storm, wave piled on wave, and foaming, whilst the sky over our heads was perfectly clear. Commenced our march up the mountain, and in about one hour arrived at the summit of this chain . . . . The summit of the Grand Peak, which was entirely bare of vegetation, and covered with snow, now appeared at the distance of fifteen or sixteen miles from us, and as high again as that we had ascended; and it would have taken a whole day's march to have arrived at its base, when I believe no human being could have ascended to its summit. This, with the condition of my soldiers, who had only light overhauls on, and no stockings, and were every way ill provided to endure the inclemency of this region, the bad prospect of killing anything to subsist on, with the further detention of two or three days which it must occasion, determined us to return . . . .

Saturday, 29th November. — Marched after a short repast, and arrived at our camp before night. Found all well . . . .

Sunday, 30th November. — We commenced our march at eleven o'clock, it snowing very fast, but my impatience to be moving would not permit me to lie still at our present camp . . . .

Monday, 1st December. — The storm still continuing with violence, we remained encamped; the snow by night was one foot deep, our horses being obliged to scrape it away to obtain their miserable pittance . . . .

Tuesday, 2d December. — It cleared off in the night . . . . Marched, and found it necessary to cross to the north side, about two miles up, as the ridge joined the river. The ford was a good one, but the ice ran very bad, and two of the men had their feet frozen, before we could get accommodated with fire, &c. . . . .

Saturday, 6th December. — . . . The Doctor and myself followed the river into the mountain, which was bounded on each side by rocks two hundred feet high, leaving a small valley of fifty or sixty feet /the Royal Gorge/ . . . .

Sunday, 7th December. — . . . two parties who were returning from exploring the two branches of the river . . . which they
reported, that they had ascended until the river was merely a brook,
bounded on both sides with perpendicular rocks, impracticable for
horses ever to pass . . . . /Pike is now convinced that the main body
of the Arkansas is below and not above; he detours north and then west
into South Park./

Saturday, 13 December. — . . . After the halt I took my gun,
and went to see what discovery I could make. After marching about
two miles north, fell on a river forty yards wide frozen over, which
after some investigation I found ran north-east. This was the occasion of much surprise, as we were taught to expect to meet with the
branches of the Red river, which should have run south-east. Query,
must it not be the head water of the River Plate? If so, the Missouri
must run much more to the west than is generally represented . . . .

Sunday, 14th December. — . . . As the geography of the
country had turned out to be so different from our expectations, we
were somewhat at a loss which course to pursue, unless we attempted
to cross the snow-capt mountains to the south-east of us, which appeared almost impossible . . . .

Thursday, 18th December. — Crossed the mountain which lay
south-west of us. In a distance of seven miles arrived at a small
spring. Some of our men observed, they supposed it to be the Red
river, to which I then gave very little credit . . . . After pointing
out the ground for the encampment, the Doctor and myself went on to
make discoveries, as was our usual custom, and in about four miles
march, struck what we supposed to be Red river, which here was
about twenty-five yards wide: ran with great rapidity, and was full
of rocks. We returned to the party with the news, which gave general pleasure . . . .

Saturday, 20th December. — . . . As there was no prospect
of killing any game, it was necessary that the party should leave this
place. I therefore determined that the Doctor and Baroney should
descend the river in the morning; that myself and two men would

47

ascend, and the rest of the party descend after the Doctor, until they obtained provision, and could wait for me.

Sunday, 21st December. — The Doctor and Baroney marched . . . . Myself, and the two men who accompanied me . . . ascended for twelve miles; and encamped on the north side of the river, continuing close to the north mountain, and running through a narrow rocky channel, in some places not more than twenty feet wide, and at least ten feet deep . . . .

Monday, 22d December. — Marched up thirteen miles farther, to a large point of the mountain, whence we had a view of at least thirty-five miles, to where the river entered the mountain, it being at that place not more than ten or fifteen feet wide . . . . From this place, after taking the course and estimating the distance, we returned to our camp . . . .

Wednesday, 24th December. — . . . About eleven o'clock met Dr. Robinson . . . who informed me that he and Baroney had been absent from the party two days, without killing anything, also without eating; but that over night they had killed four buffaloes . . . . The Doctor and myself pursued the trail and found . . . /the men/ encamped on the river's bottom. Sent out horses for the meat; shortly after, Sparks arrived, and informed us he had killed four cows. Thus, from being in a starving condition, we had at once eight beeves in our camp. We now again found ourselves all assembled together on Christmas eve, and appeared generally to be content, although all the refreshment we had to celebrate the day was buffalo flesh, without salt, or any other thing whatever.

My little excursion up the river had been undertaken with a view of establishing the geography of the sources of the (supposed) Red river, as I well knew the indefatigable researches of Dr. Hunter, Dunbar, and Freeman, had left nothing unnoticed in the extent of their voyage up that stream. I determined that its upper branches should be equally well explored . . . .

Thursday, 25th December. — The weather being stormy, and having some meat to dry, I concluded to lie by this day. Here I must take the liberty of observing that in this situation the hardships and privations we underwent, were on this day brought more fully to our minds than at any time previously. We had before been occasionally accustomed to some degree of relaxation, and extra enjoyments; but the case was now far different: eight hundred miles from the frontiers of our country, in the most inclement season of the year; not one person properly clothed for the winter, many without blankets, having been obliged to cut them up for socks and other articles; lying down too at night on the snow or wet ground, one side burning whilst the other was pierced with the cold wind; this was briefly the situation of the party; whilst some were endeavouring to make a miserable substitute of raw buffalo hide for shoes, and other covering. I will not speak of diet, as I conceive that to be beneath the serious consideration of a man on a journey of such a nature. We spent this day as agreeably as could be expected from men in our circumstances . . . .

Friday, 26th December. — Marched at two o'clock and made seven miles and a half to the entrance of the mountains . . . .

Saturday, 27th December. — Marched over an extremely rough road, our horses frequently fell and cut themselves considerably on the rocks. From there being no roads of buffaloes, or sign of horses, I am convinced that neither these animals, nor the Aborigines of the country ever take this route to go from the source of the river out of the mountains . . . .

Sunday, 28th December. — Marched over an open space, and from the appearance before us concluded we were going out of the mountains, but at night encamped at the entrance of most perpendicular precipices on both sides, through which the river ran and our course lay . . . .

Wednesday, 31st December. — Marched. Had frequently to cross the river on the ice, during our march; the horses falling down, we were obliged to pull them over on the ice. The river turned so much to the north, as almost to induce us to believe it was the Arkansaw . . . .

Thursday, 1st January, 1807. — . . . At night ascended a mountain, and discovered a prairie ahead about eight miles; the news

49

of which gave great joy to the party . . . .

Saturday, 3d January. — . . . We pursued the river, and with great difficulty made six miles, by frequently cutting roads on the ice, and covering it with earth, in order to go round precipices that projected into the course . . . .

Sunday, 4th January. — We made the prairie about three o'clock, when I detached Baroney and two soldiers with the horses, in order to find some practicable way for them to get out of the mountains without their loads. I then divided the others into two parties of two men each, to make sleges, and bring on the baggage. I determined to continue down the river along, until I could kill some provision . . . for we had now no food left . . . .

Monday, 5th January. — . . . About ten o'clock rose the highest summit of the mountain, when the unbounded extent of the prairies again presented itself to my view, and from some distant peaks, I immediately recognized our situation to be one outlet of the Arkansaw, which we had left nearly one month since. This was a great mortification, but at the same time, I consoled myself with the knowledge I had acquired of the source of the Plate and Arkansaw rivers . . . which scarcely any person but a madman would ever purposely attempt to trace any further than the entrance of these mountains, which had hitherto secured their sources from the scrutinizing eye of civilized man . . . . We proceeded to our old camp, which we had left the tenth of December, and re-occupied it . . . . This was my birth day, and most fervently did I hope never to pass another so miserably . . . .

Friday, 9th January. — . . . I now felt at considerable loss how to proceed, as any idea of service at that time from my horses was entirely preposterous. Thus, after various plans formed and rejected, and the most mature deliberation, I determined to build a small place for defence and deposit, and leave part of the baggage, horses, my interpreter, and one man; and with the remainder, with our packs of Indian presents, ammunition, tools, &c., on our backs, to cross the mountains on foot, find the Red river, and then send back a detachment to conduct the horses and baggage after us, by the most eligible route we could discover; by which time we

50

calculated our horses would be so far recovered as to be able to endure the fatigue of the march. In consequence of this determination, some were put to constructing block houses, some to hunting, some to take care of horses, &c. . . . .

Wednesday, 14th January. — We marched our party, consisting of eleven soldiers, the Doctor, and myself, each of us carrying forty-five pounds, and as much provision as he thought proper; which, with arms, &c., made on an average seventy pounds, leaving Baroney and one man, Patrick Smith, behind. We crossed the first ridge, leaving the main branch of the river to the north of us, and struck on the south fork, on which we encamped . . . .

Saturday, 17th January. — Marched about four miles, when the great White Mountain presented itself before us; in sight of which we had been for more than a month, and through which we supposed lay the long sought Red river. We now left the creek on the north of us, and bore away more east to a low place in the mountains . . . . We halted at the woods at eight o'clock for encampment, after getting fires made, we discovered that the feet of nine of our men were frozen . . . . This night we had no provision . . . .

Sunday, 18th January. — We started out two of the men least injured; the Doctor and myself (who fortunately were untouched by the frost) also went out to hunt for something to preserve existence. Near evening we wounded a buffalo . . . but had the mortification to see him run off notwithstanding . . . .

Monday, 19th January. — We again took the field . . . we discovered a gang of buffaloes coming along at some distance . . . by the greatest good luck the first shot stopped one, which we killed in three more shots, and by the dusk had cut each of us a heavy load . . . .

Tuesday, 20th January. — . . . On examining the feet of those who were frozen, we found it impossible for them to proceed. And two others only without loads by the help of a stick . . . .

Wednesday, 21st January. — . . . I went up to the foot of the mountain, to see what prospect there was of being able to cross it, but had not more than fairly arrived at its base when I found the snow four or five feet deep; this obliged me to determine to proceed and cotoyer the mountains to the south, where it appeared lower, and until we found a place where we could cross.

Thursday, 22d January. — I furnished the two poor fellows who were to remain with ammunition, and made use of every argument in my power to encourage them to have fortitude to resist their fate, and gave them assurances of my sending relief as soon as possible.

We parted, but not without tears. We pursued our march, taking merely sufficient provision for one meal, in order to leave as much as possible for the two poor fellows who remained . . . .

Saturday, 24th January. — . . . As I found all the buffaloes had left the plains, I determined to attempt the traverse of the mountains, in which we persevered, until the snow became so deep as to render it impossible to proceed; when I again turned my face to the plain, and for the first time in the journey found myself discouraged . . . .

Sunday, 25th January. — I determined never again to march with so little provision on hand; for had the storm continued one day longer, the animals would have continued in the mountains, and we should have become so weak as not to be able to hunt, and of course have perished . . . .

Tuesday, 27th January. — We proceeded on our march, determining to cross the mountains . . . . After a bad day's march through snows, some places three feet deep, we struck on a brook that led west, which I followed down, and shortly came to a small stream, running in the same direction. This we hailed with fervency, as the waters of the Red river . . . .

Wednesday, 28th January. — Followed down the ravine . . . . After marching some miles we discovered, through the lengthy vista at a distance, another chain of mountains, and nearer to us at the foot of the White Mountains, which we were then descending, sandy hills.

We marched on to the outlet of the mountain and left the sandy desert to our right; kept down between it and the mountain. When we encamped I ascended one of the largest hills of sand, and with my glass could discover a large river, flowing nearly north by west and south by east through the plain which came out of the third chain of mountains . . . . The prairie between the two chains of mountains bore nearly north and south: I returned to camp with the news of my discovery . . . .

Thursday, 29th January. — Finding the distance too great to attempt crossing immediately to the river in a direct line, we marched obliquely to a copse of woods which made down a considerable distance from the mountain . . . .

Friday, 30th January. — We marched hard and in the evening arrived on the banks of the Rio del Norte, then supposed to be the Red river . . . .

Saturday, 31st January. — As there was no timber here, we determined on descending until we found some, in order to make transports to descend the river with; where we might establish a position that four or five might defend against the insolence, cupidity or barbarity of the savages; whilst the others returned to assist on the poor fellows who were left behind at different points. We descended eighteen miles, when we met a large west branch, emptying into the main stream; up which, about five miles, we took our station . . . .

Thursday, 5th February. — The Doctor and myself went out to hunt . . . . we ascended a high hill, which lay south of our camp, from whence we had a view of all the prairie and rivers to the north of us: it was one of the most sublime and beautiful inland prospects ever presented to the eyes of man. The prairie lying nearly north and south, was probably sixty miles by forty-five . . . .

The great and lofty mountains covered with eternal snow, seemed to surround the luxuriant vale crowned with perennial flowers, like a terrestrial paradise, shut out from the view of man.

. . . In this western traverse of Louisiana, the following general observations may be made: from the Missouri to the head of the Osage river, a distance in a straight line probably of three hundred miles, the country will admit of a numerous, extensive, and

53

compact population; from thence on the rivers Kanses, La Plate, Arkansaw, and their various branches, it appears to me to be only possible to introduce a limited population. The inhabitants would find it most to their advantage to pay attention to the rearing of cattle, horses, sheep, and goats: all of which they can raise in abundance, the earth producing spontaneously sufficient for their support, both in winter and summer, by which means their herds might become immensely numerous; but the wood now in the country would not be sufficient for a moderate population more than fifteen years . . . . here a barren soil, parched and dried up for eight months in the year, presents neither moisture nor nutriment sufficient for the growth of wood. These vast plains of the western hemisphere may become in time equally celebrated with the sandy deserts of Africa, for I saw in my route, in various places, tracts of many leagues where the wind had thrown up the sand, in all the fanciful forms of the ocean's rolling waves, and on which not a speck of vegetation existed. But from these immense prairies may arise one great advantage to the United States, viz., the restriction of our population to some certain limits, and thereby a continuation of the union. Our citizens being so prone to rambling, and extending themselves on the frontiers, will, through necessity, be constrained to limit their extent on the west to the borders of the Missouri and Mississippi, while they leave the prairies, incapable of cultivation, to the wandering and uncivilized Aborigines of the country.

Friday, 6th February. — . . . We continued to go on with our stockade or breast-work . . . .

Saturday, 7th February. — The Doctor marched alone for Santa Fé. In the evening I despatched Corporal Jackson with four men to recross the mountains, in order to bring in the baggage left with the frozen men, and to see if they were yet able to proceed. This detachment left me with four men only, two of whom had their feet frozen; they were employed in finishing the stockade . . . .

Monday, 16th February. — I took one man and went out hunting; about six miles from the post shot and wounded a deer. Immediately afterwards discovered two horsemen rising the summit of a hill, about half a mile to our right. As my orders were to avoid giving alarm or offence to the Spanish government of New Mexico I endeavoured to shun them at first, but when we attempted to retreat, they pursued us at full charge flourishing their lances, and when we advanced, they would retire as fast as their horses could carry them. Seeing this we got into a small ravine, in hopes to decoy them near enough to oblige them to come to a parley, which happened agreeably to our desires. As they came on, hunting us with great caution, we suffered them to get within forty yards, where we had allured them, but were about running off again, when I ordered the soldier to lay down his arms and walk towards them, at the same time standing ready with my rifle to kill either who should lift an arm in a hostile manner. I then hallooed to them, that we were Americans and friends, which were almost the only two words I knew in the Spanish language: after which, with great signs of fear, they came up, and proved to be a Spanish dragoon and a civilized Indian; armed after their manner . . . . We were jealous of our arms on both sides, and acted with great precaution. They informed me, that was the fourth day since they had left Santa Fé; that Robinson had arrived there, and had been received with great kindness by the Governor. As I knew them to be spies, I thought it proper merely to inform them that I was about to descend the river to Natchitoches. We sat here on the ground a long time, and finding they were determined not to leave me, we arose and bade them adieu; but they demanded where our camp was, and finding they were not about to depart, I thought it most proper to take them with me, thinking we were on Red river, and of course in the territory claimed by the United States.

We took the road to my fort, and as they were on horseback, they travelled rather fast than myself. They were halted by the sentinel, and immediately retreated much surprised. When I came up I took them in and then explained to them as well as I was able, my intentions of descending the river to Natchitoches; but at the same time told them that if Governor Allencaster would send out an officer with an interpreter, who spoke French or English, I would do myself the pleasure to give his Excellency every reasonable satisfaction as to my intentions in coming on his frontiers. They informed me that on the second day they would be in Santa Fé, but were careful never to suggest an idea of my being on the Rio del Norte. As they concluded I did not think as I spoke, they were very anxious to ascertain our number, &c. Seeing only five men here, they could not believe we came without horses; to this I did not think proper to afford them any satisfaction, giving them to understand we were in many parties.

Tuesday, 17th February. — In the morning our two Spanish
visitors departed . . . . This evening the corporal and three of the
men arrived, who had been sent back to the camp of their frozen
companions. They informed me that two more would arrive the next
day . . . but the other two . . . were unable to come. They said that
they had hailed them with tears of joy, and were in despair when they
again left them with the chance of never seeing them more. They
sent on to me some of the bones taken out of their feet, and conjured
me by all that was sacred, not to leave them to perish far from the
civilized world. Oh! little did they know my heart, if they could
suspect me of conduct so ungenerous! . . . .

Wednesday, 18th February. — The other two men arrived:
in the evening I ordered the sergeant and one man to prepare to march
on the morrow for the Arkansaw, where we had left our interpreter,
horses, &c., to conduct them to us, and on his return to bring the
two invalids, who were still on the mountains . . . .

Thursday, 26th February. — In the morning was apprised by
the report of a gun from my look-out guard, of the approach of stran-
gers; immediately after two Frenchmen arrived.

My sentinel halted them, and I ordered them to be admitted
after some questions. They informed me that his excellency Governor
Allencaster, hearing it was the intention of the Utah Indians to attack
me, had detached an officer with fifty dragoons to come out and protect me, and that they would be with me in two days. To this I made
no reply; but shortly after the party hove in sight, as I afterwards
learnt; fifty dragoons and fifty mounted militia of the province, armed
in the same manner with lances, escopates, and pistols. My sentinels
halted them at the distance of about fifty yards. I had the works
manned: I thought it most proper to send out the two Frenchmen to
inform the commanding officer, that it was my request he should leave
his party in a small copse of wood where he halted, and that I would
meet him myself in the prairie, in which our work was situated; this
I did, with my sword on me only. I was thus introduced to Don Ignatio
Saltelo and Don Bartholemew Fernandez, two lieutenants; the former
the commander of the party: I gave them an invitation to enter the

56

works, but requested the troops might remain where they were. This was complied with: but when they came round and discovered that to enter they were obliged to crawl on their bellies over a small drawbridge, they appeared astonished; they however entered without further hesitation.

We first breakfasted on some deer, meal, goose, and some biscuit, which the civilized Indian who came out as a spy had brought me. After breakfast the commanding officer addressed me as follows:

"Sir, the Governor of New Mexico, being informed that you had missed your route, ordered me to offer you in his name, mules, horses, money, or whatever you may stand in need of, to conduct you to the head of Red river; as from Santa Fé, to where it is sometimes navigable, is eight days' journey, and we have guides and the routes of the traders to conduct us."

"What," interrupted I, "is not this the Red river?" "No, sir, it is the Rio del Norte." I immediately ordered my flag to be taken down and rolled up, feeling how sensibly I had committed myself in entering their territory, and was conscious that they must have positive orders to take me in. He now added, "that he had provided one hundred mules and horses to take in my party and baggage, and stated how anxious his excellency was to see me at Santa Fé." I stated to him the absence of my sergeant, the situation of the rest of the party; and that my orders would not justify my entering into the Spanish territories. He urged still further, until I began to feel myself a little heated in the argument, and told him in a peremptory style, I would not go until the arrival of my sergeant, with the remainder of my party. He replied, that there was not the least restraint to be used, only that it was necessary His Excellency should receive an explanation of my business on his frontiers; that I might go now, or on the arrival of my party; but that if none went at present he should be obliged to send in for provisions. He added, that if I would now march, he would leave an Indian interpreter and an escort of dragoons to conduct the sergeant into Santa Fé. His mildness induced me to tell him that I would march, but must leave two men in order to meet the sergeant and party to instruct him as to coming in, as he would never do so without a fight, unless ordered.

I was induced to consent to the measure, by conviction that the officer had a positive command to convey me in; and as I had no orders to engage in hostilities, and indeed had committed myself, although innocently, by violating their territory, I conceived it would appear better to shew a will to come to an explanation, rather than be any way constrained. Yet my situation was so eligible, and I could so easily have put them to defiance, that it was with great reluctance I suffered all our labour to be lost, without once trying the efficacy of it.

My compliance seemed to spread general joy through the Spanish party as soon as it was communicated. But it appeared to be different with my men, who wished to have had a little <u>dust</u>, (as they expressed themselves,) and were likewise fearful of Spanish treachery.

. . . After writing orders to my sergeant, and leaving them with my corporal and one private who were to remain, we sallied forth . . . .

FOUR: THE MOUNTAIN MEN

by Rufus Rockwell Wilson

*Even before Mexico gained her independence from Spain in 1821,
but increasingly after that, when a more liberal trade policy encouraged
such activities, Americans found important sources of profit in the
Southwestern areas. Hauling trade goods over the Santa Fe Trail was
hazardous and unpredictable, but sometimes netted nice income.
Trapping and trading for beaver furs in the western mountains was
even more profitable. The men who engaged in the trapping and trading have been called "The Mountain Men"; their work and exploits
are here described.**

*   *   *

THE MOUNTAIN MEN

From the dawn of history, mountains have ever stood as
barriers to the settlement of a new country, and, by the same
token, their reaches have been the last to know the feet and ways
of men. The pioneer is ever one whose moods and inclinings are
worlds removed from those of his homekeeping fellows; and so it
was the trapper and fur trader, loving solitude and the lure of wild
places, who first bared the secrets of the Rockies and the rugged
ranges to the east and the west of them.

These mountains had stayed the advance first of the adventurous explorers of Old Spain, then of the Mexican grandees who
fell heirs to that country's New World empire, so that, when they
finally passed to the ownership of the United States, they still belonged to the Indian and the wild animal. The pathfinders, Lewis
and Clark in 1804 and Zebulon Montgomery Pike in 1806, were the
heralds of a new order of things. After them came the trapper,
spiritual kinsman of Boone and Natty Bumppo, who, in his search
for the pelts of the beaver and other animals, made his way through

------

*from Rufus Rockwell Wilson, "The Mountain Men" from *Out of the West*, Elmira,
New York, 1940. Used with special permission of Mrs. Rufus Rockwell Wilson.

every mountain pass and traced every important stream from its source to its mouth.

While the supply lasted and until fashions changed, the skin of the beaver, finding ready buyers in the hatmakers of London, Paris, and New York, was the basis of the American fur trade. Assured running water and the edible bark of deciduous trees, the beaver flourishes at any altitude and in widely varying degrees of heat or cold, and so in the first years of the trade were found in apparently inexhaustible numbers alike in the clear-flowing streams of the Rockies and in the muddy lower reaches of the rivers which cleave the valleys of the Colorado and the Rio Grande.

Moreover, the beaver was easily caught and made ready for market, and it was not long before a number of great fur companies, with headquarters at St. Louis and other points, and backed by ample capital, were yearly dispatching carefully organized expeditions into the mountains, while a growing army of independent trappers and traders — the real mountain men . . . — ranged every stream and threaded every mountain gorge and pass from the Canadian border to the Mexican barrier of the Colorado and Rio Grande, and from the headwaters of the Missouri and Columbia to the Pacific coast . . . .

Any gathering of mountain men was pretty sure to include sundry French-Canadians and half-breeds and a few far-wandering natives of New England, but a majority of them hailed from Kentucky and Tennessee — descendants for the most part of the sturdy Scotch-Irish pioneers who in an earlier time had crossed and conquered the Alleghenies . . . . The mountain man dressed in buckskin and when on the trail wore his hair and beard long, shaving only when his rare periods of leisure and merry-making brought him for a few days and weeks into the company of women of his own race.

The mountain man's supply of food, when he left a trading post, was generally limited to meager quantities of sugar, coffee, and tobacco. As a rule he smoked only at night, and then, in order to make his dwindling store of the weed stretch over the weeks and months that must elapse before it could be replenished, he mixed his tobacco with the inner bark of the red willow . . . . The absolutely indispensable articles in his outfit were a rifle, a pistol, a long-bladed knife, half a dozen traps, a buffalo robe to lie upon, and a blanket to cover him.

Thus equipped, the mountain man was ready for the wilderness and for the perils and privations it held for him. For months at a time the meat of the animals brought down by his rifle was his only food, and, when game failed him, or his ammunition gave out, he did not scruple to find sustenance in any living thing that came his way. He would eat without complaint the stewed puppies of an Indian camp, and, when starvation threatened in the arid plains, following an example set him by the Indians of the Southwest, he would as a matter of course use the flesh of the desert rattler. Not a few of the mountain men, indeed, became close kin to the Indian, both in feeling and spirit. They did not scorn the auguries of the medicine man; many in time grew to be devout worshippers of the moon and the stars . . . . Women of his own breed had small place in the life of the mountain man. The white woman preferred ease and a fixed abode, while he was apt to regard a wife and children as incumbrances only to be taken into account with the approach of old age.

On the other hand, the squaw, whom he bought and sold as he did his horses, could be depended upon to follow wherever his wanderings led him and to do his bidding without complaint; and she could be abandoned or cast aside as the mood or convenience of her master might chance to dictate. But with the maidens of the Mexican villages of the Rio Grande region, who were blessed with good looks and knew how to submit to the male will, not a few of the mountain men formed ties that held them.

The village of Taos, then the most northerly of the Mexican settlements, and the center of one of the best beaver regions, had a charm all its own for the trappers who came there at regular intervals to buy supplies, to dance and flirt, and to spend their hard-earned dollars for liquor and at the gaming table. Many of them married Taos girls, who bore them children and kept homes to which their restless mates could return at the end of each trip into the wilds. And more than one trapper, when the looting of the streams and a fall in the price of beaver had robbed him of his calling, found a refuge in Taos and the ministrations of his Mexican wife, comforts not to be scorned in his last days.

61

Besides Taos, there were other favorite meeting places for the mountain men. One was Bent's Fort on the Arkansas, near the site of La Junta, Colorado, and another Pierre's Hole, in what is now southeastern Idaho . . . . Bent's Fort, laid out in 1828 as a trading post and outfitting point for the mountain men, was a sprawling structure with adobe walls, topped with growing cactus as a precaution against assault by Indians.

An American flag flew from these walls, and in the tower which surmounted the fort's iron-bound gate a guard, with rifle and telescope at his elbow, kept watch day and night. There was a fur press in the center of the square formed by the adobe walls, and all around it were rooms and sleeping quarters for garrison and guests. There were free meals and beds for all who needed them, a square deal for the wild tribes who came there to trade, and credit and supplies for the mountain men, many of whom, when taking the trail, left their Mexican wives with the Bents for safekeeping . . . .

Stirring memories also attach to Pierre's Hole, where, when the beaver trade had not yet fallen on evil days, hundreds of trappers and traders and whole tribes of mountain Indians frequently assembled to barter their wares. The trappers came singly or in groups, each with his three or four horses or mules bearing bales of beaver fur. The traders, many of them representatives of the great fur companies, were accompanied by pack trains loaded with beads and cloth for their Indian patrons, powder, lead, sugar, and coffee for the trappers, and generous supplies of corn whisky for any who could pay for it. The Indians, generally last to appear on the scene, reared their white tepees along the river and, clad in their finest buckskin, set off with beads and the quills of the porcupine, danced or drank themselves into a frenzy and made the night noisy with the rumble of their drums.

There were a few frugal spirits among the mountain men, but most of them, having sold their furs for whatever was offered them, bought what they needed in the way of traps and knives, powder and lead, and then made haste to squander the rest of the monies paid them for liquor and in gambling or bets on the impromptu horse races which each afternoon made the camp the noisiest and dustiest of places. Nor must mention fail to be made of the Indian girls, who, with tinkling bells about their necks and in their hair, rode up and down on their ponies and were for sale to those who would pay most for them. There were fist fights without number between those who when in their cups took to boasting of their prowess, and now and then there was a duel to the death with rifles. And at every stage the traders, who kept their wits about them and had few scruples to trouble them, dealt out liquor, indifferent to the condition of those who asked for it, or cheated and gouged Indian and trapper with impartial hand. Pierre's Hole in the last days of a rendezvous was no place for a man who loved peace and honest ways . . . .

The forgetfulness which so soon overtakes all but the greatest names has spared to us those of Jedediah Strong Smith, Thomas Fitzpatrick, and Kit Carson — the first the most unresting and venturesome, the second perhaps the ablest, and the third the most widely known of a remarkable group. Smith was born of New England parents in the Mohawk Valley in 1799, drifted to the West in his teens, and at St. Louis, in March, 1823, joined a trapping expedition about to set out for the Yellowstone country. St. Louis was then a frontier town of less than five thousand people, but already the headquarters of the Rocky Mountain fur trade. William H. Ashley, a leader in the military and political affairs of the newly created State of Missouri, was also a rising figure in the fur trade, and organizer of the party of which young Smith now became a member.

James Bridger, later to attain a leading place in the trade, was already in Ashley's employ, trapping on the Yellowstone, and among those who kept Smith company in the slow advance by keelboat up the Missouri were half a dozen young men whose names now have a meaning for every student of frontier history. Among them were James Clyman and William L. Sublette, the one from Virginia and the other from Kentucky, and both under thirty; Seth Grant, Hugh Glass, and David E. Jackson, who was later to become the partner of Smith and Sublette, and twenty-four year-old Thomas Fitzpatrick . . . .

In the last days of May, Ashley and his men passed the mouth of the Cheyenne and reached the country of the hostile and dreaded Arikaras. In a surprise attack by the Indians at sunrise of June 2, twelve of the whites were slain and as many more wounded. Ashley retreated 110 miles to the mouth of the Teton, and sent to Fort

Atkinson, just north of the present Omaha, for reinforcements. While he waited for the 250 soldiers duly dispatched to his aid, with Colonel Henry Leavenworth in command, several bands of Sioux appeared, eager to join in a campaign against their ancient enemies.

And so on August 9 a combined force of 400 whites and 700 Indians reached the neighborhood of the Arikara villages. There followed a series of mishaps which ended in a humiliating fiasco. The Arikaras, after a preliminary brush with an advance party of Sioux, took refuge behind a picket enclosure; and, while Leavenworth waited the arrival of the two six-pounders that were being brought up in keel-boats before beginning an attack, the Sioux, having plundered the Arikara cornfields and stolen a dozen horses and mules from the trappers and troopers, set out for home. After desultory skirmishes the Arikara chiefs promised good behavior and a restoration of stolen property, but in the night abandoned their villages and fled, intent when opportunity offered to resume their attacks on the whites, and bar their way to the haunts of the beaver.

However, what at the moment was regarded as a shameful disaster had unexpected issue in one of the most decisive events in the history of the fur trade. Ashley, with all his plans for the moment brought to naught, prepared to return to St. Louis, but first took steps to repair his waning fortunes. The trappers sent out from St. Louis had long been fired by the tales that came to them of the fabulous wealth of beaver to be had on the farther side of the Rockies in the valley of the Spanish or Green River in the western part of what is now Wyoming. Ashley had planned to reach and tap this source of wealth by the long and roundabout course of the Missouri, the Yellowstone, and the Big Horn, and with this avenue closed to him he decided to send a party west to the country of the Crows, and thence across the Great Divide to the Spanish River.

Ashley chose for this perilous journey into the unknown a picked body of eleven men, captained by Jedediah Strong Smith and with Thomas Fitzpatrick second in command. What remained of his original following had dropped down the Missouri to Fort Kiowa, a post of the American Fur Company not far from the present town of Chamberlain, South Dakota, and from that point in late September Smith and his ten companions set out on their historic journey. The factor at Fort Kiowa had loaned them a guide and horses, and thus equipped they had reached the upper waters of the Cheyenne, a little way south and west of the Black Hills, when their progress was halted in a startling and unexpected way.

Marching in single file with Smith at their head, they had just emerged from a strip of bushy bottom land into an open glade, when a huge grizzly pounced upon the leader and bore him to earth. Before he could be rescued and the bear killed, several of his ribs were broken and his head badly lacerated. A man of iron will, Smith submitted without murmur to the rude surgery of one of his companions, and ten days later was able to resume active command of the party. Crossing the watershed between the Cheyenne and Powder rivers, they found their first beaver in the waters of the latter stream, and trapped with profit until the middle of November.

Then, packing their furs on horseback, Smith and his companions crossed the Big Horn Range and ascended Wind River until at the northern base of what is now called Frémont's Peak they came upon a village of Crows. Here they rested and hunted buffalo, and from their hosts learned how to reach the pass that led to the Green River. Late in February, 1824, they set forth to find it. Their way led down to the mouth of Wind River, and then southward up the Popo Agie. It was bitter cold, but they pushed ahead until they reached the Sweetwater. There they found good water, timber for shelter, dry wood for fuel, and an abundance of game for food; and there they rested for a fortnight.

When they again broke camp, it was to follow the Sweetwater for a few miles and then head west toward the Great Divide. At the end of a week they came, on an early March day in 1824, upon streams flowing westward, and realized that without knowing it they had reached the summit of South Pass, which for nearly half a century was to be the most important route to the Pacific. Later in the same month they reached Green River, and during the weeks that followed piled up a store of furs. Then, in the last days of June, it was decided that Smith and most of the men should remain in the mountains ready to resume trapping in the fall, while Fitzpatrick and two others should take their peltries to the Missouri, report to Ashley, and return with supplies.

65

Fitzpatrick, after many adventures, reached Fort Atkinson in September, and soon Ashley, waiting in St. Louis, learned that Smith and his men had found a new and more direct route to the Pacific, and at the same time had laid for him the foundations of the very substantial fortune with which less than three years later he was to retire from the fur trade. Meanwhile, Smith and those who remained with him piled up stores of fur and at the same time thoroughly explored the country lying west of Green River. In the summer of 1826 Ashley transferred his interests to the newly formed firm of Smith, Jackson, and Sublette, and later in the same year the senior partner set out on another of the path-breaking journeys which was to give him enduring fame.

Starting from the rendezvous near the present Ogden, Utah, Smith with fifteen men made his way to Utah Lake, and thence late in August southwesterly to the Mohave villages on the Colorado, and across the desert by way of Cajon Pass and San Bernardino to San Gabriel Mission in southern California. After a stay in San Diego, in February, 1827, he pushed north to the Stanislaus and, leaving his party encamped on that stream, with two companions on May 20 essayed a successful crossing of the Sierras. Then braving the unknown Nevada desert, he joined his partners in the summer of 1827 at Bear Lake, near the present Laketown, Utah. Soon, with a party of nineteen men and two Indian women, he was again on his way south, retracing his route of the previous year.

In a treacherous attack by the Mohaves on the east bank of the Colorado nine of the party were slain, and the two women and all of the supplies captured. Beset by thirst, hunger, and heat, the survivors made their way over the desert, and at the end of ten days reached San Gabriel. There Smith secured fresh supplies and, leaving two of his men at the mission, in due time joined the party waiting for him on the Stanislaus. His troubles, however, were not ended, for during a visit to the mission and presidio of San Jose he was arrested, and after a fortnight's confinement conveyed to Monterey, temporary capital of the province. There some American ship captains intervened in his behalf, and when, on November 15, he bound himself to leave the country, he was released from custody. He found his combined party of twenty-one men at the presidio of San Francisco, and early in February, 1828, set out for the interior.

In mid-April he decided not to attempt a crossing of the Sierras, and instead to head for the Oregon country by way of the coast. The party moved slowly northward, gathering furs, but on July 14, 1828, on the Umpqua River in what is now Douglas County, Oregon, while Smith was absent from camp, they were attacked by Indians, whom they had regarded as friendly, and only the leader and two of his men escaped with their lives. John Turner, one of the survivors, found Smith, and after weeks of weary travel the two men succeeded in reaching Fort Vancouver on the Columbia. There they found the other survivor, Arthur Black, and there Dr. John McLoughlin of the Hudson's Bay Company gave them food, clothing, and shelter. Then Smith and Black, setting out on March 12, 1829, made their way up the Columbia to Fort Walla Walla, and thence to Pierre's Hole, the present Teton Basin, Idaho, where they were met by a party that had been sent out to search for them.

Smith, as head of the firm of Smith, Jackson, and Sublette, now took charge of its affairs and managed them to such good effect that in August, 1830, he and his partners, each with a competence at his command, were ready to leave the mountains. They sold their interests to a group headed by Fitzpatrick and Bridger, who adopted the name of the Rocky Mountain Fur Company, and, loading their supply wagons with 190 packs of furs, set out for St. Louis. There Jackson and Sublette without delay made ready to enter the Santa Fe trade, which was fast assuming substantial proportions, and on May 4, 1831, with a caravan, they left Independence on their first trip to the Southwest, a trip which was to have a tragic ending for Smith, who, having bought an outfit for two of his younger brothers, went along to help them manage the business.

Fitzpatrick, who had come from the mountains for supplies and who had fallen in with his former associates at Lexington, Missouri, kept them company as the guest of his old friend Smith. It was arranged that, when they reached Santa Fe, Fitzpatrick should buy from them the supplies he needed, along with pack animals to carry them to their destination in the north. There were eighty-seven men and twenty-three wagons in the caravan, but for all of them it was unknown country beyond the Arkansas, which they forded just west of the present Dodge City.

Ahead of them stretched the Jornada, sixty miles of waterless desert, the heat of late May giving a sharper edge to the south wind which beat full in the faces of the travelers, while to make matters worse the crisscross tramp of unnumbered thousands of buffalo had wiped out the trail made by the wagons of the previous year. On the third day after leaving the Arkansas, wracked by thirst and half blinded by wind and sun, the advance party divided, some going one and some another way in search of water. Smith and a companion headed south, following what they believed to be the trail, until they sighted, a few miles ahead of them, broken ground which to Smith's trained eye promised a spring or a water course.

And so, while Smith pushed ahead, his companion halted and waited for the main company. Spyglass in hand, he watched his friend climb a low hill and disappear from view, and that on May 31 was the last glimpse of Jedediah Smith had by any white man. Soon the main party came up, and, pushing on a few miles, reached the north fork of the Cimarron and shallow pools of water which saved the lives of all of them. Long and careful searching yielded no trace of Smith, and after a short rest the party continued on their way. When they reached Santa Fe on July 4, Mexican traders showed them Smith's rifle and silver-mounted pistols, which they had purchased from a band of Comanches. It is probable that his slayers had crept upon Smith as he and his horse were drinking from a pool in the bed of the Cimarron; that one of them had pierced him in the back with a lance, and that, although mortally wounded, he had shot one or more of them with his rifle and pistols before he sank to earth.

All contemporary accounts agree that Smith was a born leader, and there is little doubt that, had length of years been granted him, he would have played a noteworthy part in the history of the West. "He was," writes William Waldo, a fellow trader, "a bold, outspoken, and consistent Christian, the first and only one among the early Rocky Mountain trappers and hunters. No one who knew him well doubted the sincerity of his piety. He had become a communicant of the Methodist Church before leaving his home in New York, and in St. Louis he never failed to occupy a place in the church of his choice, while he gave generously to all objects connected with the religion which he professed and loved. Besides being an adventurer and a hero, a trader and a Christian, he was himself inclined to literary pursuits and had prepared a geography and atlas of the Rocky Mountain region, extending perhaps to the Pacific; but his death occurred before its publication." Despite his years in the wilderness Smith had little love for the life men led there. "Instead of finding a Leatherstocking," writes a young man who saw him in St. Louis in November, 1830, "I met a well-bred, intelligent, and Christian gentleman, who repressed my youthful ardor and fancied pleasures for the life of a trapper and mountaineer by informing me that, if I went into the Rocky Mountains, the chances were much greater in favor of meeting death than of finding restoration to health, and that, if I escaped the former and secured the latter, the probabilities were that I would be ruined for anything else in life than such things as would be agreeable to the passions of a semisavage."

Thomas Fitzpatrick, called by the Indians Broken Hand and later White Hair, was born in Ireland in 1799, and in his seventeenth year came to America. He did not remain long in New York, but soon made his way to the Middle West, where, having at command the fundamentals of a sound education, he found employment as a clerk in the Indian trade, and in the spring of 1823 joined the expedition Ashley was forming for the Yellowstone country. It has already been told how, as second in command to Smith, he played a leading part in the discovery of South Pass.

Fitzpatrick's first sojourn in the mountains covered an unbroken period of seven years. In the course of it he became master of all the arts of the trapper and trader and finally as head of the Rocky Mountain Fur Company directed the most powerful and for a time the most profitable organization of its kind. Soon, however, Fitzpatrick and his associates found their supremacy disputed by the agents and superior resources of the American Fur Company. In the end the concern with the longest purse won, and Fitzpatrick became an employee of his whilom rival, but not before he had placed to his credit one of the most stirring incidents in the history of the fur trade.

At an early stage of his career as a trapper the bursting of a rifle took off a finger and otherwise crippled his left hand. Thereafter he was known to the Indians as Broken Hand. A few years later, when his contest with the American Fur Company was nearing a climax, he one day set out alone from a point in the valley of the Sweetwater, east of South Pass, intent on reaching an appointed rendezvous at Pierre's Hole ahead of his rivals. Using two fleet horses as alternating mounts, and riding at top speed for hours at a stretch, he had crossed South Pass and the Big Sandy and was approaching Green River when he was confronted by a band of Grosventres, and knew that he must race for his life.

Fitzpatrick, always coolest in the hour of imminent peril, loosed one of his horses and on the other headed for a near-by mountain. Halfway up a steep path that led to the summit, his mount gave out under the strain. He abandoned it, and ran on, followed by the Indians, who had also dismounted and left their horses behind them. Finding a hole in the rocks, as his pursuers slowly gained on him, he crept into it, and hastily closed its mouth with sticks and leaves. The Indians passed his hiding place without finding it, and there, with furtive ventures into the open to determine if the coast was clear, he lay for a night and a day.

The second night Fitzpatrick descended the mountain, and, pushing forward until daybreak, concluded that he was beyond the range of pursuit. Hardships of the most trying sort, however, were still ahead of him. He feared to fire his rifle at game, and so pushed on with roots and berries his only food. It was days before, faint and despairing, he fell in with two half-breeds who had been sent from Pierre's Hole to find him; and when, safe in camp, he again looked into a mirror, it was to discover that his hair had turned perfectly white. And in no time to his Indian name of Broken Hand was added that of White Hair.

When his days as a trapper and trader were ended, Fitzpatrick found other important labors awaiting him. In 1835 he guided through South Pass the first missionaries and their wives sent out to Oregon, and six years later he acted as guide to the first emigrant train to follow what was soon to be known as the Oregon Trail. In 1843 he was Frémont's right hand in the Pathfinder's second expedition to the Pacific coast, and in 1846 he guided the Army of the West under Kearny on its march to Santa Fe.

Finally, in August, 1846, Fitzpatrick's pre-eminent fitness prompted his appointment as head of a newly created Indian agency. . . .

70

/His career as Indian agent is described in No. 5, below._7

Kit Carson, ten years younger than Fitzpatrick, who helped train him in wilderness ways, early became the hero of a legend, which, growing with the years, has overshadowed the fame of most of his fellows, and there is little doubt that he was for long easily the most useful man in the Southwest. Born in Madison County, Kentucky, on Christmas Day, 1809, and carried when a babe in arms to the Boone's Lick country of Missouri, he drifted while still a youth to the more remote frontier, and before he was twenty-two trapped in Arizona and parts of California with Ewing Young and the latter's followers.

At Taos in the late summer of 1831 Carson fell in with Fitz-patrick and promptly agreed to accompany him to the northern trap-ping grounds. There he quickly completed his training as a trapper, and until its great days ended about 1838 he was a figure of steadily growing note in the fur trade. One of Carson's recent biographers styles him "the happy warrior," and there is ample evidence that he was ever an eager and buoyant participant in all the labors and pas-times of his fellows. The taking of human life, when occasion demanded, he quietly accepted as an inevitable part of the day's work. He fought a quarrelsome French giant on horseback with pistols, seriously wounding if not killing his antagonist; it is known that before he was thirty-two he had slain nineteen men, and during his latter years he no doubt accounted for as many more; but he never picked a quarrel, and never took life except when his own might have been the price of doubt or delay.

Ruxton gives a graphic picture of Carson in early manhood. "Last in height," writes the Englishman, "but first in every quality that constitutes excellence in a mountaineer, whether of indomitable courage or perfect indifference to death or danger — with an iron frame capable of withstanding hunger, thirst, heat, cold, fatigue, and hardships of every kind — of wonderful presence of mind, and endless resource in time of peril — with the instinct of an animal and the moral courage of a man — who was 'taller' for his inches than Kit Carson, paragon of mountaineers? Small in stature and slenderly limbed, but with muscles of wire, with a fair complexion and quiet intelligent features, to look at Kit none would suppose that the mildlooking being before him was an incarnate devil in an Indian fight, and had raised more hair from head of Redskins than any two men in the western country; and yet thirty winters had scarcely planted a line or a furrow on his clean-shaven face."

Prior to 1832, as already noted, all the finest hats were made of beaver. In that year the silk hat was invented, and slowly yet surely caught and held the fancy of smart dressers on both sides of the sea. As a result the price of beaver fell steadily from year to year; in 1838 the skin that in an earlier time had sold for six dollars commanded only a fraction of that sum, and Carson and his fellow trappers realized that they must find other ways to earn a livelihood. Kit first became buffalo hunter for Bent's Fort, and a few years later — the Indian maiden whom he had early taken to wife without benefit of clergy having become a part of the past — he married a Mexican girl of Taos, which thereafter he regarded as his home. In 1842, and again in 1843, he served as guide to Frémont in the first two exploring expeditions which introduced the western country to the people of the East and won for their leader the title of Pathfinder; and he was Frémont's most trusted lieutenant in the expedition that in 1846 had eventful issue in the conquest of California.

The same year Carson guided Kearny in his march from New Mexico to the Pacific coast. In the winter of 1863-1864, having discharged many sizable jobs in the meanwhile, he captained a party which conquered the Navahos after three governments had failed in efforts to subdue them. To the same period belonged his appointment as agent to the New Mexican Utes, and while discharging the duties of that office he also earned money for the support of his wife and growing family by conducting a ranch on the Rayado, where he bred horses and mules for sale to the government and to traders. His last important public service was performed in November, 1864, when as a colonel of volunteers at the head of 450 odd men in what is known as the battle of Adobe Walls, on the Canadian River in the Panhandle of Texas, he fought and held off three thousand Comanches, Kiowas, and Arapahoes, bent upon the undoing of his command.

Only once during these years did Carson again enjoy to the full the delights of his youth. There is a well-authenticated tradition that in the spring of 1852 he brought together for the last time a group of his old companions of the beaver trail — eighteen in all. They rode from Taos into the mountains, there to trap many skins, for the beaver, unmolested for years, were again plentiful, and by the camp-fire of nights, during wanderings which led them to the Laramie Plains and back again to New Mexico, sang the songs, told the stories, and played the jokes that had delighted them in the days that were gone never to return. Then they disbanded, and in sober silence went their separate ways.

Carson's health, which had long been failing, broke completely in 1868, soon after the death of his wife in childbirth, and, leaving his children in the care of friends, he sought and found at Old Fort Lyon a fitting refuge for his last days. When informed the end was near, he waved aside the warnings of the post physician, ate freely of a favorite dish which he had been told would be fatal to him, and then, calling an old comrade to his bedside, calmly swapped yarns until his breath failed him. His grave is beside that of his Mexican wife at Taos . . . .

FIVE: THOMAS FITZPATRICK — INDIAN AGENT

by LeRoy R. Hafen

The region of future Colorado was still a wilderness area in the decade of the 1850s. In the San Luis Valley a few agricultural villages were settled early in the decade, on Mexican land grants. Here and there a few remnants of the fur-trading population lingered around trading posts like Bent's Fort. But, except for these, the Indians were the sole possessors of the hunting lands of the Rocky Mountain frontier. During the years that followed the Mexican War, the United States government initiated peace negotiations with the plains tribes east of the mountains, hoping to effect a reduction in their raiding of the traffic on the Santa Fe and Oregon trails. Thomas Fitzpatrick, veteran mountain man from the earlier fur era, played a major part in the negotiations. *

* * *

THOMAS FITZPATRICK — INDIAN AGENT

In the early forties, if not before, the Indian frontier along the western border of Missouri, which had been planned as a permanent institution in the days of President Monroe, fell before the pressure of Americans seeking trade or homes in the West. Those great western arteries, the Santa Fe and Oregon trails, were becoming ever more firmly established and travelers upon them, in carrying forward "manifest destiny," refused to consider themselves as intruders on Indian land. If they were breaking laws, let the laws be changed, their plans could not be altered nor their march halted. Hence, as it became more evident that relations with the western Indians must become increasingly complex and intimate, the need for an official representative among the tribes grew more apparent.

— — — — — —

*from LeRoy R. Hafen, "Thomas Fitzpatrick and the First Indian Agency in Colorado" in *The Colorado Magazine*, volume VI (March, 1929), pages 53-62. Used with permission of the State Historical Society of Colorado.

74

For some years there had been agents among the tribes immediately west of the Missouri, but prior to 1846 no agency had existed
among the wild tribes of the far western plains. In this year, however,
the region of the upper Platte and Arkansas was designated an Indian
agency and Thomas Fitzpatrick was appointed as the first agent.

For twenty-five years Fitzpatrick had been one of the outstanding fur men and guides of the Far West. As a young man, fresh from
Ireland, he entered the fur trade with William Ashley in 1822 or 1823,
and lived through the rise and fall of that pioneer industry. In the
forties he was acknowledged as the most famous guide in the Far West.
In 1841 and again in 1842, he led emigrant parties to Oregon; in 1843
he guided Fremont to Oregon and the following year continued with him
back to the states. Kearny engaged him as guide in 1845 for the First
Dragoons on their expedition to South Pass, and returning to Bent's
Fort he became guide to Abert's expedition down the Canadian. In
1846 he was again guide to Kearny, now leading the Army of the West
into New Mexico. It was while in this service that he was apprised of
his appointment as Indian agent. Returning from New Mexico he carried dispatches to Washington and on November 30, 1846, accepted the
appointment and filed his bond.

The appointment gave general satisfaction on the frontier. "A
better selection could not have been made," wrote T. M. Moore,
agent of the Upper Missouri. The St. Louis Reveille commented thus,
"This appointment will give general satisfaction; for, among both the
whites and Indians upon the frontier and the plains, Mr. Fitzpatrick
is deservedly held in high respect — the latter indeed reverence his
person, and, from this fact he has more power to control and restrain
them than even the presence of armed force."

In the spring of 1847 Agent Fitzpatrick set out from St. Louis
on his first official visit to his wards. Joining a detachment of the
First Dragoons at Fort Leavenworth, he journeyed along the Santa Fe
Trail to Pawnee Fork. Here he met traders' caravans which had
recently been attacked by the Comanche. After traveling some few
miles farther west his own party was attacked. Five soldiers were
killed, others wounded, and many of the stock were lost. Thus the
reception of the first Indians of his agency was far from reassuring
to the newly appointed agent.

Fitzpatrick continued with the troops and caravan to Santa Fe and at the earliest opportunity went to Bent's Fort on the Arkansas. Here he found white friends and well-disposed Indians. This famous post had long been a rendezvous for the Cheyenne and Arapaho, William Bent, the proprietor, having himself married a Cheyenne woman. A large band of Cheyenne who were encamped near the fort welcomed the new agent, for they had learned that agents usually distribute presents.

Procuring from the proprietors of this trading establishment a supply of bread and coffee, Fitzpatrick gave the assembled chiefs and braves the expected feast. With preliminaries over he addressed the council, explaining the kind intentions of the government towards peaceful Indians but indicating that plundering Indians would be severely punished. He reminded them of the diminution of the buffalo and advised them to turn their attention toward agriculture. Yellow Wolf, the chief, replied in friendly vein, expressing a peaceful disposition and a desire to be taught agriculture. The Arapaho present joined in a similar expression, but admitted that some of their tribe were already among the marauding Comanche.

In this council there was no thought of the formation of a treaty, only an attempt to promote friendship. Even in this, Fitzpatrick was not overconfident. Long experience had acquainted him with Indian character and made him dubious of great or rapid improvement.

One of the chief requisites for the maintenance of peace among the Indians, declared Fitzpatrick, was the abolition of the liquor traffic. The larger trading companies would gladly lend their support, for they had long since learned the inexpediency of the trade in whiskey, but the petty independent traders were the ones who kept up the trade and debauched the natives. He complained especially of the smuggling operations being conducted across the international boundary of the Arkansas River.

As to the Comanche and Kiowa who during the summer had been attacking trains on the Santa Fe Trail, Fitzpatrick recommended energetic and effective military action. Regarding their activity Colonel Gilpin, after careful inquiry, had estimated the losses sustained from these Indians during the summer of 1847 as "Americans killed, 47;

76

wagons destroyed, 330; stock plundered, 6, 500. " These Indians had asked the Cheyenne and Arapaho to join them, saying the whites were easier to kill than elk or buffalo, and that the spoils of the raid were rich.

"I am well aware, " writes Fitzpatrick, "that the intentions of the government towards the Indians are conciliatory and humane. But those of this country who know not our strength, and attribute our forbearance to dread of their great prowess, must be dealt with in precisely the opposite manner. "

One feels that the Irish agent was instinctively a military man. In his various reports advice on military matters is often presented which in its character reveals a man of positive ideas, with no little knowledge of Indian life and of effective military measures.

During the winter Fitzpatrick employed his best efforts to retain the friendship of the Cheyenne and Arapaho and prevent their joining the Comanche. Not only did he succeed, but was able to draw out from the Comanche some of the Kiowa and induce them to join the friendly Indians.

Late in February, 1848, he left Fort Bent to visit the Indians of his agency on the Platte. On the south fork he met Arapaho and Sioux who expressed friendship and promised peace. To what extent the Indian agent was able to control the liquor trade we do not know, but he does mention taking from a white trader two kegs of whiskey, which he forthwith dumped into the river.

Continuing down the Platte, Fitzpatrick journeyed eastward and reached St. Louis early in June. From here he was called to Washington. His oral report to the Department was supplemented by a written one dated Washington City, August 11. In this he recommended the immediate establishment of a fort on the Oregon and one on the Santa Fe Trail, each to be garrisoned by five hundred mounted troops and equipped with mountain howitzers. A winter campaign against the Comanche in their own country would be most effective, he said. Only ten days before this, Colonel Gilpin, after an indecisive campaign of several months, had written his report from Fort Mann, saying, "All the atrocities of a very severe Indian war may be momentarily looked for, and are certain to burst forth with the early spring." Gilpin had further recommended one thousand mounted troops and six forts for the Arkansas and its flanks, saying, "This is the minimum of force necessary."

Into a region thus threatened, Fitzpatrick was to set out on his second trip to his agency. Before leaving the frontier he made his regular annual report. In it he flayed the action of the troops, saying they had acted almost entirely on the defensive. He again warned the government that the unpunished Indians who had found marauding so profitable would not cease plundering until the government exhibited an ability and a willingness to chastise them.

Leaving St. Louis early in October, 1848, and joining a party of traders at Westport, Fitzpatrick proceeded over the Santa Fe Trail toward Bent's Fort. At Big Timbers on the Arkansas he had a talk with the assembled Indians. It was here that the adventurous Fremont, bound on his tragic fourth expedition, met his onetime guide, and with apparent satisfaction wrote Senator Benton describing Fitzpatrick among six hundred lodges of Apache, Comanche, Kiowa and Arapaho. "He is a most admirable agent," he wrote, "entirely educated for such a post, and possessing the ability and courage necessary to make his education available. He has succeeded in drawing out from among the Comanches the whole Kioway nation, with the exception of six lodges, . . . I hope you will be able to give him some support. He will be able to save lives and money for the government, ... In a few years he might have them all farming here on the Arkansas."

Of the detailed work of Fitzpatrick during the winter of 1848-49 we know little. He held several "big talks" with the Indians about Bent's Fort and assisted in securing the freedom of certain Mexican captives held among the tribes. In March, 1849, he again turned eastward. At the Big Bend of the Arkansas he met a Santa Fe bound caravan in charge of his friend, Solomon Sublette. To him he spoke of his plan to go east and ask for authorization to make a treaty with the plains Indians.

In August, 1849, Superintendent Mitchell ordered Fitzpatrick to Washington to urge in person the advisability of holding a general council with the prairie tribes. That his plan met with favor is evidenced by the sequel. He returned to St. Louis within the month with certain instructions. Five thousand dollars was provided for purchase of presents to be distributed by him among the Indians, and arrangements were made for a great council during the summer of 1850. In pursuance of the treaty plan, Superintendent Mitchell, the Indian Commissioner, and the Secretary of the Interior, each recommended in his annual report the advisability of negotiating a treaty with the prairie tribes. To the same end Senator Atchison, of Missouri, introduced a bill on March 18, 1850, authorizing an expenditure of $200,000 for effecting the purpose.

Thus Fitzpatrick returned to his agency in November, 1849, bearing with him presents and telling the Indians that their Great Father in Washington was planning to hold a great council with them the following summer. After a sojourn with the tribes during the winter he returned eastward by way of the Arkansas. At Big Timbers and again at Fort Mann he waited among the assembled tribes hoping for instructions or definite news from the east. Finally he disbanded the Indians and continued to St. Louis, only to learn that the expected law had failed of enactment. It was a keen disappointment to the agent and in his report of September 24, 1850, he stated that the Indians of that country would never again be found in better mood for treaty-making, and warned that the postponing of such matters would have a very bad effect on them.

The treaty plan met with better success at the hands of Congress in the session of 1850-51. The law of February 27, 1851, appropriated $100,000 "for expenses of holding treaties with the wild tribes of the prairie and for bringing delegates on to the seat of government." Plans could now go forward with official sanction and backing. Superintendent Mitchell and Agent Fitzpatrick were duly appointed official commissioners of the United States to negotiate a treaty with the prairie nations, and arrangements were made for execution of the project. Fitzpatrick was to go ahead, acquaint the Indians with the plan, and invite the tribes to assemble at Fort Laramie on September 1.

Westward on the Santa Fe Trail he went carrying the good news. Near the site of Fort Mann the Indians of the region were assembled and his message was given, but it did not meet with the favor hoped for. The Comanche, Kiowa, and Apache refused outright to go so far from their own country among so many strange Indians, stating with candor that they "had too many horses and mules to risk on such a journey, and among such notorious horse thieves as the Sioux and Crows." The Cheyenne and Arapaho, however, agreed to go to the meeting-place and immediately began preparations. Fitzpatrick continued through the agency inviting all Indians met with to come to the council.

Superintendent Mitchell, with an escort of Dragoons, came up the Oregon Trail after seeing that the Indian goods for the treaty council were loaded at the river. Upon reaching Fort Laramie on the last of August he found great numbers of Indians already assembled. A site at the mouth of Horse Creek, some thirty-five miles below the fort, was chosen as the treaty ground. Thither they all moved and the council opened with the firing of cannon and the raising of the flag on September 8.

It was the largest and one of the most important Indian councils ever held in the Far West. The Cheyenne, Arapaho, Snakes and several branches of the Sioux were there en masse, while the Assiniboin, Gros Ventres, Aricara and Crows were represented by delegations. Ten thousand Indians were present, and when rigged out in colorful regalia they made the council an exhibition and country fair as well as a peace meeting. . . . on the 17th the treaty was finally agreed to and the formal signing occurred. It provided for a lasting peace among the signatory tribes and with the whites; recognized the right of the United States to establish roads and military posts in the Indian territory; made depredations by Indians or whites punishable, and restitution obligatory; fixed the boundaries of the territory of the respective tribes; and provided for the payment of annuities of $50,000 in goods for a term of fifty years.

On the 20th the train of twenty-seven wagons arrived with the presents, and the goods were distributed. Father DeSmet wrote: "The great chiefs were, for the first time in their lives, pantalooned; each was arrayed in a general's uniform, a gilt sword hanging at his side. Their long, coarse hair floated above the military costume, and the whole was crowned by the burlesque solemnity of their painted faces." On the second day the distributions were completed and the Indian villages began to move off.

To impress the tribes with the white man's numbers and cities, a delegation of representative Indians was chosen to visit Washington under Fitzpatrick's escort. Superintendent Mitchell carried eastward the treaty for presentation to the United States Senate. Subsequently, when considered by the Upper House, that august body in its wisdom cut down the term of the treaty from fifty to fifteen years and the formality of a ratification of the change was later bribed from most of the signatory tribes.

In the summer of 1852, Fitzpatrick again visited his agency, carrying with him $30,000 worth of goods to be distributed as annuities . . . .

In the spring of 1853, Fitzpatrick was called to Washington and was appointed sole commissioner on the part of the United States to negotiate a treaty with the wild Comanche, Kiowa and Apache who had refused to treat at Fort Laramie, and had never yet had treaty relations with the United States. Having sent messengers ahead to call in the tribes, Fitzpatrick found large numbers assembled upon his arrival at Fort Atkinson. Three of the largest bands of the Comanche and Apache were assembled en masse, while the Kiowa were represented by their principal chiefs.

"At first," wrote Fitzpatrick, "almost insurmountable difficulties presented themselves, in the distant and suspicious bearing of the chiefs, and the utter impossibility of obtaining any interpreters who understood their intricate languages. But little intercourse had ever existed between them and the white race, and that usually of the most unfriendly character . . . ." But finally the Indians were induced to bring forth some of their Mexican prisoners and through the medium of the Spanish language communication was established.

Fitzpatrick remarked the keen intelligence with which these desert warriors replied to propositions submitted to them. A right of way through their territory — a privilege already long enjoyed — was readily assented to, but on matters such as establishment of military posts and cessation of hostilities against Mexico more vigorous opposition was encountered. The treaty, as finally agreed upon, bound the three tribes to maintain peace among themselves and the United States. It recognized the right of the United States to lay off roads,

81

locate depots for railroad purposes, and establish military posts in the region . . . .

The usual inducement for signing the agreement was at hand in the form of presents. When the chiefs had marked their respective crosses on the treaty, the distribution of goods took place. Gay trappings for the chiefs, blankets, beads, trinkets, and the whole gamut of Indian goods, useful or ornamental, were passed out and produced the usual effect of jollity, good will, and expressions of good intentions.

This mission successfully performed, Fitzpatrick set out from Fort Atkinson to visit other of his wards, get the changes in the Fort Laramie Treaty ratified, and distribute the annuities.

As he journeyed up the Arkansas he was impressed, perhaps more than ever before, with the good soil and rank vegetation along the stream. In several respects he was the advance agent of a new day for this region. In the heart of the area which Major Long had labeled the "Great American Desert" he saw the dawn breaking. "My course led through rich alluvial bottom lands," he wrote, "rank with vegetation, and skirted heavily with cottonwood, near the margin of the stream. Fine soils prevail in these low grounds; and on the high table lands a short but nutritious grass affords excellent grazing, and will cause this country to be some day much prized for pastoral purposes." He thus saw the great cattle herds that were to speck the plains two or three decades hence, even though he may not have visioned fully the day and reign of the cantaloupe and the sugar beet.

From the Pueblo he turned northward up Fountain Creek and crossed the divide to the South Platte drainage. Again the gray-haired pioneer peered into the future. "Indications of mineral wealth," he wrote, "abound in the sands of the water courses, and the gorges and canons from which they issue; and should public attention ever be strongly directed to this section of our territory, and free access be obtained, the inducements which it holds out will soon people it with thousands of citizens, and cause it to rise speedily into a flourishing mountain state." He spoke almost better than he knew, for following his track but five years after, came the famous Russell party of prospectors who panned gold from these same streams and inaugurated the famous stampede which had "Pike's Peak or Bust" as its motto.

Here speedily arose the "mountain state" he visioned, assuming first the name of Jefferson, and then that of Colorado.

In the vicinity of Fort St. Vrain he met the Cheyenne and Arapaho, gave them their annuities and induced them to accept the Senate amendments to the Fort Laramie treaty. Continuing northward he met the Sioux at Fort Laramie and a similar procedure was followed.

Now turning his face to the east and leaving for the last time the far western mountains and plains that for thirty years had been his home, he journeyed down the Platte and to St. Louis. Here he wrote his last report, paragraphs of which are in the spirit of a valedictory. "After mature reflection, . . . I am constrained to think that but one course remains which promises any permanent relief to them (the Indians), . . . That is simply to make such modifications in the 'intercourse laws' as will invite the residence of traders amongst them, and open the whole Indian territory to settlement . . . . Trade is the only civilizer of the Indian. It has been the precursor of all civilization heretofore, and it will be of all hereafter. It teaches the Indian the value of other things besides the spoils of the chase, and offers to him other pursuits and excitement than those of war."

In the winter of 1853-54 Fitzpatrick was ordered to Washington for consultation relative to the treaty he had negotiated with the Comanche, Kiowa, and Apache. It was while on this mission that he died of pneumonia in Washington, February 7, 1854.

SIX: THE GOLD RUSH

by James F. Willard

In 1848-1849 the people of the United States experienced the excitement of the first large-scale gold rush in their nation's history when the precious metal, in quantity, was discovered in the newly-won province of California. After that, any rumor of gold in the western reaches could be believed. When, exactly a decade later, news of gold discoveries in the Pike's Peak region began to appear in newspaper columns, the "Rush to the Rockies" began. That which the Spaniards had sought and failed to find, now brought to the Colorado region its first sizable white population, and ushered in a new era.*

*   *   *

THE GOLD RUSH

Small quantities of placer gold had been found from time to time in what is now the State of Colorado before the discoveries that led to the gold rush of 1858-1859. William Gilpin, who had visited the mountains with Frémont and who later became Territorial Governor of Colorado, had told stories of gold in the Rockies to an unmoved world; others had found gold, though little of it, and then, in 1858, wise after the event, told of their discoveries. Some men doubtless invented their tales in order to share in the publicity given to the early Peakers. As none of these finds of gold led to active exploitation of the streams and mountains they may be left without further mention in this brief sketch.

The movement toward the Rocky Mountains in search of gold owed its origin to the reputed great success of a company that reached the district surrounding the present site of Denver in June, 1858. This

*from James F. Willard, "The Gold Rush and After" in *Colorado: Short Studies of Its Past and Present,* by Junius Henderson and others, Boulder, 1927, pages 101-116, 121. Used with permission of the University of Colorado Press.

company, composed of Georgians, Missourians, Kansans and Cherokee Indians, is known in Colorado history as the Russell Company. Shortly after this company reached the mountains another, of independent origin, known as the Lawrence Company, reached the vicinity of Pike's Peak in search of gold. The movement that followed was stimulated by hard times in the Mississippi Valley, the result of the panic of 1857.

It is necessary to keep in mind when reading of the movements of the early gold hunters that they did not enter into an entirely unknown land. Nor did they venture into an uninhabited wilderness. There were a number of trappers and traders in the Rocky Mountains and along their eastern slope. There was one trading post, Bent's Fort, near Pike's Peak. By Fort Laramie, which lay to the north of the gold region, went the wagons of emigrants bound for Utah or the Northwest and the fort with traders, trappers, and visiting Indians formed a centre of gossip for the mountain district. Along the Arkansas by Bent's Fort went a part of the Santa Fé trade. What is more there was cross traffic between the northern and southern routes along the base of the mountains. When the early companies reached the foothills of the Rockies they met mountain men from whom they learned the names of the streams and of the peaks. After they had discovered gold these same mountain men and other wayfarers carried the news to Fort Laramie from whence it sped down river to the towns of the Missouri Valley and westward to Utah. Others carried the news to Taos and the New Mexican country. To one who reads of the rapidity with which the news spread it seems as though within the snowy range of the mountains there was a powerful station broadcasting in every direction hundreds of miles across the hills and mountain valleys.

The Russell Company journeyed toward the mountains to investigate a report of gold found at Ralston Creek. The reason why that particular stream formed their goal is not easy to discover. Rumors of gold in the Rockies were afloat in the Missouri Valley in 1857, but they were far from definite. The Lawrence Company which was influenced by these rumors went to Pike's Peak to find gold. It may be that the Russell Company owed its more definite information to John Beck, a Cherokee Indian and a returned Californian who had been to the base of the mountains and found gold there. Whatever the reason William Green Russell and his brothers decided in 1857 to organize a company to prospect for gold during the following summer. The Russells got together a party in Georgia, Beck organized a group of Cherokees and a few white men in the Indian Territory, and a small party was formed in Missouri of men from Ray and Bates counties and a scattering few from elsewhere. These parties came together in May and June, 1858, on the southern route to the mountains. Luke Tierney, one of the members of the company gives the total number of gold seekers as one hundred and four and divides them as follows: Georgia, 19; Missouri, 27; Cherokee Nation, 58.

On the twenty-fourth in the evening, or the twenty-fifth of June, the former is Tierney's statement, the company reached its destination, Ralston Creek, near the present site of Denver. "Here," writes Tierney, "according to the statements of the returned Californians, we were in the immediate vicinity of the gold mines." The members of the company prospected the region and were promptly disillusioned, for they found only a few particles of gold. Several days of anxious search brought no better results and the majority of the men were so discouraged by the fourth of July that they determined to return home. They went, leaving about thirty to continue the search. This number was soon reduced to thirteen and this small group, known as the Georgia Company, made the first discoveries of gold in reasonably paying quantity. Gold was found in several places but the name of Cherry Creek was prominent in the stories carried to the outside world despite the fact that it yielded little placer gold. It was the news of these discoveries in July that spread through the mountains and the Missouri Valley and caused the excitement of the autumn months. Curiously enough Oliver P. Goodwin is reported in the Weekly Kansas Herald of the twenty-fourth of July as having arrived on the preceding Wednesday, from Fort Bridger with the following news: "On the head waters of the South Fork of Platte, near Long's Peak, gold mines have been discovered and 500 persons are now working there." The distorted news of the earliest meagre finds of the Russell Company had found a credulous host.

The Lawrence Company was organized in April, 1858, and left the city on the 24th and 25th of May for Pike's Peak. Following the southern route it arrived at Bent's Fort on the 28th of June. On the fifth of July the company met two wagons of the Russell Company deserters and learned from them the discouraging results of the first expedition. During the months of July and August they prospected in the southern part of the reputed gold region. Hearing of the discoveries on the South Platte they moved northward and arrived at the new diggings on the second of September. William B. Parsons, one of the company, tells the story: "There we found five or six men engaged in mining, and, although they had very inferior tools, they were making respectable wages. We immediately went to work, and found that although things had been considerably exaggerated, we could do well, and had a good prospect for the future."

Gold had been found in the streams near the present site of Denver in July and the following weeks and it did not take long for the news to reach the Missouri Valley. The exaggerated account from the Weekly Kansas Herald, quoted above, seems to have received no attention in the papers. Then in August came more definite news. The Missouri Republican, of St. Louis, published an item from the St. Joseph Gazette on the twenty-fifth of August on discoveries near Fort Laramie, and doubted the story. Four days later the same paper published a despatch from Kansas City dated August 26 chronicling the arrival of Monsieur Bordeau and party from Pike's Peak. They came for outfits to work in the mines on Cherry Creek. A few days more and most of the doubters were silenced, for a letter came down from a man who had visited the mines, a specimen of gold was brought into Rulo, Nebraska, and Mr. John Cantrell arrived in person with three ounces "which he dug with a hatchet in Cherry Creek and washed out with a frying pan."

There was immediate and unreasoning excitement in the river towns for times were still hard in the valley and the New Eldorado promised relief from all financial worries. Some of the earlier reports promised great riches. On the thirty-first of August the St. Louis Republican sent forth to the world the story, emanating from Leavenworth, that two men had "washed out $600 in one week." Much less modest sums were soon to figure in the newspapers.

As the news spread men from the relatively near-by points of Fort Laramie and the towns in New Mexico and Utah hastened to the mines. Then the more distant towns of the Missouri Valley fell into line. Mr. Buttan, a member of the Lawrence party, left the mines on the twentieth of September and reported that there were already about one hundred men there and more arriving daily. He stated that on his way down he met from seven hundred to one thousand emigrants. This statement is found in the Lawrence Republican of the 28th of October. There are notices of parties forming and departing from various places in Kansas, Nebraska, Missouri, Iowa, Ohio, and even far away Michigan. In several instances a member of the company agreed to write to the home paper about the adventures of the group. William O'Donnall wrote of the activities of a second Lawrence Company, General William Larimer about the Leavenworth men, and A. A. Brookfield and others about the Nebraska City boys. Some of these men continued to write during the winter and ensuing spring. There were many volunteer correspondents. Thus the western country was kept well informed of the progress of the first migration.

With the advance of cold weather there was a cessation in the movement westward, and the same weather conditions caused a number of the gold seekers to leave the mines. They came down to the Missouri Valley towns to purchase supplies for the next season or because they had had enough of placer mining and all its ways. The optimists were in the majority and some of them told great tales. Mr. Cantrell said that he could make $17 to $20 a day with pick and pan; others reported $10 to $30 a day as the results of their mining; but the usual estimates of returns ran from $3 or $5 to $10 or $12 a day, with emphasis upon the larger sums. The largest sum reported as having been taken by an individual in the mines was $6,000, and $3,000 and $2,000 were also mentioned. It is perhaps unnecessary to add that these large sums were purely apocryphal and that the large sum noted would probably cover all the gold washed out by all the miners during the autumn and early winter months. However, gold was brought down from the mines, flake gold as it was called, shown to everyone on the way, and later exhibited in drug stores, newspaper offices and saloons. Who could doubt the stories when they had actually seen and handled the gold dust? The newspapers spread the glad tidings and everywhere in the West and Middle West men began to prepare for the spring migration to Cherry Creek. Some of the discontented who had been to the mines and had found the situation there far from roseate, called the whole affair a humbug, even a damned humbug. They were answered with vigor by the optimists; the newspaper editors of the river towns were glad to support the cause of the latter, for a great migration meant prosperity to the merchants in the struggling settlements on the Missouri.

The late winter months were spent in preparation for the spring rush to the mining district. Companies were organized not only in the Missouri Valley but also throughout the region east of the Mississippi. The newspapers were full of sage advice concerning the proper outfits for the prospective miners. Guides and maps of the routes were published. Of the guides, that issued by William B. Parsons in Lawrence during the month of December seems to have been the earliest. Others followed. The maps were more or less accurate according to the knowledge or bias of their makers. As many of the maps were local products, issued in order to attract attention to one town and one route, they were at times very indefinite in their designation of other towns and routes. A map drawn up by E. L. Berthoud in Leavenworth shows the various routes, but of the rival towns notes only Lawrence. The Lawrence Republican of the third of March, 1859, grew indignant over the entire omission of Lawrence from Pearman's map of the gold regions. Each of the river towns put forward a claim during the winter and spring to be the best outfitting point for the prospective miners. Even St. Louis, far down the river, modestly claimed that its goods were the cheapest and that the up-river merchants charged exorbitant prices for everything they had to sell.

The battle of the routes, which was directly connected with outfitting, was one of the most interesting events of the period preceding and following the opening of the spring migration. Though bloodless it was of vital interest to all concerned. The various towns lying on the Missouri as it turns to the north could be reached by steamboat or railroad, and then arose the problem of the selection of the route westward. From the southern part of the bend of the river there led the Southern Route by the Santa Fé road, and also by way of Kansas and Smoky Hill Fork, the Smoky Hill route. From points farther north there lay the route by the Republican Fork and the Northern or Platte Route. Each town claimed the best or shortest road to Fort Riley or Fort Kearney, which were the assembling points on these routes, and then expatiated on the advantages of the roads to the mines. Nebraska City made much of its Great Central Route to Fort Kearney and unquestionably it stood at one end of the shortest route from the Missouri to the fort. Most of the towns laid emphasis upon the cheapness of their supplies and the advantages of their western route. Atchison and St. Joseph favored the North Route; Lawrence the Smoky Hill Route and Kansas City the Southern Route. The battle went on merrily during

the winter and spring over the distance to the mines, the condition
of the roads, the best supplies of wood, water, and grass. Then the
Peakers came and decided the matter for themselves. Leavenworth,
from which men could take with comfort any but the Northern route,
and they could even go by that highway, had, if not the best arguments,
at least the greatest success in the warfare. Soon its position as an
outfitting and starting point was made doubly secure by its selection
as the eastern end of the route followed by the Leavenworth and Pike's
Peak Express. This stage line chose a route almost midway between
the Republican and Smoky Hill routes, avoiding so it was thought the
disadvantages of each.

While the merchants laid in stores, the wheelwrights built wagons
and the newspapers wrangled over the merits of their respective routes.
At the same time companies were organizing in the East preparatory to
the spring migration as soon as the roads opened and the steamers could
bring them to their starting points. While all this excitement prevailed
in the "States" the miners in the West settled down for the winter.

A considerable number of the men who had reached the mines in
the late summer or autumn returned to the valley as winter approached,
but many remained to mine a little, to form towns and build houses, to
take up farms, and to discuss mining and politics when they could not
work. It is clear that mining languished during the winter, but that
house and town building flourished. Scores and even hundreds of log
cabins were built in the new towns, not only for the accommodation of
the builders, but also to sell or rent to the men who were sure to come
in the spring. Of the towns the earliest was Montana, the work of the
Lawrence men. It was started early in September, 1858, on the Platte
to the north of the Denver of today. During the following months
Auraria, St. Charles and Denver City were all founded on the present
site of Denver. Arapahoe City was laid out near the site of the present Golden and El Paso to the south where Colorado City now stands.
El Dorado City and Fountain City both in the southern district were
begun and to the north in February Boulder City started on its career.
In connection with the latter event A. A. Brookfield, one of the founders
wrote in March, 1859, "I did not come out here for town speculation but
after we made what are considered by far the best discoveries of the
'precious metal' we thought as the weather would not permit us to mine,
we would lay out and commence building what may be an important town,

90

provided the mines prove of the richness we expect." Though some of the miners had left for home, while others had gone to Laramie, or to the building of the old St. Vrain's Fort, even to New Mexico, there remained in the mining district during the winter about five hundred of the more optimistic or the more farsighted. Mining might not pay well, but house building had a potential value and selling shares in the town companies was attractive and might prove remunerative.

The first groups of the gold hunters of the spring migration were those formed in the Missouri Valley towns. As early as February, 1859, a small company called a "packing company", using Indian ponies instead of wagons for the transportation of their goods, left Lawrence for Cherry Creek. In March the rush began, despite the warning of old timers, and increased in volume during the months of April and May. What a rush it was! Every boat that came up the river to the starting points was filled with Peakers. As they landed they were greeted by the merchants, or runners for the merchants, who wished to sell them rifles, provisions, mining utensils, tents, oxen, the inevitable whiskey, and all other things needed on the plains and in the mines. The pages of the newspapers bore startling or attractive Pike's Peak advertisements of all sorts and, so it is said, in Leavenworth and elsewhere, hotels, saloons, and other establishments, by their signs and placards, tried to draw to themselves the attention of the gold seekers. Many of the latter placed the slogan Pike's Peak on the sides of their wagons and so carried the tale across the plains.

By the several routes a motely lot of men and conveyances started toward the mines in the spring of 1859. The earlier gold seekers had been organized into companies and had set forth in the dignified large wagon, with its white top, drawn by oxen or mules. The men who went out in the rush of the following spring were in a hurry; they went in companies or small groups and many were without the money with which to purchase an expensive outfit. So there were all kinds of means of conveyance from the prairie schooner to the pack on the back of a pedestrian. There are many references to the heavy and slow wagon. Along side of these went light wagons of various sorts drawn by horses or mules. Some men rode on horseback across the plains. There were many hand carts, large and small, drawn by the Peakers themselves. Most of these seem to have had crews of eight men, serving two at a time. A hand cart is thus described in April: "The cart is constructed pretty much after the fashion of a 'go-cart', only being minus the legs or supports in front to keep it level while standing. A cross-piece is attached to the ends of the shafts, while the space between is occupied by the locomotive powers, who push against the cross-rod." In most cases, however, the hand carts are said to have been pulled or drawn. A few men pushed wheelbarrows with all their worldly goods loaded on them. There are at least two references to light wagons drawn by dogs toward the mines. Decidedly the most curious conveyance invented was the Westport Wind Wagon. With wheels some twenty feet in diameter, and large sails, its omnibus body was to accommodate over twenty people. It is perhaps needless to say that it was a failure. The number of men who started for the mines with handbags, black carpetbags, or packs on their backs was large, how large it is impossible to state. One contemporary observer writes: "Those who observed the character of this emigration this spring, must have noticed the vast number who were totally unprepared for an expedition of this kind. A black carpetbag, an extra pair of boots, and a substantial suit of clothes, with, in every case almost, a rifle and gun, and perhaps six-shooter, generally constituted their outfit for a trip of one thousand miles. Of mining implements, or anything to aid in separating the particles of gold from the earth, the exhibition was a scanty one." Through the accounts of and by the Peakers there runs a thread of exaggeration and burlesque, yet even sober observers were wont to lay stress upon the bizarre equipment of many of the emigrants and upon the medley of means of transportation. Many observers record that, by the month of May, an emigrant train was but rarely out of sight of others either to the east or the west.

The goal of most of the emigrants was the Cherry Creek district, though some were attracted by the mines to the north and south. When they reached Denver City or Auraria in April and May they found towns with many log houses, a number of saloons and stores. These, like the other towns of the mining district were decidedly frontier towns with the roughness and enthusiasm of their kind. The residents of the embryonic cities were glad to greet the newcomers and to sell them town lots and whatever they might need. Some of the Peakers were convinced that the majority of the inhabitants of Denver and Auraria were speculators in town lots. One who returned home in May is reported to have stated that, "As soon as he and his party arrived at

Denver City they were surrounded by town speculators, all eager to make them rich by selling them lots at low figures. This seems to be the whole and sole business of the inhabitants of Denver City and Auraria". Allowing for the exaggeration of a disappointed gold hunter, the rivalry between the Denver City and Auraria lot-holders seems to have been intense. In the month of May, when the hopes of many of the men who were seeking gold had been dashed to the ground, there was much disorder in the frontier towns. Prices were high, provisions scarce and hard times the order of the day. The disillusioned, who had expected to reap a rich harvest with little effort, were discontented and ripe for disorder.

From the towns the gold seekers went to the mines in the vicinity. The methods of placer mining used by those who had reached the mines during the autumn and early winter were crude and unsatisfactory. What is more most of the men were inexperienced. The usual plan of operations was that of pick, shovel, and pan, and the pans were those used in cooking. From the start the yield of gold was estimated by the pan. In October, 1858, it is reported that James Rooker had made a rough rocker out of a split hollow log and that he was doing well. In November the Russell Company is said to have been using quicksilver. More rough log rockers are mentioned before the winter set in. During the winter many long sluices and the shorter Long Tom, which was a sluice box, were made in the mining district. The spring migration brought many men unprepared for mining despite the efforts of the stores in the border towns to sell them a complete equipment including Long Toms, rockers, and gold pans. But by that time a large number were using better implements, even hydraulic pumps and pipe lines, and quicksilver.

The gold that was found was placer gold, called scale, float or drift gold. It was very fine and was found in the creek beds and in the South Platte bottom. The broad and sandy beds of the rivers and streams flowing out of the mountains offered a wide field of operations. In these beds the miners dug trenches or holes seeking for the bed rock above which the gold was found. The estimates of the depth at which the gold bearing sand or "dirt" was found vary from two to fifteen feet. As the streams were small in the spring the miners had often to carry their pans of "dirt" many yards before they reached the water needed for washing it. By the winter at least claims were staked out, the usual size, so it is stated, being fifty by one hundred feet.

Mining was hard work, much harder work than that to which many of the emigrants were accustomed, and it was soon found that it did not pay. After a day's labor in April and May a miner might have but a few cents to show for all his pains. When the first day's yield was matched by that of several more the men became discouraged. Mr. Barney, who arrived in May, describes his own experience with his usual inimitable humor: "I have had three day's experience in gold digging. The first didn't reach the auriferous color, though I washed about a thousand panfuls. The second day about the same number with a shade of yellow dirt, which inspired courage. Third day, near as I can judge, having no means of measuring or weighing, I secured about the sixteenth part of a new cent's worth of the genuine article". To most, not gifted with Barney's sense of humor, such a result was a tragedy. With little or no money, their hopes blasted, the disappointed men turned back toward home. To the Missouri Valley came the news that the Pike's Peak gold region was a humbug and this news was reinforced late in April and in May by the appearance of those who had failed to make their fortunes.

The return of the miners, which began in April, 1859, was a stampede in May. Down the routes went disappointed and angry men who spread the bad news as they traveled. A few went down the Platte in small flatbottomed boats. To the men on their way to the mines the news they received from the returning miners spelled disaster and many gave up long before they came in sight of the mountains. Those who went on had hardships to face, for a large number were unprepared for a long journey. Along the Smoky Hill Route especially there was suffering and even starvation. The month of May seemed, therefore, to mark the beginning of the end of the gold excitement. Even the optimistic editors of the papers in the river towns began to doubt the richness of the mines and some were convinced that the Pike's Peak bubble had "busted".

At the time when the discouragement of the gold seekers was approaching its nadir there came the news of discoveries of exceeding richness in the mountains. Many of the early miners had noticed, as they worked up the streams toward the foothills, that there was or

94

seemed to be more gold dust. They had, therefore, predicted that with the coming of spring the rich deposits would be found in the Rockies. A few had ventured into the mountains in the autumn and winter in an attempt to verify these predictions only to be deterred by the snow and ice. It remained for George A. Jackson and John H. Gregory to realize the hopes of the miners.

During the first week of May there came to the towns in the mining district first rumors and then direct evidence of the discoveries of Jackson and Gregory. Jackson's Diggings were what were called bar diggings, true placer mines, and were located on Chicago Creek as it empties into Clear Creek at Idaho Springs. Gregory's discovery was made on the hillside of a small ravine between the present Black Hawk and Central City in the valley of the North Fork of Clear Creek. The mines there were called quartz mines. The miners found at first rotten or disintegrated quartz on the sides of the hills and worked downwards along the lodes until they reached the hard rock. Then their troubles began. Up to that time they broke up the loose quartz, carried the ore in sacks or otherwise down to the streams, washed it in sluices and collected the gold with the aid of quicksilver. Of the two districts Gregory's became immediately the more renowned and was the goal of the majority of the gold hunters.

The news of the new discoveries caused the desertion of the little towns along the mountains by their inhabitants. Then, rather slowly at first, the glad tidings were carried down the routes. On the tenth of June the Pike's Peak Express coach reached Leavenworth. On that day the Leavenworth Times issued an extra. In it under the heading IMMENSE GOLD DISCOVERIES! PIKE'S PEAK A GLORIOUS REALITY! was printed a long letter from Henry Villard telling of the discoveries, of the rush to the Gregory district, and of the marvelous yields of the quartz leads. Gregory himself is said to have taken out $1,100 in five days. From Leavenworth the news was sent by telegraph to St. Louis and from there to the East. Though some editors were sceptical because of what had happened before, the arrival of gold dust in fairly large quantities soon dispelled their doubts. The march of the Peakers to the Rockies was resumed.

The population of the mountain mining region grew by leaps and bounds. When William N. Byers, editor of the Rocky Mountain News, reached the Gregory Diggings on the twentieth of May, he found about twenty men there and only two quartz leads had been opened. About two weeks later he estimated that there were about three thousand men in the mines, about thirty leads satisfactorily prospected, and several hundred claims being worked. Henry Villard, writing on the eleventh of June, states that there were about six thousand men in the mountains. During the following weeks the estimates run as high as ten thousand men and in July one observer notes that there were about fifteen thousand in the mountain districts. The hillsides were in the first weeks dotted with the tents or rude shacks of the miners, but cabins quickly appeared. Horace Greeley visited the Gregory Diggings in early June and notes in his Overland Journey that about one hundred cabins were being built and "three or four hundred in immediate contemplation". "As yet", he adds, "the entire population of the valley sleep in tents, or under booths of pine boughs, cooking and eating in the open air. I doubt that there is as yet a table or chair in these diggings, eating being done around a cloth spread on the ground, while each one sits or reclines on mother earth". Sluices lined the creeks, to which the busy miners carried their loads of "dirt". In the midst of the Gregory Diggings, Mountain City was founded late in May. It is described in June as containing over two hundred dwellings. "The pine trees are being levelled to the ground, streets opened, and the axe and hammer sounding in every direction . . .". Stores appeared, saloons and gambling houses, hotels, express offices and a printing office. Lawyers' and physicians' signs were hung up. Town life had invaded the mining district. Within a short time Central City, the successor of Mountain City, was an established town with substantial buildings and a prosperous air. The foundations of several considerable fortunes were laid in the district about it.

While many succeeded in the mines, and while there are verified stories of rich yields, there were numerous cases of failure. James Robinson and five other men reached the mines late in May. In Jackson's Diggings they worked for six days and made just six cents. In the Gregory Diggings they averaged twenty-five cents a day. Others had similar tales to tell. One man reported that the "mines will not pay as well as staying at home with one's wife". The work of mining was hard work, the leads though numerous, were not sufficient to provide everyone in the crowded district with a paying claim, and many miners did not know how to get out the gold. Byers writing from Omaha on the tenth of July, advised no one to think of going to the mines without serious consideration. But many lazy, ignorant or thoughtless persons went, failed and returned to their homes in the autumn of the year 1859, went to work for other men, or went off to other diggings.

Within a very short time after the opening of the mining districts in the mountains it was found that some sort of organization must be adopted if confusion in the matter of claims was to be avoided. On the ninth of May a miners' meeting was called in the Jackson Diggings. The assembled miners drew up a set of by-laws regulating the size of claims, and the method of marking them. Officers were chosen. On the eighth of June the miners in the Gregory Diggings met, defined the boundaries of their district, and passed a series of resolutions relating to claims, water rights and the settlement of disputes. * On the sixteenth a more formal set of laws was adopted. During the winter months a miners' court was created. Other mining districts were quickly formed with codes of laws, elected officers and courts. The names of most of the districts were undistinguished. Some were named after the original discoverers, Jackson, Gregory, and Russell, others were given place names, Pleasant Valley and Spring Gulch, while still others were named Wisconsin, Bay State, Eureka, Independent. The Shirt Tail District, in Clear Creek County, bears a name that carries with it the flavor of pioneer days. As the months passed the codes of law became more comprehensive. At times considerable attention was devoted to criminal matters. It is interesting to note that some districts excluded lawyers from practicing in the courts, and that some forbade saloons or gambling halls within their limits. There was a strain of puritanism in the mining camps at first along side of the independence and wild ways that charm present day writers of western tales.

Though the interest of the miners during the year 1859 was first centered about Cherry Creek and later in the districts just noted, there was a considerable broadening of the field of mining operations as the year passed. Both the early and late discoveries already described soon failed to satisfy the desires of the multitude. What is more the original districts were soon overcrowded. There was,

— — — — — —

*These resolutions are included in Number Eight, below.

therefore, a considerable number of unemployed or adventurous spirits, men ready to move anywhere in response to the news of rich finds and almost as ready to give up quickly if their hopes of quick returns were not realized. There were several minor stampedes during the year in consequence of the presence of these men in the camps.

Early in the year "shot" gold, which was coarser than "flake" or "float" gold, was found in Boulder Creek. So a number of miners went there. A. A. Brookfield wrote from Boulder City on March sixth "Our mines are all the talk of Auraria and Denver". The Boulder placer mines like many others soon disappointed the miners. As the spring advanced the miners continued to move into the mountains and in June quartz gold was discovered in Gold Hill. The Horsfal lode proved to be rich and the district prospered.

During the spring months some men crossed the Continental Divide into South Park and as early as May there were stories of shot gold there, but also of frozen ground and cold weather. Gold was soon found across the range in paying quantities on the South Fork of the South Platte, near where Como stands, near at hand at Fairplay, on the Blue River near the present Breckenridge, and on the Swan River. These were all placer mines and some of them proved to be rich. The news of the discoveries in South Park, on the headwaters of the Platte, came to Denver and the mining camps late in July and there was great excitement. More reports arrived and one writer reports that on his arrival in Denver City on the sixteenth of August "The whole community was in a perfect stir in regard to the new discoveries on the head of the South Platte and Colorado." The emigration across the Divide was estimated by the same writer to number about five thousand men, of which number all but about five hundred returned. As it was with this migration so it was with most of the others. When rumors of returns as large as one hundred to one thousand dollars a day in other places were in the air the adventurers could not rest content with the small individual earnings they were able to make where they were . . . .

Most of the mining towns of early days are now mere shadows of their former selves. A number have been completely deserted, others still hold on to a semblance of life despite boarded up houses, and deserted stores; only a few are active and reasonably prosperous.

98

Yet in the lobbies of the hotels of the moribund towns and in other gathering places a visitor may still hear of new discoveries by hopeful miners, of the Mother Lode that is just about to be found, and of the return of prosperity to the camp "next year". Prospectors are still grub-staked to search for gold and silver and wander through the mountains seeking for lost mines and the end of the rainbow. Some day they may find what they seek.

SEVEN: LIFE IN THE GOLD TOWNS

by Colin B. Goodykoontz

Life in a mining camp was a mixture of many things. While some men mined, others sought profits by supplying the miners with goods and services. In every mining camp and supply town, part of the population hoped that the embryo village would become a permanent city, and on the basis of such hopes, investments were made in land and buildings and improvements. The population of the early mining districts tended to be highly mobile, largely male, and at times given to violence. But the towns were also viewed as an attractive field for religious endeavor and the composite picture of life in the gold towns that follows was constructed from the reports of one missionary who labored for the Lord in the Colorado region.*

*   *   *

LIFE IN THE GOLD TOWNS

In 1863 the Reverend William Crawford of Massachusetts, an Andover graduate, came out to Colorado as a missionary and field agent for the American Home Missionary Society, one of the oldest and most important missionary organizations in this country and, at that time, the chief home missionary agency of the Congregational Church. Mr. Crawford was not the first minister of the gospel or missionary to visit the Pike's Peak country, but he was the first one sent there by his society. His first duty was to preach and to organize a church; naturally his letters and reports were concerned primarily with his problems, failures, and achievements as a home missionary. But he was interested also in locating other ministers of his denomination in important camps and towns in the Rocky Mountain region. If the officers of the American Home Missionary

- - - - - -
*from Colin B. Goodykoontz, "Colorado as Seen by a Home Missionary, 1863-1868" in *The Colorado Magazine*, volume XII (March, 1935), pages 60 to 69. Used with permission of the State Historical Society of Colorado.

100

Society were to act wisely and promptly in sending out other men, they must be furnished with specific and accurate information about material as well as spiritual affairs. They must know about the establishment of towns and their prospects; they must be informed about mining activities, business opportunities, living conditions, the climate, and Indian relations. The future of Colorado depended on these points. As the society's first representative in the region, it was incumbent on Mr. Crawford to supply as much of that information as he could. Hence, much space in his missionary reports was devoted to mundane matters.

At least twenty-eight of these reports are to be found in the papers of the American Home Missionary Society, which are now in the custody of the Chicago Theological Seminary. From these letters, most of which were written at Central City, I have taken several extracts to illustrate the way in which they throw light on conditions in Colorado during the five years, 1863 to 1868, in which Mr. Crawford lived in this territory . . . .

The first letter from Colorado naturally contained an account of the trip across the plains. On June 30, 1863, less than a week after his arrival in Denver, Mr. Crawford wrote as follows:

"From Omaha to Denver I came by coach — six days and nights of constant traveling. No other conveyance offered except by the slow trains. I stopped over Sabbath at Julesburg — 200 miles east of Denver. The ride was not so bad in reality as in anticipation. Fare $75.00 and for meals by the way 75 cents each. Should another missionary come out, it would be a matter of both comfort and economy for him to get a basket of provisions before leaving the river. The Stage Co. allow passengers to carry only 25 pounds of baggage except at an extra cost of 30 or 40 cents per pound. I think, however, that provisions are excepted. The quickest and cheapest route is by Atchison instead of Omaha. Going by Omaha saves about 75 miles of staging. In warm weather, when the air on the boat is close and hot, this might be no great saving. The best stations for resting, on the road, are Fort Kearney, Julesburg, and Spring Hill. Stopping at any one of them would not be a positive good but only the 'lesser of two evils.' At Fort Kearney there would be an opportunity to preach on the Sabbath.

"Baggage is brought through by teams at from 5 to 7 cents per pound. Mine has not yet arrived. My expenses thus far, with rigid economy, have amounted to about $150.00. They would have been higher had I not obtained a pass from Hannibal to Omaha by courtesy of Col. Hayward.

"Coming through by some light wagon would be preferable to the coach. A better way still would be . . . to buy a wagon and horses, as both would sell readily for more than the original cost (I mean for a family) . . . ."

In a letter of April 29, 1864, he referred again to travel by stage coach:

"The coach from Atchison to Denver is now crowded continually and many have to wait a long time at Atchison. Anyone coming from New York would do well to see Mr. Holliday, the proprietor, and to telegraph to Atchison for a seat. It is better to come by Atchison than Omaha, because the passengers from Omaha must wait at Fort Kearney till there is an empty seat in the Atchison coach, which may be some weeks. The fare from the river to Denver is now $100.00."

In the summer of 1865 Mr. Crawford visited the East in the interest of the Colorado mission field. He returned with three additional helpers, Messrs. Goodrich, Thompson, and Mellis. Again in the letters we find information about the overland journey to Denver. The following extract is taken from a report of November 17, 1865:

"Our expenses in coming out were much larger than we anticipated — I had a letter from the Butterfield Overland Dispatch Co. stating that their coaches would carry passengers from Atchison to Denver for $100.00 and allow 100 pounds of baggage. When we reached Atchison, however, we found that the coaches were poor affairs, that only 25 pounds of baggage were allowed, and 50 cents a pound charged for extra baggage, and that the trip would occupy from ten to fifteen days. As meals would cost from $1.50 to $2.00 each it was plain to see that the expense would be very great before we reached Denver. Add to this that the Indians had just attacked and burned one coach and that passengers who had been turned back were then at Atchison, trying in vain to recover their money from the Butterfield company, and you

102

will see that it would have been very unwise to go by that route. What we did was to take a Holliday coach, going through in 5 1/2 days, fare $150.00 and baggage over 25 pounds at 50 cents per pound. Of course your missionaries had a heavy bill to pay before they got through."

The terminus of the stage lines was Denver. Our missionary did not find it a pleasant place when he first arrived in the summer of 1863. On July 13 of that year he wrote:

"And now a word about Denver. I spent last Sabbath week there, and several days following, attending, in the meantime, the first general S. S. convention held in the territory. Perhaps I ought not to try to give a description of Denver, as this is a 'year of drought.' The country for miles around, the river bottoms only excepted, is as dry and bare (almost) as if the fire had passed over it. The air is hot and stifling, and the dust so thick that a man cannot keep himself in respectable order. It cannot be said there that 'cleanliness is akin to piety.' The only trees are a few scattered cottonwoods, 'the most worthless of fair-sized trees.' I preached for Mr. Day /Presbyterian minister/ in the morning, and was strongly tempted to give out that hymn of Watts:

> Lord, what a wretched land is this,
> Which yields us no supply,
> No cheering fruits, no wholesome trees,
> No streams of living joy.

"Yet some of the Denverites think they have found the best spot on earth. Poor, deluded mortals! The population of the place is now about four thousand. Much of the society is good, business is brisk, and many of the buildings really fine for so young a city. It will probably retain the commanding position it has already gained."

Somewhat more complimentary were the references to Denver seven months later. After a visit to that rising metropolis in February, 1864, Mr. Crawford wrote (Feb. 11, 1864):

"Denver has improved very much since my visit last July. The ground swept by the fire a year ago has been built up with substantial and elegant brick blocks, the occupants of which seem to be doing a thriving business. The U.S. mint is finished — an ornament to the city, but a burden to the government . . . . Denver is fast becoming a stylish place, and a rough pioneer preacher would not meet the demand."

The letter from which the above extract was taken was written in Golden, a place which had little charm for our informant. Golden's only advantage, he wrote, "seems to be a rather pleasant location. There are no mines, and but little arable land to give it importance. Nominally it is the capital of the Territory, but the legislature which met here last week showed their estimate of the place by adjourning to Denver." He predicted that it would soon be nothing but a decayed city "consisting of a stage station and a few scattered families." Two years later he was much more hopeful about the future of "Golden City" and in a letter of April 2, 1866, recommended to the American Home Missionary Society that it station a minister there. The reason he gave for the promise of better things was the discovery of mines of iron and oil springs in the vicinity.

Idaho Springs was characterized in a letter of August 7, 1863, as "a place which has seen better days, and is likely to see better days again. It is a beautiful 'bar' — a bed of smooth drift extending across the valley — and the mountain scenery is unusually fine. The population is about 200 . . . . The town is now drooping for want of capital. The gulch mining pays well, and the lodes give a good 'prospect.' There are some medicinal springs near by, which may yet make the place a resort for invalids."

Mr. Crawford made his headquarters at Central City. In one of his early reports he gave the following description of that great mining camp and its environs (July 13, 1863):

"The three places, Black Hawk, Central City and Nevada, are one continuous settlement extending along the narrow gulches about three miles, having three centers where population is denser than at other points. Mountain City between Central City and Black Hawk was originally the place of principal importance but is now under eclipse. The lodes and quartz mills are at Black Hawk and Nevada while the best stores, hotels, theatres, saloons, etc., are at Central City. Black Hawk has the advantage of the best water power, and the best class of people, and is, in my opinion, the most promising place of the three. Nevada is the least aristocratic in character and pretensions. Just at present its prospects are better than for some time past, owing to the influx of capital from the East. The only attractions which any of these places can present is the opportunity to make money, or to do good. The soil is barren, utterly so, quite unlike the mountain regions of New England. The pines in this immediate vicinity have all been swept off by fire or cut down for fuel. A few little poplars, starting up in <u>their</u> place, are all the green objects one can see, unless it be in the gulches which have not been dug for gold, where one can get a cheerful green by looking <u>aslant the grass</u>, and not directly down upon it. There is some compensation to be found in the flowers, which are really abundant and beautiful. The sides of the mountains are riddled with shafts, tunnels, and 'prospect holes.' The buildings are mostly of the first growth, about half of them of logs, and half frame buildings. There are few dwellings which can make any pretensions of elegance. Very few intend to make a permanent residence here. They mean to get their 'pile,' they say, and then go back to 'the states.' Hence they prefer to build a shanty rather than a more expensive house. There are some, however, who intend to make a <u>home</u> here, and the number is increasing. There will doubtless be a constant and, perhaps, rapid increase of population for a long time to come, but it will be, to a large extent, a <u>floating</u> population, as it has been from the first. The number now here, in a circle of four miles diameter, taking Central City as the center, is variously estimated at from five to ten thousand. With my not very sanguine temperament, I should <u>guess</u> there were six thousand. There are a great many cultivated and pious people, and a great many who are <u>not</u>. The places of business are generally open on the Sabbath, and many of the mills in full blast. A change of public opinion for the better is now taking place. Violence and bloodshed are not common. There has been a great improvement, the people tell me, within a year. There is room for more."

Returning to the question of the character of the people at Central City, Mr. Crawford wrote in a letter of September 18, 1863:

"Perhaps there are some who think our society is so rude and wicked that there is no living here in comfort. Wicked enough, and rough enough it is, but not wholly so. In few places will one meet

105

with more well-informed and cultivated people, or with pleasanter families. Our people demand and can appreciate good preaching. Many of them have been accustomed to the best. "

Naturally these letters contain many references to costs and living conditions. Our missionary had to live; he was dependent upon his Society for the difference between his expenses and his receipts from the people among whom he labored. In a letter of August 7, 1863, he suggested places to which other missionaries might be sent, and added this comment:

"Whenever you send men to Colorado, you will have to pay a large portion of their support. We cannot live here on a small salary, and the people cannot pay us a large one. The money is not in the hands of Christians, and we cannot get it from others. "

In November, 1863, after he had been six months in Colorado, Mr. Crawford wrote:

"I am boarding myself, or 'baching it, ' as the phrase is. I do this partly from choice, partly for the sake of economy.

"Table board is now eight dollars a week. Flour is $15.00 a sack, that is $30.00 a barrel; butter 75 to 85 cents per pound; eggs $1.50 per dozen; potatoes 12 1/2 cents per pound; milk 30 cents per quart; hay $120 to $125 per ton; and other things in proportion. Interest is from five to fifteen per cent a month. You will see it is rather hard to live if one has money, and very hard if one has not. The rise in provisions is due partly to a heavy fall of snow and partly to a rise in freights. We expect that prices will keep up to about the present rates until spring. "

One year later, November 16, 1864, he reported that:

"The cost of living is enormously high — Flour is $25.00 a sack ($50.00 per barrel), butter $2.00 per pound, eggs $2.00 per dozen, potatoes 15 cents per pound, table board from $10.00 to $15.00 per week, pine wood $12.00 per cord and other things in proportion. "

Conditions grew worse instead of better for those who had to buy

106

their food as is indicated by the following comment in a letter of
November 17, 1865:

"The past season has been a bad one for farmers as well as
miners. The crops were principally consumed by the grasshoppers
which seem to have rivalled the locusts of the East. As a natural
consequence provisions are held at a high figure. The cost of living
has not been so great since I have been here as it is today — I have
been driven to boarding myself for the sake of economy. Don't pub-
lish it, however, as I never want to receive so much commiseration
again as I did after you had published a former letter."

The high prices of 1864 and 1865 were due in part to the increase
in freight rates across the plains because of the Indian disturbances of
those years . . . . The Reverend Mr. Crawford's comments on the
Indian problem are interesting and illustrative of the frontier view-
point. He wrote as follows on September 25, 1864:

"Of the Indian troubles which for some time have interrupted our
communications with the states, you are doubtless already well informed. The coaches running between Denver and the River /Missouri/
were taken off about six weeks ago, but will be put on again this week.
It is said that the proprietor exaggerated the real danger in order to
secure the new mail contract on more favorable terms; and this, though
we would not vouch for its truth, is a very credible report to us who
know how the affairs of the 'Overland Stage Co.' are usually conducted.
At any rate that company will be the gainers by our misfortunes. Not
only will they receive a larger remuneration for carrying the mail, but
for every traveler who passes over their line they will receive one hundred and fifty dollars, instead of one hundred dollars as heretofore.

"We are now at open war with nearly all the Indians on the plains
— the Sioux, the Cheyennes, the Kiowas, the Arapahoes, the Comanches, etc. General Curtis with a considerable force is marching toward their homes, supposed to be on the Blue River, while a regiment
of one hundred days men are at Denver, awaiting orders, and independent companies are out on the plains. The Indians avoid open battles,
and only fall upon little parties of emigrants, and unprotected ranches.
The loss they have occasioned in property and life cannot well be estimated. A gentleman who has just come through from the River, thinks

that as many as seventy-five persons have been killed. Denver has several times been thrown into consternation by the report that the Indians were advancing upon the city. Martial law was in force for several days, and fortifications were commenced. The alarm has now subsided and business has returned to its usual channels. The usual emigration of families to the states, before winter sets in, has begun. They travel entirely in large trains for mutual protection.

"Probably our friends at the East, who have not heard from us for several weeks, may be concerned for our safety. Let them be assured that we can defend ourselvs against any attack which may be made. But we do not apprehend any attack. We may have alarms and preparations, but we do not anticipate anything more serious.

"There is but one sentiment in regard to the final disposition which shall be made of the Indians: 'Let them be exterminated, men, women, and children together.' They are regarded as a race ac-cursed, like the ancient Canaanites, and like them, devoted of the Almighty to utter destruction. Of course, I do not myself share in such views; at the same time my feelings have greatly changed since I studied the character of the ideal Indian in the works of Cooper, Irving and other novelists. We who have seen live Indians know that, as a whole, they are a filthy, lazy, treacherous, revengeful race of vagabonds. It would be difficult for us to shed many tears over their wrongs. Nor can we entertain any strong hope of their being reclaimed from the savage state and brought under the blessings of the Gospel. 'Nurture will not stick' upon them. The grace of God may indeed be sufficient for them; and yet, humanly speaking, there seems to be no better destiny in store for them, than to fade away before the white man."

As might be expected, these letters written from one of the greatest of the Colorado mining camps contain many references to prospecting, to veins, lodes, and processes, and to the capital so necessary to the successful prosecution of a costly business. The letters of 1863 reflect a depression in mining because of lack of cap-ital and the shifting of interest to rival camps in Idaho — a region then so vast as to include our Wyoming and Montana as well as the present state of Idaho. But in 1864 the Crawford letters indicate that the Clear Creek and Gregory camps had taken a new lease on life.

For example, this optimistic note is sounded in a letter of February 13, 1864:

"Notwithstanding the stampede to Bannock, our prospects are better than ever before. Large stock companies formed in the East will commence operations in the spring and with processes far superior to those hitherto employed. Probably four times as much gold will be saved as heretofore, at the same expense. The value of mining property has been quadrupled during the last six months. Capitalists who wish to make sure investments with large returns would do well to look at our lodes . . . ."

It might appear that this man of the cloth had become a Colorado "booster," but he was well aware of the way in which his work as a preacher would be affected by the mining excitement of the time and place as is shown by these sentences taken from a report of April 12, 1864:

"The fever of speculation now runs very high. A large amount of mining property is bonded for sale in the New York market, and a large amount has already been sold. The mountains have been prospected anew, and many very rich lodes discovered. The recorder's office is crowded every day by those who are entering new claims, and looking up their old, and hitherto, worthless, property. How long the excitement will continue it is impossible to say. The mines are so rich and extensive, and so much capital has already been invested, that we do not look for any serious and damaging reaction, such as has occurred in the history of most of the western states.

"Of course, the excitement is unfavorable to the progress of spiritual religion. Those who live in the quiet towns of New England, do not know what we have to contend with. All minds are so occupied with the one idea of getting rich, that there is no room for religion."

What about the climate of Colorado? Obviously it had been described to Mr. Crawford before his arrival as "ideal," or "very fine," or as "good for sick people," for in one of his first letters (July 13, 1863), he made this observation:

"The climate does not meet the representations which have been

109

made of it. Sickness and death are here as well as elsewhere. A reliable physician in Central City tells me that there have been more cases of lung disease this last spring than he ever knew elsewhere, five to one. This may have been epidemic. Consumptives and those who have heart disease should not come here. Rheumatism is common in the mountains and fever and erysipelas both here and in Denver. Now I am not saying that the climate is worse here than in other places, but only that I doubt whether it has the salubrity which has been claimed for it."

It would be unfortunate if I gave the impression by these extracts from Mr. Crawford's letters that his interests were mainly secular. He was first of all a missionary and a preacher. He organized the first Congregational Church in Colorado at Central City and he was the missionary pastor of this church until he left the Territory in 1868. He organized the Congregational Church in Boulder, now the oldest church of that denomination in the state. He was also instrumental in founding the first Congregational Church in Denver, and through his efforts three other Congregational ministers came to Colorado in 1865. He was frankly interested in furthering the interests of his own denomination, as well as those of Christianity in general, in the Rocky Mountain region. It was a period of strong denominational rivalry on the frontiers. Each of the major Protestant religious bodies was striving to establish itself in as many of the promising new western towns as possible. The result, of course, was duplication of effort and the planting of too many small struggling churches in the western states and territories. In his zeal for his own denomination, Mr. Crawford was exemplifying a point of view and methods that were usual among religious leaders of the period. In this respect he was probably not different from his fellow ministers of other creeds and faiths. Moreover, he believed that it would be good for the West to come under "the good old New England influences." The planting of Congregational churches would be one method of achieving that result. Two extracts from the letters will suffice to illustrate the point of view here set forth and the importunate nature of appeals to the authorities of the American Home Missionary Society. The first is from a letter of April 12, 1864:

"I cannot too strongly urge upon you to send some more men at once. When I say at once I mean it. Don't wait for warmer weather.

The traveling is as good now as it ever will be, and the necessity is urgent so far as the interests of our denomination are concerned. The openings are probably better now than they will be for some time to come."

About a month later (May 19, 1864), he again implored his Society to send reinforcements:

"We are expecting two or three Presbyterian ministers every day — one for Black Hawk, and one for Central City. Rev. Mr. Willard of Denver, presiding elder of that district, has just gone East for a reinforcement of Methodist ministers. I cannot too strongly urge you to obtain some more ministers for us at once . . . . I hope you will do all that you possibly can for us. Give us four new ministers now and we will secure Colorado for New England, but omit this opportunity and we can make no promises."

In January, 1868, Mr. Crawford closed his work at Central City and returned to New England . . . .

EIGHT: LEGAL BEGINNINGS AND A MINER'S CODE

by Thomas Maitland Marshall

The gold-seekers of the Pike's Peak region found themselves geographically removed from regular governing agencies, and one of their earliest endeavors was to correct that situation. A variety of indigenous organizations were formed: mining districts, claims clubs, peoples' courts, and the extralegal territory called Jefferson. Not until the spring of 1861, after Congress created Colorado Territory, did an effective and legal government exist for the miners. But, in the meantime, their own creative agencies filled the gap. A short statement of the problem is here followed by an example of an early mining district code.*

*   *   *

LEGAL BEGINNINGS AND A MINERS' CODE

When the gold rush began the Pike's Peak Country fell within the Territories of Kansas and Nebraska. The region east of the Continental Divide and south of the fortieth parallel was within the Territory of Kansas, and the territory north of the fortieth parallel and east of the summit of the Rocky Mountains fell within the boundaries of Nebraska. The principal mining camps were in Arapahoe County, Kansas, a county which had never been fully organized.

It became evident to the settlers that they were too far from the settled areas of Kansas to obtain the benefits of its established government. Before the close of 1858 men at Auraria conceived the idea of asking Congress for a territorial organization. On November 6 Hiram J. Graham was elected delegate to Congress. Upon his arrival at Washington he found that a bill had been introduced to

_ _ _ _ _ _

*from *Early Records of Gilpin County, Colorado, 1859-1861* edited by Thomas Maitland Marshall, Boulder, 1920, pages xii-xiv; 10-12. Used with permission of the University of Colorado Press.

organize the "Territory of Colona" in the Pike's Peak Country. Another bill was also pushed forward to organize a temporary government for the "Territory of Jefferson." Neither bill passed.

The Pike's Peakers took steps to get in touch with the Kansas government by electing A. J. Smith to represent them. In February, 1859, the Kansas Assembly abolished Arapahoe County and created five counties in its place.

The settlers foresaw the necessity of immediate provision for maintaining law, order, and property rights, and accordingly took matters into their own hands. In April, 1859, a convention was held at Auraria which resolved that the "State of Jefferson" be created. The boundaries as laid down by the convention embraced a larger area than the present State of Colorado, including portions of the modern States of Nebraska, Wyoming, and Utah as well as Colorado, about 177,000 square miles in all.

On June 6 delegates met in Denver for the purpose of drawing up a constitution, but the convention adjourned before its work was completed. A sentiment favoring a territorial organization soon developed. The convention, which came together on August 1, completed a state constitution and submitted to the voters the question of whether the new government was to be that of a state or a territory. On September 5 the people voted in favor of territorial government, and October 10-12 a convention perfected a provisional government for the Territory of Jefferson. Many people believed that the Territory of Jefferson was illegal and an election was called to elect officers under the laws of Kansas. Captain Richard Sopris was elected a representative and eventually took his seat in the Kansas Legislature. The real government of the Pike's Peak Country, however, was administered under the laws of the Territory of Jefferson, although many transactions were conducted in accordance with the laws of Kansas. The Territory of Jefferson existed until superseded by the Territory of Colorado, which was created by act of Congress on February 28, 1861.

As soon as the miners began to penetrate the mountains, they found it necessary to establish local governments. They took matters into their own hands, laid off mining districts, organized governments, and enacted laws . . . .

113

/The following are the early laws of Gregory District, Gilpin
County.7

MINERS' MEETING

At a meeting of the miners of Gregory Diggings on the North
Fork of Clear creek, K. T., on the evening of the 8th inst., /June 8,
1859/ Wilk Defrees was elected President and Joseph Casto, Secretary.

1st. Resolved that this Mining District shall be bounded as follows: Commencing at the mouth of the North Fork of Clear creek, and
following the divide between said stream and Rallston Creek running
seven miles up the last named stream to a point known as Miners Camp.
Thence South West to the Divide between the North Fork of Clear Creek
and the South Branch of the Same to place of beginning.

2nd. Resolved that no miner shall hold more than one claim except by purchase or discovery, and in any case of purchase the same
shall be attested by at least two disinterested witnesses and shall be
recorded by the Secretary and the Secretary shall receive in compensation a fee of one dollar.

3rd. Resolved, that no claim which has or may be made shall
be good and valid unless it be staked off with the owner's name, giving
the direction length, breadth also the date when said claim was made,
and when held by a company the name of each member shall appear
conspicuously.

4. Resolved that each miner shall be entitled to hold one mountain claim, one gulch claim and one creek claim for the purpose of
washing, the first to be 100 feet long and fifty feet wide, the second
100 feet up and down the river or gulch and extending from bank to bank.

5. Resolved that Mountain claims shall be worked within ten
days from the time they are staked off, otherwise forfeited.

6. Resolved that when members of a company constituted of two
or more, shall be at work on one claim of the company the rest shall
be considered as worked by putting a notice of the same on the
claim.

7. Resolved, each discovery claim shall be marked as such, and shall be safely held whether worked or not.

8. Resolved, that in all cases priority of claim when honestly carried out shall be respected.

9. Resolved, that when two parties wishing to use water on the same stream or ravine for quartz mining purposes, no person shall be entitled to the use of more than one half of the water.

10. Resolved, that when disputes shall arise between parties in regard to claims the party agrieved shall call upon the Secretary, who shall designate nine miners being disinterested persons from whose number the parties shall alternately strike off one untill the names of three remain who shall at once proceed to hear and try the case, and should any miner refuse to obey such decision, the Secretary shall call a meeting of the miners and if their decision is the same the party refusing to obey shall not be entitled to hold another claim in this district, the party against whom the decision is given shall pay to the Secretary and referees the sum of $5.00 each for their services.

11. Resolved, that the proceedings of this meeting be published in the Rocky Mountain News, and a collection be taken up to pay for 100 extra copies for the use of the miners.

Joseph Casto, Sec.   Wilk Defree, Pres't.

NINE: A COUNCIL ON WAR AND PEACE

The isolation of the Pike's Peak mining camps exposed them, from the beginning, to the dangers of Indian depredations. The Cheyenne and Arapahoe tribes, whose lands the gold seekers had invaded, agreed to amendments of the Fort Laramie settlement in 1861, accepting a large triangular reservation in southeastern Colorado. Then, the coming of the Civil War in the east and the resulting obviously weak defensive posture of the whites, presented to the Indians what seemed to many their last opportunity to stem the tide of white encroachment. Sporadic fighting in the years 1862 to 1864 kept the whites in nervous expectations of a general attack that never quite developed. Alternately pursuing policies of peace and retaliatory warfare, Governor John Evans, in June, 1864, offered protection for those Indians who would come in to the military posts in the region. Not until late summer was there a favorable response from the tribes. Then, escorted from Fort Lyon on the Arkansas to Denver, a group of Cheyenne and Arapahoe chiefs held the following council with Governor Evans and his aides.*

* * *

A COUNCIL ON WAR AND PEACE

CAMP WELD, DENVER, Wednesday, Sept. 28, 1864

PRESENT — Gov. John Evans, Col. Chivington, Comd'g Dist. Colorado, Col. Geo. L. Shoup, Third Colorado Volunteer Cavalry, Maj. E. Wynkoop, Colorado First, S. Whiteley, U. S. Ind. Agt.

Black Kettle, leading Cheyenne Chief. White Antelope, Chief central Cheyenne band. Bull Bear, leader of Dog Soldiers, /Cheyenne./

– – – – –

*from "Report of Council with Cheyenne and Arapahoe Chiefs and Warriors, Brought to Denver by Major Wynkoop; Taken Down by U.S. Indian Agent Simeon Whiteley as it Progressed," Appendix (pages 1-4), *Reply of Governor Evans, of the Territory of Colorado. To That Part Referring to Him, of the Report of "The Committee on the Conduct of the War," Headed "Massacre of Cheyenne Indians."* n.p., n.d.

Neva, sub-Arapahoe Chief, (who was in Washington.) Bosse, sub-Arapahoe Chief. Heap of Buffalo, Arapahoe Chief. Na-ta-nee, Arapahoe Chief.

The Arapahoes are all relatives of Left Hand, Chief of the Arapahoes, and are sent by him in his stead.

John Smith, Interpreter to the Upper Arkansas Agency, and many other citizens and officers.

His Excellency Gov. Evans asked the Indians what they had to say.

Black Kettle then said: On sight of your circular of June 27th, 1864, I took hold of the matter, and have now come to talk to you about it. I told Mr. Bent, who brought it, that I accepted it, but it would take some time to get all my people together — many of my young men being absent — and I have done everything in my power, since then, to keep peace with the whites. As soon as I could get my people together, we held a council, and got a half-breed who was with them, to write a letter to inform Major Wynkoop, or other military officer nearest to them, of their intention to comply with the terms of the circular. Major Wynkoop was kind enough to receive the letter, and visited them in camp, to whom they delivered four white prisoners — one other (Mrs. Snyder,) having killed herself; that there are two women and one child yet in their camp, whom they will deliver up as soon as they can get them in: Laura Roper, 16 or 17 years; Ambrose Asher, 7 or 8 years; Daniel Marble, 7 or 8 years, Isabel Ubanks, 4 or 5 years. The prisoners still with them /are7 Mrs. Ubanks and babe, and a Mrs. Morton, who was taken on the Platte. Mrs. Snyder is the name of the woman who hung herself. The boys were taken between Fort Kearney and the Blue.

I followed Maj. Wynkoop to Fort Lyon, and Major Wynkoop proposed that we come up to see you. We have come with our eyes shut, following his handful of men, like coming through the fire. All we ask is that we may have peace with the whites. We want to hold you by the hand. You are our father. We have been traveling through a cloud. The sky has been dark ever since the war began. These braves who are with me are all willing to do what I say. We want to take good tidings home to our people, that they may sleep in peace. I want you to give all these chiefs of the soldiers here to understand that we are for peace, and that we have made peace, that we may not be mistaken by them for enemies. I have not come here with a little wolf bark, but have come to talk plain with you. We must live near the buffalo, or starve. When we came here we came free, without any apprehension, to see you, and when I go home and tell my people that I have taken your hand, and the hands of all the chiefs here in Denver, they will feel well, and so will all the different tribes of Indians on the plains, after we have eaten and drank with them.

Gov. Evans replied: I am sorry you did not respond to my appeal at once. You have gone into an alliance with the Sioux, who were at war with us. You have done a great deal of damage — have stolen stock, and now have possession of it. However much a few individuals may have tried to keep the peace, as a nation you have gone to war. While we have been spending thousands of dollars in opening farms for you, and making preparations to feed, protect, and make you comfortable, you have joined our enemies and gone to war. Hearing, last fall, that they were dissatisfied, the Great Father at Washington sent me out on the plains to talk with you and make it all right. I sent messengers out to tell you that I had presents, and would make you a feast, but you sent word to me that you did not want to have anything to do with me, and to the Great Father at Washington that you could get along without him. Bull Bear wanted to come in to see me, at the head of the Republican, but his people held a council and would not let him come.

Black Kettle — That is true.

Gov. Evans — I was under the necessity, after all my trouble, and all the expense I was at, of returning home without seeing them. Instead of this, your people went away and smoke the war pipe with our enemies.

Black Kettle — I don't know who could have told you this.

Gov. Evans — No matter who said this, but your conduct has proved to my satisfaction that was the case.

118

Several Indians — This is a mistake. We have made no alliance with the Sioux or any one else.

Gov. Evans explained that smoking the war pipe was a figurative term, but their conduct had been such as to show they had an understanding with other tribes.

Several Indians — We acknowledge that our actions have given you reason to believe this.

Gov. Evans — So far as making a treaty now, is concerned, we are in no condition to do it. Your young men are on the war path. My soldiers are preparing for the fight. You, so far, have had the advantage; but the time is near at hand when the plains will swarm with United States soldiers. I understand that these men who have come to see me now, have been opposed to the war all the time, but that their people have controlled them and they could not help themselves. Is this so?

All the Indians — It has been so.

Gov. Evans — The fact that they have not been able to prevent their people from going to war in the past spring, when there was plenty of grass and game, makes me believe that they will not be able to make a peace which will last longer than until winter is past.

White Antelope — I will answer that after a time.

Gov. Evans — The time when you can make war best, is in the summer time; when I can make war best, is in the winter. You, so far, have had the advantage; my time is just coming. I have learned that you understand that as the whites are at war among themselves, you think you can now drive the whites from this country. But this reliance is false. The Great Father at Washington has men enough to drive all the Indians off the plains, and whip the rebels at the same time. Now the war with the whites is nearly through, and the Great Father will not know what to do with all his soldiers, except to send them after the Indians on the plains. My proposition to the friendly Indians has gone out; I shall be glad to have them all come in, under it. I have no new propositions to make. Another reason that I am not

119

in a condition to make a treaty, is, that war is begun, and the power to make a treaty of peace has passed from me to the great War Chief. My advice to you, is, to turn on the side of the government, and show, by your acts, that friendly disposition you profess to me. It is utterly out of the question for you to be at peace with us, while living with our enemies, and being on friendly terms with them.

Inquiry made by one Indian — What was meant by being on the side of the government?

Explanation being made, all gave assent, saying "All right."

Gov. Evans — The only way you can show this friendship is by making some arrangement with the soldiers to help them.

Black Kettle — We will return with Major Wynkoop to Fort Lyon; we will then proceed to our village, and take back word to my young men, every word you say. I cannot answer for all of them, but think there will be but little difficulty in getting them to assent to help the soldiers.

Major Wynkoop — Did not the Dog Soldiers agree, when I had my council with you, to do whatever you said, after you had been here?

Black Kettle — Yes.

Gov. Evans explained that if the Indians did not keep with the U.S. soldiers, or have an arrangement with them, they would be all treated as enemies. You understand, if you are at peace with us it is necessary to keep away from our enemies. But I hand you over to the military, one of the chiefs of which is here to-day, and can speak for himself, to them, if he chooses.

White Antelope — I understand every word you have said, and will hold on to it. I will give you an answer directly. The Cheyennes, all of them, have their eyes open this way, and they will hear what you say. He is proud to have seen the chief of all the whites in this country. He will tell his people. Ever since he went to Washington and received this medal, I have called all white men as my brothers. But other Indians have since been to Washington, and got medals, and now the soldiers do not shake hands, but seek to kill me. What do you mean by us fighting your enemies? Who are they?

Gov. Evans — All Indians who are fighting us.

White Antelope — How can we be protected from the soldiers on the plains?

Gov. Evans — You must make that arrangement with the Military Chief.

White Antelope — I fear that these new soldiers who have gone out, may kill some of my people while I am here.

Gov. Evans — There is great danger of it.

White Antelope — When we sent out letter to Major Wynkoop, it was like going through a strong fire or blast, for Major Wynkoop's men to come to our camp; it was the same for us to come to see you. We have our doubts whether the Indians south of the Arkansas, or those north of the Platte, will do as you say. A large number of Sioux have crossed the Platte, in the vicinity of the Junction, into their country. When Major Wynkoop came, we proposed to make peace. He said he had no power to make a peace, except to bring them here and return them safe.

Gov. Evans — Again, whatever peace they make, must be with the soldiers, and not with me.

Gov. Evans — Are the Apaches at war with the whites?

White Antelope — Yes, and the Camanches and Kiowas as well: also a tribe of Indians from Texas, whose names we do not know. There are thirteen different bands of Sioux who have crossed the Platte and are in alliance with the others named.

Gov. Evans — How many warriors with the Apaches, Kiowas and Camanches?

White Antelope — A good many. Don't know.

Gov. Evans — How many of the Sioux?

White Antelope — Don't know, but many more than of the southern tribes.

Gov. Evans — Who committed the depredation on the trains near the Junction, about the 1st of August?

White Antelope — Do not know — did not know any was committed. Have taken you by the hand, and will tell the truth, keeping back nothing.

Gov. Evans — Who committed the murder of the Hungate family, on Running Creek?

Neva — The Arapahoes; a party of the northern band who was passing north. It was Medicine Man, or Roman Nose, and three others. I am satisfied from the time he left a certain camp for the north, that it was this party of four persons.

Agent Whiteley — That cannot be true.

Gov. Evans — Where is Roman Nose?

Neva — You ought to know better than me. You have been nearer to him.

Gov. Evans — Who killed the man and boy at the head of Cherry Creek?

Neva — (After consultation) — Kiowas and Camanches.

Gov. Evans — Who stole soldier's horses and mules from Jimmy's Camp, twenty-seven days ago?

Neva — Fourteen Cheyennes and Arapahoes, together.

Gov. Evans — What were their names?

Neva — Powder Face and Whirlwind, who are now in our camp,

were the leaders.

Col. Shoup — I counted twenty Indians, on that occasion.

Gov. Evans — Who stole Charley Autobee's horses?

Neva — Raven's son.

Gov. Evans — Who took the stock from Fremont's Orchard, and had the first fight with the soldiers this spring, north of there?

White Antelope — Before answering this question I would like for you to know that this was the beginning of war, and I should like to know what it was for, a soldier fired first.

Gov. Evans — The Indians had stolen about forty horses, the soldiers went to recover them, and the Indians fired a volley into their ranks.

White Antelope — This is all a mistake. They were coming down the Bijou, and found one horse and one mule. They returned one horse before they got to Geary's, to a man, then went to Geary's, expecting to turn the other one over to some one. They then heard that the soldiers and Indians were fighting, somewhere down the Platte; then they took fright and all fled.

Gov. Evans — Who were the Indians who had the fight?

White Antelope — They were headed by the Fool Badger's son, a young man, one of the greatest of the Cheyenne warriors, who was wounded, and though still alive he will never recover.

Neva — I want to say something. It makes me feel bad to be talking about these things and opening old sores.

Gov. Evans — Let him speak.

Neva — Mr. Smith has known me ever since I was a child. Has he ever known me commit depredations on the whites? I went to Washington last year — received good council. I hold on to it. I determined

123

to always keep peace with the whites. Now, when I shake hands with them they seem to pull away. I came here to seek peace and nothing else.

Gov. Evans — We feel that they have, by their stealing and murdering, done us great damage. They come here and say they will tell me all, and that is what I am trying to get.

Neva — The Camanches, Kiowas and Sioux have done much more injury than we have. We will tell what we know, but cannot speak for others.

Gov. Evans — I suppose you acknowledge the depredations on the Little Blue, as you have the prisoners then taken, in your possession.

White Antelope — We (the Cheyennes) took two prisoners, west of Fort Kearney, and destroyed the trains.

Gov. Evans — Who committed depredations at Cottonwood?

White Antelope — The Sioux. What band, we do not know.

Gov. Evans — What are the Sioux going to do next?

Bull Bear — Their plan is to clean out all this country. They are angry, and will do all the damage to the whites they can. I am with you and the troops to fight all those who have no ears to listen to what you say. Who are they? Show them to me. I am not yet old — I am young. I have never hurt a white man. I am pushing for something good. I am always going to be friends with the whites — they can do me good.

Gov. Evans — Where are the Sioux?

Bull Bear — Down on the Republican, where it opens out.

Gov. Evans — Do you know that they intend to attack the trains this week?

Bull Bear — Yes. About one-half of all the Missouri River Sioux and Yanktons, who were driven from Minnesota, are those who have crossed the Platte. I am young and can fight. I have given my word to fight with the whites. I am willing to die in the same way, and expect to do so.

Neva — I know the value of the presents which we receive from Washington. We cannot live without them. That is why I try so hard to keep peace with the whites.

Gov. Evans — I cannot say anything about those things, now.

Neva — I can speak for all the Arapahoes under Left Hand. Raven has sent no one here to speak for him. Raven has fought the whites.

Gov. Evans — Are there any white men among your people?

Neva — There are none except Keith, who is now in the store at Fort Larned.

Col. Chivington — I am not a big war chief, but all the soldiers in this country are at my command. My rule of fighting white men or Indians is to fight them until they lay down their arms and submit to military authority. They are nearer Major Wynkoop than any one else, and they can go to him when they get ready to do that.

The Council then adjourned.

TEN: SAND CREEK

by Robert L. Perkin

The ominous sound of the words of the last speaker at the Denver council was probably not fully comprehended by any person present, unless it was Colonel John Chivington himself. For it developed that the military officer, to whom Governor Evans had presented the problem of procedures, would write the next chapter in the history of Indian relations in the Territory. That chapter is still one of the most controversial in Colorado's development. It begins at the point when the Indians left the Denver meeting.*

*   *   *

SAND CREEK

The chiefs led their bands back to Fort Lyon, where they turned in their arms and were given food. A few days later the rifles were returned to them for hunting use. Officers at the fort said the guns were so old as to be almost worthless. The authorities at Lyon also told the Indians to move out away from the fort. So Black Kettle moved his mixed village up to the open prairie of the Arapaho-Cheyenne reservation and camped about forty miles north of the fort on the big bend of Sand Creek. He assumed he was still complying with Governor Evans' order to remain where he could be watched.

In Denver, meanwhile, the 3rd Colorado had been filled. The "100 Dazers" were eager for action and rankled under the taunt of "Bloodless Third." Their colonel was George L. Shoup, who had served with the 1st Colorados in New Mexico. Horses, arms and other equipment arrived at Camp Weld early in October, and the regiment of six hundred and fifty men sallied out into the Bijou basin east of Denver.

------

*from Robert L. Perkin, *The First Hundred Years: An Informal History of Denver and the Rocky Mountain News*, New York, 1959, pages 268-281. Copyright by the Denver Publishing Company. Used with special permission of the author and Mr. Jack Foster.

126

/John/ Chivington assumed personal command, outranking Shoup by virtue of his position as commander of the Colorado Military District. The big, black-bearded colonel, described by Jerome Smiley as "a fine example of the preacher militant," was determined to lead his troups to glory — and vault himself into Congress — by hitting the Indians a blow which would be hailed by everyone as decisive. Late in August he had delivered an address, either as a sermon or a campaign speech, in which he declared his policy was to "kill and scalp all, little and big," because "nits make lice." He was warmly applauded, and the phrase became a fighting slogan for the 3rd. "Nits make lice."

In November, through two feet of snow, Chivington led his "Bloodless Third" southward. Units of the veteran 1st, now a cavalry regiment, what was left of it, joined him. As the column jogged down into the Arkansas Valley the ground cleared and the cold eased, but there were still white patches of snow out among the yucca clumps on the gray-brown prairie. The troopers huddled down in their new army-issue overcoats and cursed the maggoty hardtack given them for breakfast. They were saddle-sore, cold, and already sick of soldiering, with the first hostile redskin yet to be encountered.

There had not been a depredation within two hundred miles for two months, and the settlers were beginning to move back to their farms and ranches to harvest corn and try to round up scattered stock. John Dailey's Company A had been on a detached mission to Fort Garland, in the San Luis Valley, where he found the colonel in charge "d-k all day, as usual." Company A moved up to join the main column and lingered pleasantly and informally at Pueblo, where, Dailey's diary indicates, the "100 Dazers" faithfully observed the riotous traditions of the 1st Colorados. He records a wild and wonderful account of chicken and melon stealing, casual AWOLs, late sleeping, trout fishing, bitching, drunken officers, saloon fights, and tumbles in the hay with country maidens much impressed by new blue cavalry uniforms. Hangovers considered, it must have been rigorous duty for the officers. No one wanted to drill, guard duty was ignored, and none of the volunteers, apparently, obeyed any order unless the mood was on him and the tone of the command suitably civil.

Company A joined the main column, which then swung east down the river.

Chivington was getting the scent, and his tense excitement mounted. Two hundred and fifty pounds of six-foot fighting man, he forked his beautiful black horse like an emperor on parade. Imperiously he halted the United States mails. No one must know he was coming. In sudden, slashing movements to left and right he dispatched squadrons to nearby ranches to place occupants under house arrest until the command had moved far down the road beyond danger that word of its coming would pass on ahead. Out in advance of the spearpoint of the force rode Jim Beckwourth, the old mountain man, pressed into service as guide and scout. Poker-faced and stoic, Jim rode with his rifle cradled across his arms and one leg hooked up over the saddle for comfort. His passive brown eyes took in everything and seemed to see nothing.

The column surprised the small garrison of 1st Regiment troops and New Mexico volunteers at Fort Lyon. The black-bearded colonel was pleased when the garrison officers told him they had not known the 3rd had left the Bijou. He was more than life-sized. "Hero of Gloriéta," congressional candidate, and now author of a model cavalry maneuver across two hundred and fifty miles of open plains with a large body of troops in complete secrecy. Surely Washington could not long withhold his brigadier's stars.

Chivington routed out his men before dawn on November 28, and they had trotted into Fort Lyon at 9 A.M. They went into camp, but not before the colonel had circled the fort with a strong line of pickets. No one was to leave. Colonel's orders.

It now became apparent what was afoot. Some of Chivington's officers said later that they remonstrated with him against the plan, but their claims well may have been self-serving, as was so much of the testimony that would be given. Even if they did protest, it was of no consequence one way or the other. Chivington's mind, the mind of a popular hero and an ambitious man, was set. As leader of the "First Indian Expedition," he knew precisely what he was doing. As commanding officer of the Colorado Military District, he also knew, as well as any man could, where the Indians were. Any Christian scruples he may have felt had long since been conquered.

He knew where Black Kettle's village was. He and Evans had

sent them there. He knew about what Indians he would find; they had been to visit him and hear his blusterings. He knew they were friendly. Or, at minimum, they professed friendship, had sought out, made themselves subject to, and now relied upon the protection of the Fort Lyon troops. They would not suspect a thing.

Chivington also knew the work ahead would be bloody and easy. His force was far larger, better armed, better equipped than anything he would meet, and perhaps he had planned it that way a long time ago. Just when his design was laid can only be conjecture, but possibly it had been fermenting in his mind in September when he had told these chiefs exactly where to go and what to do to put themselves under the eye and command of his forces at Fort Lyon. Yet none of this need appear in public accounts. Chivington obviously was confident he could make it all seem to be a fiercely fought and glorious victory. The hysterical town of Denver, whipped up by the dispatches and editorials in the /Rocky Mountain7 News, would support him in anything he did so long as Indians were killed. He could count on that.

By nightfall of November 28 all was in readiness. Three days' cooked rations in each man's saddlebags. Horses rested and fed. The bulk of the Fort Lyon garrison added to the force. At 8 P.M., under cover of darkness, Chivington moved out. All told, he had at his command about nine hundred and fifty mostly raw but well-equipped and emotionally aroused men, along with a battery of four 12-pounder mountain howitzers armed with grape and canister. The men were not told where they were going, except that there would be an Indian fight at the end of the march. Only the officers knew Chivington's secret.

Jim Beckwourth guided the long column of fours off to the north through the frosty night. Although Jim once was confused briefly by a low pool of fog lying in a swale like a lake, the course was straight and true. He brought the command to the top of a rise just as the eastern sky began to pale off to grays and yellows. There in the wide bottoms of white sand was Black Kettle's village, a few over a hundred lodges, most of them Cheyenne, eight or ten of them occupied by Left Hand's Arapahoes. The first morning smoke was just beginning to curl out of the wings of the tipis.

Chivington halted his column and rode back down the line.

"Off with your coats, men," the commander ordered. "You can fight better without them. Take no prisoners. Remember the slaughtered white women and children! Remember the Hungates!"

Beckwourth said he heard it this way: "I don't tell you to kill all ages and sex, but look back on the plains of the Platte, where your mothers, fathers, brothers, sisters have been slain, and their blood saturating the sands on the Platte."

According to his aide, Captain A. J. Gill, Chivington said: "Now boys, I shan't say who you shall kill, but remember our murdered women and children."

Then, at sunrise, the attack began.

It lasted eight hours or longer, and it presents as brain-splitting a picture of fiendish savagery as exists in the records of the human race. The day of November 29, 1864, ran deep with blood and rocked the heavens with insanity.

The village was totally surprised and wholly confused by the treachery. If reliable estimates can be found in the tangle of perjured testimony which came later, the lodges contained between five and six hundred Indians. At least two thirds of these were women and small children. Many of the others were old men, like Black Kettle and White Antelope themselves. Altogether there were perhaps a hundred warriors, armed with bows and arrows, lances and guns which had been turned back to them as worthless.

Other considerations aside for the moment, the battle was a horrible botch as a military operation. Those hundred ill-armed warriors kept nearly a thousand soldiers, mounted and supported by artillery, busy until midafternoon. Meanwhile nearly five hundred Indians escaped across the prairie, most of them on foot, through lines which supposedly encircled the camp. The "enemy" commander, Black Kettle, was among those who got away. Fighting was confused, disordered, entirely undisciplined. Command was lost early in the day and never recovered until after the last shot was fired. Soldiers caught each other in their own cross fire. Some of the eight killed and forty wounded were not victims of the Indians. Orders were lost, countermanded, or frankly disobeyed. If Chivington had displayed any military aptitude at Apache Cañon, he showed not a glimmer at Sand Creek.

Those of the Indians who could not flee died on the spot. The most credible estimates place the number at something under two hundred, though Chivington would claim five to six hundred killed out of a "hostile" force of nine hundred to a thousand. Two thirds of the bodies counted later were women and children.

White Antelope was among the first to go down. Soon after the firing began he advanced from his lodge toward the troopers with both hands upraised, palms forward, in the traditional sign of peace. Shots kicked up sand around him. He stopped, folded his arms, and began to chant his death song:

> "Nothing lives long,
> Except the earth and the mountains . . ."

At last the excited volunteers found the range. The Lincoln peace medal on the old warrior's chest bounced and he pitched face forward to the ground.

As he had been instructed to do, Black Kettle flew the Stars and Stripes on a pole over his lodge. The flag had been given to him by an Indian commissioner some years earlier. Under it he flew a white flag. Neither was recognized. The chief took his wife and began to flee. She was shot and went down. Troopers rode over her, putting eight more bullets in her body. But she was still alive, and Black Kettle, far past his prime as a brave, put her over his shoulder and ran. They got through the lines.

A three-year-old Indian child, perfectly naked, toddled out on the sands of the dry creek bed. Three troopers dismounted seventy yards away and assumed the position shown in the cavalry manual for kneeling fire. One carbine cracked and sand spurted at the child's heels. "Let me try the little son of a bitch," the second trooper demanded. He, too, fired and missed. "Hell," spat the third soldier, "you boys couldn't hit the side of a mountain." He took aim and squeezed. The baby dropped. One nit that would never make a louse.

131

Out of one of the lodges came running old "Uncle John" Smith, one of the founders of Denver, the squawman who had helped build the city's first house. He had been sent to the Indian camp a few days earlier to trade and report on what the savages were doing. His orders had come from Major Scott J. Anthony, who now led a portion of the attack.

Smith ran toward the troops and was greeted by fire. He was recognized. "Shoot the old son of a bitch," someone shouted; "he's no better than an Indian." Bullets spattered around him. The gray-haired man hesitated and then scuttled back toward his lodge. "Run here, Uncle John," Chivington himself called. "You are all right." Smith cast a glance back at the lodges, turned, and scampered toward the troops. He climbed on the caisson of one of the howitzers and was safe. So low had one of the founding fathers fallen for running with the redskin.

Smith's half-breed son Jack didn't fare as well. He was captured, held prisoner for twenty-four hours in a lodge, and then killed by a shot from a pistol thrust through a cut in the stretched buffalo hide of the tipi. Officers reported they were unable to ascertain who fired the shot. Chivington had been told that his troopers planned to kill Jack Smith. He had shrugged. His orders, he said, had been to take no prisoners; he couldn't change them now.

As the fight progressed madness seized the battlefield. The troopers had knives out and were scalping everything that fell, "one week to 80 years" of age. Children were shot at their mothers' breasts. The victims of the scalping were not always quite dead. One old squaw wandered sightless through the carnage. Her entire scalp had been taken, and the skin of her forehead fell down over her eyes to blind her. Several troopers got into a quarrel over who should have the honor of scalping one body. The issue could not be decided; so all took scalps from the same carcass.

Nor was the scalping the worst of it. The "Bloodless Third-sters" would show the Indians a thing or two about barbarity and the finer points of mutilation.

A group of soldiers paused amid the firing to take turns profaning the body of a comely young squaw, very dead. The nose and ears, as well as the scalp, of White Antelope were cut off. Indians' fingers were hacked away to get their rings as souvenirs. One soldier trotted about with a heart impaled on a stick. Others carried off the genitals of braves. Someone had the notion that it would be artistic work to slice away the breasts of the Indian women. One breast was worn as a cap, another was seen stretched over the bow of a saddle. In Denver, many years later, there was a persistent rumor that one of the surviving Thirdsters had a tanned Indian breast that he carried in his pocket as a coin purse.

The catalogue of atrocities could go on and on. All except the ghoulish purse and the blinded squaw are from the sworn testimony presented to the two investigations into the affair ordered by Congress. The record of those proceedings forms what is possibly the most shocking document in the American archives. How much of the testimony is truth and how much lie, no one can say; for it is obvious that otherwise honorable men, on both sides, perjured themselves repeatedly under oath. Partisanship was at white heat, and neither investigation was unprejudiced against Chivington. It is unlikely that he could have received a calm hearing, in Colorado or elsewhere, for a quarter century after that November day of 1864. Nearly halfway into the twentieth century Denver still remembered Sand Creek with shame. When someone, thinking of the valiant fight at La Gloriéta, proposed that a street be named Chivington, a storm of protest blew up and the boulevard got another designation. (Hale Parkway, for a Spanish-American War hero.)

Testimony at the hearings indicates that Chivington said he was out "after scalps," that he would give the Indians "a lively buffalo hunt," and that he "longed to be wading in gore." Others testified he "issued an order that he would hang any 'son of a bitch' who would bury the bodies or bones" of prisoners who were killed and that he asserted "he believed it right or honorable to use any means under God's heaven to kill Indians that would kill women and children, and 'damn any man that was in sympathy with Indians.'" It is probable the big colonel said these, or similar, things. Before Sand Creek, Denver was clamoring in almost one voice for extermination of the Indians, good or bad, and Chivington knew he had the city behind him.

133

When word of his victory reached Denver on December 7 the
/Rocky Mountain/ News carried a bulletin:

BIG INDIAN FIGHT.

The First and Third Regiments have had a battle
with the Indians on Sand Creek, a short distance north-
east of Fort Lyon. Five hundred Indians are reported
killed and six hundred horses captured. Captain Baxter
and Lieutenant Pierce are reported killed. No further
particulars. A messenger is hourly expected with full
details. Bully for the Colorado boys.

Next day the official report to Major General S. R. Curtis,
commanding the Department of Kansas at Fort Leavenworth and
Chivington's superior, was in. For the second time the colonel
deliberately had disobeyed the orders of his commanding officer;
Curtis in a general order had instructed all troops under his command to spare Indian women and children. Chivington did not
admit his disobedience, however. He reported to Curtis:

Headquarters District of Colorado

In the field, on Big Bend of Sandy Creek, Col. Ter.,
Nov. 29, 1864

Sir: I have not the time to give you a detailed history of our engagement to-day, or to mention those officers and men who distinguished themselves in one of the
most bloody Indian battles ever fought on these plains.
You will find enclosed the report of my surgeon in charge,
which will bring to many friends the sad fate of loved ones
who are and have been risking everything to avenge the
horrid deeds of those savages we have so severely handled. We made a forced march of forty miles, and surprised, at break of day, one of the most powerful villages
of the Cheyenne nation, and captured over five hundred
animals; killing the celebrated chiefs One Eye, White
Antelope, Knock Kno /Knee/, Black Kettle, and Little

134

Robe, with about five hundred of their people, destroying all their lodges and equipage, making almost an annihilation of the entire tribe.

I shall leave here, as soon as I can see our wounded safely on the way to the hospital at Fort Lyon, for the villages of the Sioux, which are reported about eighty miles from here, on the Smoky Hill, and three thousand strong; so look out for more fighting. I will state, for the consideration of gentlemen who are opposed to fighting these red scoundrels, that I was shown, by my chief surgeon, the scalp of a white man taken from the lodge of one of the chiefs, which could not have been more than two or three days taken; and I could mention many more things to show how these Indians, who have been drawing government rations at Fort Lyon, are and have been acting.

Very respectfully, your obedient servant,

J. M. Chivington

Col. Comd'g. Colorado Expedition against Indians on Plains

The News published the text of the report on December 8 and went on editorially:

This noted, needed whipping of the "red skins" by our "First Indian Expedition," particulars of which appear elsewhere, was the chief subject of comment and glorification through town today. The members of the Third, and First, and the First New Mexico, who collectively "cleaned out" the confederate savages on Sand Creek, have won for themselves and their commanders, from Colonel down to corporal, the eternal gratitude of dwellers of these plains. This brave beginning will bring down the hauteur of the treacherous tribes, all round, so that, should there not be even another similar defeat enacted on them through this

135

season, our people may rest easy in the belief that outrages by small bands are at an end, on routes where troops are stationed. Having tasted of the "bitter end," the news of which will quickly be dispatched among the others, the supremacy of our power will be seriously considered, and a surrender or a sueing for peace be perhaps very soon proclaimed. This plan of attacking them in their villages is the only one available, while it is certainly as advantageous to the Indians as they justly dare desire, if they're in for a fair fight.

Despite his brave declarations to General Curtis, Chivington moved his command not an inch nearer the big camp of hostile Cheyennes and Sioux eighty miles away on the headwaters of the Smoky Hill River. Instead he boldly scouted back in the direction of Fort Lyon and then east down the Arkansas. He reported he found no hostiles in that quarter. Along the way, he neglected to report, the Indian baby that had been thrown into the feed box of one of the wagons was abandoned on the prairie.

The hundred-day enlistments of his Thirdsters were now about to expire; so the colonel wheeled his column to the homeward road. They arrived in Denver December 22, and the News of that date tells of a big parade and a glorious homecoming. The "Bloodless Third" boasted that it was the "Bloody Third," and the whole town smiled proudly and applauded the boast.

The boys brought along "hundreds" of Cheyenne scalps, and the News confessed itself somewhat confused by the trophies. Every soldier, it said, "gives a different version" and "each has the scalp of the chiefs." The "local" editor commented: "Cheyenne scalps are getting as thick here now as toads in Egypt. Everybody has got one, and is anxious to get another to send east."

In addition to the scalps, the 3rd had brought home other spoils: three small Cheyenne children, two girls and a boy. The children were shoved out onto the stage of the Denver Theatre between acts to be exhibited as curiosities along with a rope of a hundred scalps.

The captives shared the bill with "Seignor Franco, the great stone-eater, and Mons. Malakoff, the celebrated sword swallower," and big posters printed by the News were plastered up around town.

As late as December 16, Chivington was still contending in his official messages that he had attacked a hostile camp of nine hundred to a thousand Indians and killed five to six hundred of them. And on December 17 the News was still standing staunchly behind him:

> Among the brilliant feats of arms in Indian warfare, the recent campaign of our Colorado volunteers will stand in history with few rivals, and none to exceed it in final results . . . .
>
> Whether viewed as a march or as a battle, the exploit has few, if any, parallels. A march of 260 miles in but a fraction more than five days, with deep snow, scanty forage, and no road, is a remarkable feat, whilst the utter surprise of a large Indian village is unprecedented. In no single battle in North America, we believe, have so many Indians been slain . . . .
>
> A thousand incidents of individual daring and the passing events of the day might be told, but space forbids. We leave the task for eyewitnesses to chronicle. All acquitted themselves well, and Colorado soldiers have again covered themselves with glory.

Space also prevented mention of the fact that Indian women and children were killed, although the paper admitted "there were neither wounded nor prisoners."

Other and differing reports were being made, however, and the aroused Eastern press was demanding facts about the "massacre." Pressure was put on Congress to investigate. On December 30 the News printed a Washington dispatch saying that an investigation would be conducted on the strength of "letters received from high officials in Colorado" reporting that "the Indians were killed after surrendering,

137

and that a large proportion of them were women and children." In the space immediately below the Washington dispatch the paper loosed its best irony on the "high officials":

Indignation was loudly and unequivocally expressed, and some less considerate of the boys were very persistent in their inquiries as to who those "high officials" were, with a mild intimation that they had half a mind to "go for them." This talk about "friendly Indians" and a "surrendered" village will do to "tell to marines," but to us out here it is all bosh.

The confessed murderers of the Hungate family — a man and wife and their two little babies, whose scalped and mutilated remains were seen by all our citizens — were "friendly Indians," we suppose, in the eyes of these "high officials." They fell in the Sand creek battle.

The confessed participants in a score of other murders of peaceful settlers and inoffensive travellers upon our borders and along our roads in the past six months must have been friendly, or else the "high officials" wouldn't say so . . . .

Possibly those scalps of white men, women and children, one of them fresh, not three days taken, found drying in their lodges, were taken in a friendly, playful manner; or possibly those Indian saddle-blankets trimmed with the scalps of white women, and with braids and fringes of their hair, were kept simply as mementoes of their owners' high affection for the pale face. At any rate, these delicate and tasteful ornaments could not have been taken from the heads of the wives, sisters or daughters of these "high officials." . . .

The House of Representatives went ahead anyway and on January 10, 1865, ordered an investigation which began in March. Clippings from the News were read into the record as comments from

138

"the organ of Governor Evans." Governor Evans himself was called as a witness and masterfully side-stepped questions to the great annoyance of committee members. At the conclusion of its hearings the committee issued a blistering report. It said in part:

> . . . From the suckling babe to the old warrior, all who were overtaken were deliberately murdered. Not content with killing women and children, who were incapable of offering any resistance, the soldiers indulged in acts of barbarity of the most revolting character; such, it is hoped, as never before disgraced the acts of men claiming to be civilized . . . .

> It is difficult to believe that beings in the form of men, and disgracing the uniform of United States soldiers and officers, could commit or countenance the commission of such acts of cruelty and barbarity . . . .

> His /Governor Evans'_7 testimony before your committee was characterized by such prevarication and shuffling as has been shown by no witness they have examined during the four years they have been engaged in their investigations /of the conduct of the Civil War_7; and for the evident purpose of avoiding the admission that he was fully aware that the Indians massacred so brutally at Sand creek, were then, and had been, actuated by the most friendly feelings towards the whites, and had done all in their power to restrain those less friendly disposed . . . .

> As to Colonel Chivington, your committee can hardly find fitting terms to describe his conduct . . . he deliberately planned and executed a foul and dastardly massacre which would have disgraced the veriest savage among those who were the victims of his cruelty . . . .

Almost concurrently with the Washington investigation a three-man military commission met for seventy-six days in Denver and at Fort Lyon to hear duplicating but more extensive testimony.

139

Chivington, now a civilian, appeared before the commission with attorneys in an effort to defend his actions. The commission made no finding, but the evidence it heard was damning. During the course of its inquiry one of the principal witnesses against Chivington, Captain Silas S. Soule, was assassinated in the streets of Denver. His killer, a soldier of the 2nd Colorado Cavalry named Squires, admitted the slaying, then was reported to have escaped. Squires was not seen in Denver again.

Byer /of the Rocky Mountain News7 lost the fight to save his friend Chivington. The Methodist Church forced his resignation as presiding elder, and the big man left town stripped of honor, his political dreams shattered. He returned to Denver years later to die.

Nor was time kind to the predictions of the News that the affair at Sand Creek would bring peace to the plains. Outrages did not come to an end. Hauteur was not decreased. There was no surrender or suing for peace. Instead of striking terror, the "bully" work of the "Bloody Third" kindled a towering anger that scorched the prairies from Montana to Texas for twenty years to come. When Custer and his men went down on the Little Big Horn in 1876, Cheyenne and Arapahoe warriors were leading the charges.

Fugitives from Sand Creek had scarcely been sheltered in the Cheyenne-Sioux camp at the head of the Smoky Hill before the war pipe was making its rounds. Cheyenne pipe bearers fanned out to the northern tribes, and all the chiefs they visited smoked.

On January 6, little more than a month after Sand Creek, the Indians hit Julesburg with a force of one thousand warriors. The News reported the attack on January 7 and offered:

A SUGGESTION.

Since it is a settled fact that the friendly — peaceable — surrendered — hightoned — gentle-minded — quiet — inoffensive savages are again "on it" down the Platte, we respectfully suggest that a small select battalion of "high officials" be permitted to go down

140

instanter to pacify the devils, receive their arms and
negotiate a treaty by which they will bind themselves
not to massacre any but the outside settlements this
winter, and also to let an occasional train come through
with bread and meat. We have no doubt that the gentlemen are ready, willing and waiting to enter upon the
pleasant duty of proceeding under the protection of a
white flag, with olive branches in their hands, to the
country residences of Messrs. Black Kettle, White
Antelope & Co., where it will be their pleasure to fix
things to suit them.

Three days later another Indian force struck on the Arkansas,
and so it went through the 1860s and into the '70s. Exposed settlers,
wagon freighters, fort garrisons, railroad builders, and cavalrymen
paid the price for Chivington's moment of glory. Jim Beckwourth
told the military inquiry that he made a private attempt in January of
1865 to mediate. Jim, known to the Cheyennes as "Medicine Calf,"
set out alone from Denver and rode boldly into a camp on White Man's
Fork. He told the commission:

I went into the lodge of Leg-in-the-Water. When I
went in he raised up and he said, "Medicine Calf, what
have you come here for; have you fetched the white man
to finish killing our families again?" I told him I had
come to talk to him; call in your council. They came
in a short time afterwards, and wanted to know what I
had come for. I told them I had come to persuade them
to make peace with the whites, as there was not enough
of them to fight the white, as they were as numerous
as the leaves of the trees. "We know it," was the general response of the council. But what do we want to
live for? The white man has taken our country, killed
all of our game; was not satisfied with that, but killed
our wives and children. Now no peace. We want to go
and meet our families in the spirit land. We loved the
whites until we found out they lied to us, and robbed us
of what we had. We have raised the battle-axe until
death . . . .

141

In October of 1865 two men who should have been listened to backed off and took a long-range view of the flaming plains. Their summary and suggestions, ranged against the violent temper of the times, stand out as singularly wise and prescient. Both knew what they were talking about, if any men in the West did. They were Colonel Christopher (Kit) Carson and Colonel William W. Bent of Bent's Fort, whose 'breed son, incidentally, had been among the Indians wounded at Sand Creek. In a letter to Major General John Pope, Carson and Bent wrote:

. . . For a number of years the policy of our Government has been to remove our Indians Westward, before the steady advancing tide of Eastern progress, but now emigration leaps forward from the West itself, swarming over the Eastern slope of the Sierra Nevada, and will probably soon make the Rocky Mountains resound throughout its entire length to the hum of busy life . . . gradually encircling them /the Indians7 with its ever advancing stride, civilization presses them on all sides, their ancient homes forcibly abandoned, their old hunting grounds destroyed by the requirements of industrious and civilized life, how pitiable a prospect is presented for the preservation of any portion of those vast numbers of aboriginals that swarmed through the interior of our continent the happy possessors of a country full of game, and replete with everything that tended to realize their ignorant ideas of happiness and comfort. The cruel or the thoughtless, might leave to this steady advance of a superior race, the ultimate destruction of the various Indian tribes, that it would occur from this cause alone is certain, but humanity shudders at the picture presented by the destruction of hundreds of thousands of our fellow creatures, until every effort shall have been tried for their redemption and found useless, by dispossessing them of their country, we have assumed their stewardship, and the manner in which this duty is performed will add a glorious record to all American history, or a damning blot and reproach for all future time . . . .

142

ELEVEN: THE DENVER AND RIO GRANDE RAILWAY

by Robert G. Athearn

Throughout the first decade of empire building in the Pike's Peak region, the lack of adequate transportation proved a serious handicap. Only railroads would solve the problem, and they were slow in arriving. A major set-back threatened the Coloradans when the Union Pacific selected the Wyoming area for its crossing of the Great Divide. But, by 1870, the Denver Pacific provided a connection with the transcontinental at Cheyenne and in that same year the Kansas Pacific linked the Colorado capital directly with the Missouri River. Something different in western railroading arrived about the same time, when General William Jackson Palmer began organizing the Denver and Rio Grande Railway, the "Baby Road" that would become intimately associated with Colorado's development. *

*   *   *

THE DENVER AND RIO GRANDE RAILWAY

At precisely eight o'clock on a bright autumn morning, in 1871, the people of Denver watched a shiny, new train move along the edge of the city, pause at F /Fifteenth7 and Larimer Streets, then disappear southward along the Platte River. As it passed they could see the name "Montezuma" painted on the cab of the thirty-nine foot engine and the words "Denver & Rio Grande" spread the full length of its tender. Then came a baggage car followed by "two elegant passenger coaches," one bearing the name "Denver," the other, "El Paso." In that fleeting moment a whole story of railroad enterprise passed them in review. The words on the coaches and tender explained the road's projected termini while the engine's name revealed a hope that it would one day enter the city of the Aztec kings. But on this twenty-

– – – – – –

*from Robert G. Athearn, "The Denver and Rio Grande Railway: Colorado's 'Baby Road'" in *The Colorado Magazine*, volume XXXV (January, 1958), pages 35 to 50. Used with permission of the State Historical Society of Colorado.

sixth day of October the train was going only to Colorado Springs — a village that was barely three months old.

The passengers were neither the paying variety, nor just ordinary folk. This was "show day," and to display its accomplishments the management invited a number of regional editors to enjoy an excursion, at its expense. Among them were men like Nathan C. Meeker, of the Greeley Tribune, O. J. Goldrick, Denver's first schoolmaster, now of the Denver Herald, and Rocky Mountain News editor W. N. Byers, an ardent supporter of all Colorado enterprises.

As the train moved along at a steady fifteen miles per hour, the News reporter admired the clear, blue atmosphere, marred only by a few thunder-heads that sulked harmlessly in the distance, and indulged himself in a brief, but glowing, essay on Colorado's climate. Meanwhile, the little engine, weighing only twenty-five thousand pounds, tugged its load along a grade that gradually increased to seventy-five feet to the mile as it scaled what was known as "Lake Pass." Beyond the right of way were stands of excellent timber, and piled along the road lay a half million feet of lumber awaiting shipment.

Five hours, and seventy-six miles, south of Denver they came to a station labelled Colorado Springs where a railroad chef had a meal ready. Their host, young and genial road President William Jackson Palmer and his right-hand man, former Territorial Governor Alexander C. Hunt, were waiting to escort the party to the site of Colorado Springs. After lunch members of the excursion inspected the tract, upon which the first house had been built that August, and then went back to the railroad cars for the return trip to Denver. Perhaps the most enthusiastic member of the group was W. N. Byers, whose newspaper became a strong supporter of Palmer and his project. The editor had a great admiration for such enterprising newcomers and he did all he could to lend assistance through the columns of the News.

During these years there were a number of young men like Palmer in the plains and Rocky Mountain West — veterans of the Civil War, in search of fresh economic opportunities in a land that was new and as yet relatively undeveloped. Some of them sought the gold fields as a source of sudden wealth, others aspired to the title of cattle baron or merchant prince, but Palmer cast his lot with the railroad builders, believing that transportation was the key to success in the limitless stretches of public domain beyond the Missouri. Like General Grenville Dodge, chief engineer of construction on the Union Pacific, or former Confederate General Thomas L. Rosser, who had a similar position with the Northern Pacific, General Palmer was anxious to start life anew with what appeared to be a very promising western industry.

Few, if any, of the former soldiers returned to civilian life with better prospects. Using his previous railway experience as private secretary to J. Edgar Thomson, of the Pennsylvania Railroad, Palmer made himself available to a business whose expansion would match any other in the post-war boom. It was with careful consideration that he chose the Union Pacific's Eastern Division, a road being built across the plains of Kansas, and one that soon would adopt the optimistic name of Kansas Pacific. He foresaw, quite correctly, that the West offered enormous opportunities for enterprising individuals who were qualified to act as agents for eastern capitalists and, accordingly, he accepted the treasurership of the road, along with the post of secretary-treasurer of the construction company that proposed to build it.

Originally, it was planned that the Union Pacific's Eastern Division would connect with the main line at the 100th parallel, somewhere in the vicinity of Fort Kearny, Nebraska, but the enthusiasm of the road builders, spurred by the pleas of Denver for a direct connection with the East, resulted in the decision to build to that mining capital. During 1867 surveys were made across the plains, and that fall two more parties, over which Palmer had general charge, were sent forth to choose a route west of the Rio Grande to the Pacific coast in anticipation of a transcontinental road. It was here, while trying to choose between a route along the Thirty-Second parallel or the Thirty-Fifth parallel, that he became acquainted with the country of southern Colorado and northern New Mexico. Enthusiastically he reported that while the population of these parts was still small the potential was great. Certainly, he urged, a line built through a country that was possessed of both agricultural and mining resources would be profitable.

Congress did not share the road projectors' enthusiasms and declined to provide the necessary subsidy to build on to the Pacific along the Thirty-Fifth parallel, as Palmer had urged. Nevertheless, by the fall of 1870 Denver welcomed the tracks of the Kansas Pacific and realized its ambition of a connection with the Missouri River. The "Queen City of the Plains" would have to wait another sixty-four years for the opening of a line due west to San Francisco. Meanwhile, the Kansas Pacific people were obliged to satisfy their desires for a transcontinental route by making a connection with the Union Pacific, at Cheyenne.

Palmer now cut himself loose from his employers and struck out on his own. His almost passionate defense of the country south of Denver, offered in the official report on the Thirty-Fifth parallel route, had revealed him as a man of vision reminiscent of Colorado's former Governor Gilpin who had for years talked in glowing terms of railroad opportunities in the West. In Palmer the business leaders of Denver found a friend and an enthusiastic booster. Men like Governor A. C. Hunt and former Governor John Evans welcomed him and shared his excitement over the prospects for Colorado.

Palmer's desire to build a road along the mountain front south of Denver was revealed privately months before the Kansas Pacific line reached that city. After trying, without avail, to persuade the directors of the company to build up the rich Arkansas valley to Pueblo and then north to Denver, the youthful promoter determined to stake out the claim for himself. In the spring of 1870, accompanied by William P. Mellen, a wealthy easterner, his daughter, Queen, and Colonel William H. Greenwood, chief engineer of the Kansas Pacific, Palmer visited Colorado City near the future location of Colorado Springs. It became clear to him that a railroad along the canyon mouths that opened from the mountains onto the plains, with branch lines into the valleys, was certain to catch the traffic passing to and from the mines. Convinced he was right, he went forward with his grand scheme for a mountain railroad.

When the party returned to Denver, Palmer persuaded his friends, A. C. Hunt, F. Z. Salomon, and Irving Howbert to organize a dummy railway company to hold the field for him until he was in a position to perfect his own plans. Next, he turned to the acquisition of land. Much of the country along the mountains was "offered land," that is, subject to private entry, and on some of it people had already taken up claims.

146

Since land, the value of which would rise with the coming of a road, was to be one of the bases for financial support of the whole project, it was necessary to acquire title to as much of it as possible before publicly announcing his plan. Accordingly, Hunt and Howbert covered the ground between Denver and Colorado City, to determine what part of it would be valuable, after which the latter embarked upon a buying trip, obtaining the necessary relinquishments for next to nothing. Then the property was purchased from the federal government with agricultural scrip which was also very cheap. The land upon which Colorado Springs was built sold for eighty cents an acre. The right of way for the road bed itself was gained from the United States government by a direct charter conveying to the company a strip two hundred feet wide with twenty acre-tracts for depot purposes at ten mile intervals.

By the late summer of 1870, with the Kansas Pacific finished to Denver, Palmer was ready to pursue actively his plans for the construction of his own railroad running south of Denver to El Paso. On October 24, he wrote to William Mellen, "We are determined to put through the N. and S. Line immediately . . . ; I have a very tempting plan of Pool ready, and will vouch for the ready paying from the start; expecting to live along this line and to make a speciality of this railroad system, I shall undertake to make it a success." To show he had something more to offer than enthusiasm, Palmer revealed that Wilson Waddingham, a New Mexico land speculator, had just called upon him at which time the young railroader "invited him to put in his money, which he did at once to the extent of $50,000, and authorized me besides to sell his Maxwell /Land Grant/ stock while abroad and put the proceeds into our little railroad." This would raise perhaps another quarter of a million dollars, enough to assure a successful beginning.

Palmer promised to be in Philadelphia on November 5, when the promoters, calling themselves "Colorado Construction Company, Friends," would meet to discuss the progress of their proposed road. Dr. William A. Bell, who had become well acquainted with Palmer during the Kansas Pacific surveys, and was now associated in the new venture, was hard at work raising money in Europe. Using the influence of his father, a prominent English physician with a wealthy clientele, Bell hoped to raise a half million dollars to build up a proposed colony near Colorado City, which would, in turn, help to support the railroad venture. From the financial standpoint, the picture seemed very bright.

Before leaving for the East, where he not only would attend the November 5 meeting, but two days later would marry Queen Mellen and take a honeymoon trip to Europe, Palmer busied himself with final details of the projected road to Colorado. His close friend and associate, W. H. Greenwood, who would also leave the Kansas Pacific to join the new venture, assured him that the grand plan for a North-South railroad was both feasible and logical. The Rocky Mountain front, said the engineer, would cause all transcontinental railroads, except the Union Pacific, to alter their westbound direction in seeking an outlet to the Pacific. The new railroad, lying athwart these routes, would be in a perfect position to collect both through and local traffic from the large lines. It should be of three-foot gauge, he further explained, because it would run through mining country where some of its branches must, of necessity, be constructed by the mining companies. For economic and topographical reasons the narrow gauge was the best. By so constructing the entire line there would be no break in service between points of supply and the mines. Aside from these considerations, the narrow gauge was thought to be superior because it would reduce the cost of tunnels and cuts in a complex and tortuous terrain. Since there were no other roads south of Denver, Greenwood supposed that the initial use of the narrow gauge by the Denver and Rio Grande Railway Company, as the road was to be known, would dictate its use by all subsequent lines in the region.

Alexander C. Hunt, now removed as territorial governor to make room for one of President Grant's favorites, but still very close to Palmer, supported Greenwood's notion that the country south of Denver was ideally situated for a railroad. From it came much of the lumber used in the city as well as along the other railroads entering that place. Not only did the route intersect numerous roads into the gold mines but along it were deposits of gypsum from which plaster of Paris was made, as well as known coal veins. The climate, varying sharply as one proceeded south, was bound to attract pleasure seekers and it certainly would yield a wide range of agricultural products. Finally, the line would tap the southern cattle ranges and offer transportation to remote military posts. Hunt, whose enthusiasm matched that of Palmer, was quite excited about the promise of Colorado's future.

Determined to overlook nothing that might frustrate his plans, Palmer also solicited the advice of Samuel E. Brown, attorney, and engaged him to study the articles of incorporation to make sure no conflicting interests might rise up to complicate his plan. The field was clear, Brown reported. The Denver and Rio Grande had complied with the law and there were no legal obstacles in its path. Satisfied, Palmer proceeded with formal organization.

On October 27, 1870, the certificate of incorporation for the railroad was filed. It had a capital stock of $2,500,000 and the main office was located at Denver. The Board of Directors consisted of William P. Mellen, New York; Robert Henry Lamborn, a Philadelphian who had served with Palmer during the war; Alexander Cameron Hunt, Denver; Captain Howard Schuyler, closely associated with Palmer during Kansas Pacific construction days; and Palmer himself. The announced route of the main line — to be very important in later litigation — was south from Denver to the Arkansas River near Pueblo, westward through the "Big Canon of the Arkansas," across Poncha Pass into the San Luis Valley to the Rio Grande River and thence along it to El Paso. Seven branches were proposed, covering a good portion of the mining country, and including one through to Salt Lake City.

A contract to build was let to the North and South Construction Company, of Philadelphia, on December 1, 1870. During that month it was succeeded by the Union Contract Company, a firm chartered by the Pennsylvania legislature and headed by Palmer's wartime friend, Charles S. Hinchman. In return for building the estimated 875 miles between Denver and El Paso, the Union Contract Company was to receive $14,000,000 in first mortgage seven per cent gold bonds, less $16,000 for each mile it failed to complete. It was agreed that the Denver and Rio Grande could also pay in its own capital stock or in any municipal, county, state or federal bonds it could secure.

Energetically the management of the new road set about its task. Dr. Bell, busily seeking out prospective investors abroad, wrote to the English land speculator, William Blackmore, in January, 1871, "We are thoroughly in earnest about this enterprise, the grading has already commenced . . . ."

During the same month Palmer published in London a twenty-nine

149

page pamphlet entitled <u>The Denver and Rio Grande Railway of Colorado and New Mexico</u>, in which he told potential stockholders about the advantages of his railroad. The land along the Rockies was arable and well-watered. It also contained coal, iron ore, fire-clay, limestone and building materials, not to mention the well-known deposits of precious metals. The road was bound to be valuable in supplying miners. "A population engaged in mining," he explained, "is by far the most profitable of any to a railway. A hundred miners, from their wandering habits and many wants, are better customers than four times that number otherwise employed." The high price of foodstuffs paid by these men would make farming very profitable to those who would come to till the soil.

Due to delay in receiving iron rails from England, the first spike was not driven until July 28, 1871. Appropriately, it was Colonel Greenwood, general manager of construction, who put it down, after which solicitor Samuel Brown, rather defensively, told the gathering that the rest of the nation's railroad builders were using too broad a gauge. He predicted that in twenty years the three-foot width would be standard.

Now track laying began in earnest. By the first of September the little iron rails, weighing only thirty pounds to the yard, reached out from Denver twenty-three miles. On October 21, they came to the brand new colony town of Colorado Springs, and the seventy-six mile first division of the Denver and Rio Grande presumably was ready for business. All it needed was traffic.

Palmer had already thought about that matter. From the outset he planned to participate in the establishment of a colony town near Colorado City and to use it in support of his project. On June 21, 1871, he signed an agreement with General R. A. Cameron, lately of the Greeley Colony, providing for the establishment of a joint stock company with a capital stock of $300,000, to be divided into shares of $100 each. Property at and around the Springs, owned by Palmer, was then to be sold to the new company, which, in turn would sell a thousand shares for cash and pay the proceeds to Palmer, who promised to loan one-half of it to the company for three years at seven per cent. The president of the Colorado Springs Company was William Jackson Palmer.

The colony's pamphlet propaganda was so successful, particularly in England, that soon the new village would be dubbed "Little London." So rapidly did the newcomers arrive that the manager Cameron had to send a rush order to Chicago for a hundred and fifty portable houses to prevent suffering during the first winter.

By early 1872, two months after the completion of the road's first division, Colorado Springs claimed a population of almost eight hundred. Already there were a number of business houses, a newspaper, two churches, a reading room and a proposed schoolhouse.

As they watched the Colorado Springs colony grow the promoters made plans to duplicate the success all along the line. During 1872, A. C. Hunt reminded Palmer that "We have connected with our own enterprise, over a million and a half acres of land. The ostensible purpose for which these lands were purchased was for colonization." Why not send agents abroad, to Switzerland, Sweden, Germany, and particularly to troubled Alsace-Lorraine, to seek out "hardy husbandmen" for further colonization? Follow the example of the Mormons, Hunt advised. Offer the newcomers half-fare tickets, cheap lands, a healthy climate, rich soil and a place to settle among friends. He thought company holdings along the Arkansas and in the upper Rio Grande country ideally situated for the land-hungry farmers of Europe.

Regular business on the small railroad began on the first day of 1872, when the Union Contract Company turned it over to the new owners. It was an immediate success.

Before the day of rail travel a tri-weekly stagecoach, carrying an average of five passengers per trip, ran between Denver and the Colorado Springs area. During 1872 the Denver and Rio Grande carried 25,168 passengers, an average of 484 weekly. With a great deal of pride General Palmer pointed out that this was an increase of fifteen hundred per cent. During that year the road hauled over forty-six thousand tons of freight, most of which was commercial, the rest, construction materials. Among the freight items hauled were wool, hides, furniture, hay, wagons, agricultural implements, groceries, iron, nails, hardware, grain, lumber, cordwood, stone, lime, cattle, sheep, coal and mining machinery. The pineries along the divide, south of Denver, added a good deal to the traffic, Palmer wrote. "Their produce

151

is shipped both ways over the railroad, and the demand is rapidly increasing for all the requirements of a new country without trees on the plain, and rapidly filling up with towns and farm-houses. There are about 20 saw-mills along the completed line." Then, there were the coal mines near Canon City, not quite reached during 1872. They held great promise as a source of locomotive fuel. Palmer never tired of essaying upon Colorado's resources and its brilliant future.

The General had a right to boast. When he began his project, in 1870, Denver was a small place of 4,800 people. North and west of the City lay Golden and Boulder, little towns that would grow slowly. To the south there was Colorado City, with perhaps three hundred residents, with another five or six hundred scattered along the mountain base toward Trinidad. The region's real metropolis was Santa Fe, an old and well established commercial point of around 8,000 residents.

By the end of 1872 Palmer made the claim that in two years Pueblo's population had jumped from five hundred to thirty-five hundred, and that Colorado Springs was already a thriving city of fifteen hundred, having grown almost a hundred per cent during the year. Trinidad, he said, now had eleven hundred people, while Denver was a relatively large city of fifteen thousand. Allowing for some exaggeration on the promoter's part, population figures had mounted noticeably with the coming of the major railroads to the Denver area. Unquestionably, the plans of the Rio Grande and the excellence of its projectors' salesmanship had advertised the region south of Denver. All over the West emigrant families followed the rail routes to make their new homes. They would come, in great numbers, to live along the little narrow gauge.

Newcomers watched the operations of the new road with interest. It gave them a feeling of satisfaction to see the tiny "Montezuma" or the "Cortez" moving across the foothills, pulling their thirty-five foot long by seven-foot passenger cars. Divided into two apartments, the cars had double seats on one side of the aisle and single seats on the other, with the arrangement reversed in each apartment to preserve balance. They weighed only twelve thousand pounds. Interesting also were the somewhat larger freight engines, bearing names like "Tabiwachi," "Ouray," "Shou-wa-no," costing $8,500 each. They pulled either the eight-wheeled truck-type freight car, twenty-four feet in

152

length, or the tiny, twelve-foot, four-wheeled cars. Because of the lightness of the cars and the small amount of rolling stock owned in the initial period, the railroad's first switch engine was a mule, a fact that probably seemed less quaint at the time than it does today.

These were small beginnings, but Coloradoans were proud of what they called "The Baby Road." Even though it had a mule for a switch engine and its first schedule was no more than a plain piece of paper upon which the Superintendent of the road himself affixed departure and arrival times, a start had been made. And it was not an easy beginning. Tracklaying to Colorado Springs was completed in the fall of 1871, but before the roadbed could be ballasted or surfaced severe winter weather had stopped the work. Even after the first of the year, when trains began running regularly, the roadbed was soft and unreliable. Added to these difficulties the gradient on the first division was heavy and the curvature sharp. The ascent of two thousand feet and descent of thirteen hundred made construction more costly than had been anticipated. The newness of track, the experimental character of the rolling stock, high shop and other labor costs, and the expensive, inferior coal that had to be used before the Canon City area mines were reached, added to the complexities surrounding the initiation of the venture.

On January 1, 1872, the day regular service to Colorado Springs was inaugurated, grading commenced on the second division toward Pueblo, 118 miles south of Denver. Connection with Pueblo was not an announced part of the original plan. The charter talked of building south toward the Arkansas River, to the Labran coal fields in the vicinity of Canon City and "near Pueblo," after which the rails would pass through the Grand Canon of the Arkansas, and seek the headwaters of the Rio Grande. Even after grading south of Colorado Springs began, the railroad company declined to reveal publicly its next immediate goal.

For over a year, Palmer and his associates had studied the country to the south. Meanwhile, in March, 1871, a mass meeting was held in Pueblo to discuss the possibility of a rail connection with Denver by means of the new line. Townsmen were agitated when they listened to a letter, written by A. C. Hunt, explaining that Pueblo was not on the main line because it would lengthen the route by twenty-five

153

miles. The inference was clear that if they wanted a road, they would have to do something about raising money to assist in its building.

During that summer, as southern Colorado pondered its railroad future, Palmer and Hunt continued their appraisal of the situation. In November, Palmer, Mellen, Lamborn, Greenwood and Josiah C. Reiff organized a new land company called The Central Colorado Improvement Company, the purpose of which was to buy the Nolan Grant and other land. This large tract lying south of the Arkansas River, near Pueblo, originally was granted to Gervacio Nolan by Mexico. On July 1, 1870, Congress confirmed its title, but only to the extent of some forty thousand acres. Palmer and his associates bought it from Charles Goodnight, Peter K. Dotson and Charles Blake.

Excited by the knowledge that Canon City had approved a $50,000 bond issue to bring the road from Colorado Springs, and fearful of being left out, the people of Pueblo went to the polls in late June, 1871, and overwhelmingly voted to assist the Denver and Rio Grande. During the following months, as the railroad officials negotiated for the Nolan Grant, nothing was said about the direction of their proposed construction. Stories made the rounds that the $100,000 voted in June by Pueblo was not a large enough sum. When a committee was appointed to press for a decision, and word leaked out that it might even flirt with other railroads, Palmer was forced into action. Toward the end of November, Hunt came to Pueblo and announced that the narrow gauge would build into that city if another $50,000 in municipal bonds was forthcoming. This, he said, was needed to build a branch line to the Labran (Florence) coal fields. Reluctantly, on January 30, 1872, voters agreed to the final stipulation.

Meanwhile, apparently certain of a favorable vote, the railroad had, on January first, arranged with the Union Contract Company for the laying of tracks to within a mile of the Pueblo Courthouse. On June 19, 1872, the first train entered the old Santa Fe Trail trading center. Shamefacedly the Colorado Chieftain confessed that the Rio Grande's arrival was "accomplished so quickly and so cleverly, that but few of our citizens were aware that the road had reached town." Pueblo, however, made up for its civic laxity on July 3, when an excursion train filled with Denver dignitaries arrived amidst a thunder of welcome. The passengers were promptly escorted to the Courthouse

154

where a banquet was served and for those who could stay on, there was a grand ball. The whole affair, said the paper, "served to place Pueblo and Denver in closer and more endearing bonds of fellowship."

The bonds of fellowship did not get a chance to cement. Palmer's organization, now in possession of the Nolan Grant, decided to move the Pueblo depot across the river to a new and favored company town called South Pueblo. Deeply angered by what they regarded as both an act of duplicity and a breach of agreement, the people of the county declined to honor the promised bonds. The railroad at once instituted suit, but the decision was unfavorable to it and the delivery of the bonds was never made.

Despite what they felt to be a betrayal, Pueblo business men had to admit that the road was highly beneficial. With its approach that sleepy municipality sprang into life and experienced a sharp boom. During 1872 a hundred and eighty-five new buildings, worth approximately $621,000, were built. Forty acres on the north side of town were brought into the city, and South Pueblo, that child of the Central Colorado Improvement Company, brought new settlers into the community. The latter addition was particularly stimulated by the railroad extension to the coal fields of Fremont county.

Building the branch to the Labran coal mines, near Canon City, was commenced before the main line reached Pueblo. At a meeting on May 1, 1872, it was agreed that the Central Colorado Improvement Company would purchase a million and forty thousand dollars worth of the railroad's bonds and pay, upon receipt thereof, $825,000.00 in cash, or just under eighty per cent of the face value. The road builders promised to construct a sixty-five mile railroad and telegraph line from Canon City, down the Arkansas Valley to the mouth of the Huerfano, east of Pueblo. That portion between Pueblo and the coal mines was to be in operation within a year; the remainder, by May 1, 1874. The Rio Grande further agreed to haul coal for the Improvement Company for fifteen per cent less than that charged anyone else for coal haulage over its tracks for a period of thirty years.

Dirt flew, and by the end of October, 1872, a thirty-six mile spur called the Canon Coal Railway Company reached the coal fields, fulfilling the long desired connection with fuel supplies and an

155

additional source of traffic. But the Denver and Rio Grande's eyes were bigger than its pocketbook. When the Union Contract Company prepared to turn over the new branch, Palmer and Company could not pay, so the contract company retained possession of this spur until 1874. It was the construction company, using its own funds, that finally finished the stretch into Canon City.

Completion of the branch to Labran in 1872 ought to have made the residents of Canon City happy. It did not. They complained bitterly that instead of building on into the city, the Rio Grande graded the road that far and then with what appeared to be stubborn arbitrariness, refused to lay the necessary rails, apparently wishing to spend the money capturing new and unclaimed territory elsewhere. Palmer, of course, would not confess to them that he was unable to pay for the already constructed part of the branch.

For about a year and a half Canon City experienced a depression and, like a man dying of thirst with water just beyond his reach, its people angrily viewed the nine mile stretch of graded but trackless space that separated them from a rail connection with Pueblo. Fremont County, which in 1871 had voted a $50,000 bond issue, now was asked to confirm that decision and to add a like amount, as the price of rail service. Rural inhabitants doubted that a railroad into Canon City was worth that much, and even some of the townsmen objected to the railroad's tactics. Nevertheless, in March, 1873, a county election was held and while the result was favorable, the county commissioners did not regard a majority of two votes as sufficient popular enthusiasm to give their approval. Finally, in March of 1874, the city held its own election and agreed to the railroad's demands: $50,000 in bonds and $50,000 worth of adjacent lands. Four months later, on July 6, the first locomotive entered Canon City. The Rio Grande had held out for its price and it had been paid, albeit with great reluctance.

Two of southern Colorado's important cities now had rail service. But in gaining it a good many people in that part of the country felt they had paid dearly. Time would reveal that the Denver and Rio Grande's greediness was expensive, for the decision to go south through Pueblo deeply disappointed Canon City. The die was cast at a meeting of the Board of Directors, held January 30, 1872, when William Mellen offered a resolution to the effect that at least a

156

hundred miles could be saved in building the main line by running south from Pueblo across the Spanish range, near the headwaters of the Huerfano or Purgatoire, instead of "going by the route originally contemplated up the Arkansas River by Canon City."

Within a half dozen years the whole picture would change, and the Rio Grande, then extremely anxious to lay its tracks through the Grand Canon of the Arkansas, or what was later called the "Royal Gorge," would discover that it had few friends in Canon City. Confronted by vicious competition from the Atchison, Topeka & Santa Fe, Palmer would have to make the fight of his life to retain the narrow defile that offered the only logical passageway into the mountains for some distance. When the General looked back upon the events surrounding the entrance of his road into Pueblo and Canon City, he may have recalled a remark he made in a letter written to his wife during their courtship days: "One thing I feel certain of — that amidst all the hot competition of this American business life there is a great temptation to be a little unscrupulous." Southern Colorado felt that he had indeed yielded to the temptation.

TWELVE: UNION COLONY'S FIRST YEAR

A unique chapter in the story of the settlement of Colorado could be written only after the advent of the iron horse. Then, when railroad companies eagerly advertised their land-grant acres for sale, and sought agricultural settlers who would produce surplus crops to make up freight cargoes, the "colony" era of settlement began. A wide variety of experiences were encountered as various groups collectively took up lands and attempted to create model communities in the fast-fading frontier of Colorado. The following excerpts report the plans and progress of the colonists at Greeley during their first year in Colorado. *

*   *   *

THE UNION COLONY

Organization and Plans of the Colony

The Daily Colorado Tribune
April 9, 1870

The definite location of what is commonly known as the "Meeker Colony", renders a description of its organization and purposes, appropriate. We accordingly will attempt to do this, as we understand it.

If we are not mistaken, the idea of such a colony as this, was a pet one of Horace Greeley's, on the strength of whose wishes and requests, Mr. N.C. Meeker of the Tribune staff, commenced to travel in the search for the kind of country desired. He went through half a dozen or more Southern States, and found nothing, and then came west. He visited Kansas and Colorado, and returned to New York, where the colony was organized on the 23rd of December, 1869. Mr. Meeker was elected President, Gen. Cameron Vice President, and Horace Greeley Treasurer.

------

*from James F. Willard, editor, *The Union Colony at Greeley, 1869-1871*, Boulder, 1918, pages 240-242; 254-257; 264-266; 297; 358-562. Used with permission of the University of Colorado Press.

A locating committee was then appointed, who visited Colorado, Nebraska, Kansas, Wyoming and Utah, and they were unanimous in the opinion that no where was there anything to compare with Colorado in advantages. Upon so reporting to the colony they were sent back to secure lands, which has now been done. Seventy thousand acres in all have been obtained, including 50,000 acres of railroad lands, and 20,000 entered under the pre-emption and homestead laws, and bought of private parties. The town has been named Greeley, and by the 4th of July, when Mr. Greeley is going to address them, they expect to have a city in something more than name.

Five hundred members of the society, most of them being heads of families, have paid in the sum of $150 each, as all other members will have to, before receiving any of the benefits of the society. To provide against speculators, who might otherwise pay their fee and obtain a portion of the lands without settling upon them and contributing to the general improvement, the lands are placed in trust of Horace Greeley, to be deeded only upon occupation and improvement. The society will organize under our general incorporation act, as "The Colony of Colorado," and will make themselves a permanent society for the encouragement of emigration to their midst. An office will be kept permanently in the Tribune building, New York, and a proper person kept in charge. The results of this will be seen in the addition of thousands of the best kind of people to our Territory.

It is perhaps known to some of our readers that there are two cities in the United States where liquor cannot be and never has been purchased. Those cities are Vineland, New Jersey, and Evanston, Illinois. The latter was named in honor of our Ex-Governor Evans. Deeds for property in these places contain a provision that no intoxicating liquors shall ever be sold on the premises or words to that effect. Greeley will be the third city of that kind.

The members of the colony will now be soon arriving. Special arrangements have been made over all the roads, so that each member comes on a special ticket as soon as he is ready. It is expected that in addition to the erection of their houses, and public buildings, such as school house and church, they will raise a part of a crop during the present year.

The five hundred members include workmen of all trades and professions, besides men of capital for carrying on manufacturing, &c. There are also among them fancy stock and fruit growers, and some who will introduce a new business into the Territory--that of growing mint, burgamont, &c., for their essential oils.

The committee now here estimate that most of the trading of the colony will for the first year, at least, be done in Denver. They inform us that their estimate is, that the 500 families will at least average $200 each during the year, amounting to $100,000. Our opinion is, that it will be much larger, but those are the figures arived at in New York.

We have thus given a brief statement of some of the more important facts connected with the colony, and we expect in future issues to chronicle its rapid success. We have no doubt but that it will be the most important in its grand results that ever located in the west, and its effect upon Colorado can be no more measured at the present time than can that which will follow the two rairoads about to reach us.

The Colonists Begin to Move Westward

Daily Rocky Mountain News
May 4, 1870

From Monday's Cheyenne Leader: A large number of colonists, en route for Greeley, Colorado, arrived on yesterday's train from the east. The Denver Pacific company had provided an extra train, which took the new comers out without detention.

A Disgruntled Colonist

Daily Rocky Mountain News
May 14, 1870

Some sore-headed Union colonist who expected to find a
finished town at Greeley, with manufactories, churches and
street cars awaiting him, telegraphed to the Missouri Democrat,
and his special was published this morning, to the effect that the
Union Colony is all broken up and the members scattering in
every direction. The statement is false. There are only a few
of that kind of fellows in the colony--probably three or four--
and they had better go back to Illinois at once. They are not
wanted in a new country--unless it be to start grave yards.

A Good Account from Greeley

Daily Rocky Mountain News
May 25, 1870

We understand that reports have been circulated that the
Union colony had been broken up and that the members had left.
Could those who have sent such reports visit our colony, and see
the improvements made during the last week, and converse with
our best men, they would come to a very different conclusion. It
is true that there has been some dissatisfaction, but the most of
it has arisen from a misunderstanding in regard to our situation.
Some have come, expecting to obtain an eighty or one hundred and
sixty acre tract of land immediately adjoining the town site, and
were dissatisfied because they could not. Others came wholly unprepared as to clothing and shelter, and of course felt some privations to which they were unaccustomed, and were thus disappointed.

Lumber has now become more plenty, and as we have two
large buildings and nine tents for present shelter, we have no
more trouble of this kind.

Another class, and the most troublesome, have come expecting great chances for individual speculations, and because they found
that such was not the case, and that they could not obtain positions as

161

officers, they have left us--for which we are very thankful.

The town of Greeley will be built; and those who have
borne the brunt of the labor will have occasion to be proud of
their work. Some of our members have been to the mountains and
purchased logs, which they will send down the river during high
water. They have sent a man to Chicago for the machinery for
a good saw mill, which we expect will be in operation in a few
weeks. Good clay has been discovered for brick, and a yard will
probably be started soon. A fine bed of clay for pottery ware has
also been discovered and will be used. Parties are on the ground
ready to contract to put up grout and adobe buildings at about the
same price as wooden ones will cost. A company for mining coal
has been organized, and will proceed to immediate work. They
expect to obtain plenty of coal on the colony grounds. We have
found fair stone within six miles of the town and hope to find some
nearer.

At church, yesterday, there were present by actual count,
two hundred and fifteen persons--twenty-three being women. We
have at least four hundred persons on the ground, and all are doing their best to build up the place and are working in general
harmony. The clouds are passing away and the sun of prosperity
is shining brightly.

Population, Business Houses, Government, Irrigation

Daily Rocky Mountain News
June 1, 1870

Greeley, at present date, contains seventy houses and 460
inhabitants, many of them still living in tents. This infant town
is now four weeks old and growing vigorously; thereby, is entitled
to rank as one of our western cities. She expects soon to shake
hands across the Platte with Denver, and be her rival friend, with
a friendship strong as the iron band, which in four weeks is to
bring them so near together.

The places of business now open are three general provision stores, two bakeries, two meat markets, one hotel, neatly kept, with board and lodging at $10 per week; one boarding house; a blind, sash, and paint shop; a furniture room; an artist's room (landscape and portrait painter); a bank of exchange; a post office and depot; also a telegraph office, soon to be in operation.

...Municipal authority is in the hands of the people. The trustees have the direction of irrigation, road-making, mining, &c. The executive committee have charge of the division and distribution of lands. The first survey, or survey of the town and five acre lots, is nearly complete. All the blocks are 400 feet square and divided into sixteen, eight, or four lots, according to the distance from the depot. One hundred and thirty-five acre lots lie immediately about the town. Nearly all this land is taken, except that reserved for persons coming next fall.

Cache-a-la-Poudre river runs closely along the northern boundary of Greeley, touches it on the north-eastern corner and passes off to the south-east, leaving a fring of cottonwood trees to relieve the view in two directions. The irrigating canal passes through the south-west corner and forms a southern boundary. Hundreds of fruit and forest trees have been set out and much land plowed and planted in "good faith" that irrigation will shower its benefits on us in a few days. The workmen are now engaged upon the last of the nine miles of digging but "the way the water comes down at" our door remains to be demonstrated through all the lines, angles and curves of the whole distance. The trees meantime are watered from three or four wells; a Herculean task indeed. It remains for the future to decide whether energy now manifested by this colony is real unflagging enterprise, or merely enthusiasm.

It would be a seven days wonder, if "all went merry as a marriage bell," if there were no one to find fault, no one to make blunders or to be disappointed, if every one found all his air castles without a blemish. There is no such seven days wonder here. Many are disappointed, some on very reasonable and others on very unreasonable grounds. Some very wisely, others very unwisely decide to go away. Perhaps fifty have left. Most of them young men who

163

hoped to get clerkships. One man remained in Greeley nearly
an hour, and shaking the sand of the desert, and the prickly pears
from his feet, departed on the next train. Long's Peak blinked
and beckoned in vain. He did not like the look of things.

Improved health is the rule and not the exception. Sick-
headache, asthma and catarrh are very timid. A good moral
tone pervades: no brawls, no drunkenness; not even a dog has
been known to fight, so powerful is the moral influence. Public
religious service is held twice on each Sabbath. It is proposed
to build a Union church for present needs. No schools are talked
of yet, further than to reserve good grounds for them.

The Indians treat us with silent contempt. We do not even
pique their curiosity.

<u>Whiskey in Greeley</u>

<u>Daily</u> <u>Rocky</u> <u>Mountain</u> <u>News</u>
October 25, 1870

It has been known for some time that whisky was sold at
two stores in this place. A member of the Good Templars has
boasted of buying liquor at one of the places mentioned, yet no
steps were taken toward abolishing the evil.

Early on last Sunday morning a German came up from Evans
and opened a saloon within the town limits, on a ranch partially
owned by the Colony. Certain persons repaired to the saloon and
"loaded up" preparatory to attending morning service at the church.
Before the benediction had been pronounced, a committee was appointed to interview the saloon keeper. About two hundred persons
gathered around the liquor establishment, soon after the committee
arrived. The proprietor said that he had paid $200 for the use of
the building, which was claimed by one Smith, of Evans, and he
meant to stay until the lease expired. One of the committee got
possession of the key and locked the door. The committee finally
agreed to pay the whisky dealer $200 for his lease, and to cart the
liquor to a place of safety. Many were clamorous to burn the shanty

and destroy the brandy casks. The den was soon afterwards discovered to be on fire. Then the committee made a grand rush
and succeeded in extinguishing the flames, besides saving the
rum, with the card tables, decanters and dice-boxes.

While the members of the committee were congratulating
themselves on this feat, the building was discovered to be on fire
again, but the flames were subdued only to break out again on the
outside of the shanty, and this last conflagration entirely destroyed it.

The next move was to preserve the brandy. A team was
sent for, and after a slight remonstrance, the proprietor with
his brandy, card tables and dice boxes, was escorted to Colony
Hall.

Here the committee parted with a sigh of relief, and felt
that their mission had been nobly and faithfully performed.

Completion of the First Year

Daily Rocky Mountain News
April 19, 1871

The Union colony of Colorado has now completed its first
year. From a review of its history and its progress important
information may be gained, as well as encouragement for a con-
tinuance of the new system of immigration which it inaugurated.
The Union colony was an experiment. Immigration by colonization was a new idea, and like all new ideas its value had to be
demonstrated by practice, and its utility by success. In full faith
that the practical workings of the system would more than realize
the claims of the theory the colony was founded, and at the close
of the first year success has placed its imprint not only upon the
organization itself, but has illustrated the correctness of the idea,
and fully demonstrated its claims as the most practical and efficient
method of peopling the great west, and of opening up and developing the vast and varied resources which here abound, and which
await only the hand of industry to be turned into productive wealth.

The Union colony is a pioneer, and whatever of value, whatever of information, whatever of encouragement is derived from
the first year of its history, should be gratefully acknowledged,
and the same honor yielded as would be given to the individual
who manfully wins and deserves success in a new and untried
field of thought or of endeavor.

...The results of the first year's labor are eminently satisfactory, and show an industrial, financial and social progress
which is most gratifying to all friends of the west. Thirty-six
miles of main irrigating canals have been constructed, which
place an aggregate of 60,000 acres of land under the influence of
water, and insure an abundant supply for all time to come. A
simple and efficient system of lateral ditches has been begun,
which gives a full and equal distribution to all portions of the
colony domain. Two thousand acres of land are now plowed and
being placed under cultivation, and it is safe to assert that before the end of the season at least 2,500 or 3,000 acres will be
planted with grains and vegetables and this year yield renumera-
tive returns to the husbandman. A thriving and flourishing town
has been built up, in which are stores which are carrying on a
growing business in all the departments of trade, a bank whose
operations indicate a sound and healthy state of finances, churches,
schools, societies, and all the various elements which constitute
a community. From January 1st to April 15th, inclusive the
freight received at the depot of the Denver Pacific railway, amounted to 258 car loads, or 6,414,386 pounds on which was paid a
total of $30,096.87. The local ticket sales for the same time
were $1,072.80. There is also a large express and telegraph
business. The receipts of the post office for the various quarters
since the organization of the town are as follows: For the quarter
ending June 30, 1870 (55 days) $4.25; ending September 30, $322.50;
ending December 31, $478.06; ending March 31, 1871, $598.94.
The number of papers and periodicals received is 441, of which
131 are copies of the weekly New York Tribune, and 50 copies of
the Weekly Rocky Mountain News. There have been given 422
deeds on improved property, and 2,954 shares of stock issued.
The present population of the colony is between 1,200 and 1,500,
which are the extremes of the different statements.

THIRTEEN: LURING THE HEALTH-SEEKER

by F. J. Bancroft

Much of the literature circulated by the Territorial Board of Immigration naturally concerned economic opportunities awaiting the newcomer in Colorado's mines and fields. But the climate of the area, and its effects upon health and disease, were also of interest to a generation that lacked the miracle drugs and medical knowledge of today. In many of the Board's publications, sections were included that were designed to extol the virtues of the Territory as a health-inducing area. The following extract is an example of such advertisements, written at the request of the Immigration Board by a pioneer Colorado physician. *

*   *   *

LURING THE HEALTH-SEEKER

Denver, Colorado, November 15, 1873.

To the Board of Immigration:

GENTLEMEN: — In complying with your request to furnish you with facts in regard to Colorado as a Sanitarium, I must necessarily repeat in substance what I have stated upon the same subject in former papers. The altitude and geographical characteristics of different portions of Colorado have a marked effect upon the climate, and its adaptability to the various diseases and conditions of the human system; and therefore the Territory may be considered as climatically divided into two distinct parts, viz.: mountains and plains. The former comprising about one-half the area of the Territory, and forming its western portion, consists of a succession of perpetually snow-clad ranges and peaks, separated by beautiful and fertile valleys and parks, which are from seven to nine thousand feet

_ _ _ _ _ _

*from *Report of the Board of Immigration of Colorado Territory For the Two Years Ending December 31, 1873.* Denver, 1874. Pages 10-12; 14-18.

167

above sea-level, while many of the peaks attain an altitude of nearly fifteen thousand feet. It is well watered by clear, cold rivers and streams, which are rapid in their course, and abound with speckled trout. The forests are composed principally of pine and fir, which give a delightful and healthful aroma to the air.

Hot and cold mineral springs, possessing a great variety of medicinal virtues, are found in many localities. The atmosphere is a little moister than that of the plains, and is rare, clear, cool, and charged with an unusual amount of electricity. This region is unsurpassed in its endless variety of grand and beautiful natural scenery, by any place in America. Persons desiring to escape the fatal diseases incident to large towns and cities in the summer months, may here gain not only health and comfort, but pleasure; those who are fond of botany may find in the abundant flora many of the rare and most beautiful plants and flowers, while those who have a taste for mineralogy, may also here find deposited almost every variety of the base and precious metals, from crude iron ore to the delicate frosted wire gold. Notwithstanding thousands of veins of the different kinds of minerals have been opened and worked, there still remain tens of thousands more hidden away in our hills and mountains, unfound and unclaimed. Primitive granite, hard enough for mill-stones, is stored here in mass, while upon the hillsides and valleys are found many precious stones, as white crystal, moss agate, topaz, onyx, opal, garnet, and amethyst.

Those of a sporting turn of mind can find amusement either in angling for the wary trout, or in hunting the swift-winged grouse, the nimble deer and mountain sheep, the stately elk, or the aggressive grizzly bear. It is here that the chest expands to its fullest extent, and the lungs fill to their utmost capacity at every inspiration, in order to secure sufficient oxygen for the aeration of the blood; and owing to the lessened atmospheric pressure upon the body, capillary circulation is increased, and hence elimination and nutrition become more active.

With these qualities in such a climate, — its bright days inducing out-door sports; its cool nights bringing refreshing slumber, — it can be readily understood that even a short residence therein would cause the narrow in chest to become broad, the relaxed in muscle to grow strong, the thin in flesh to gain weight, and thoroughly regenerate those suffering from the bilious diseases caused by prolonged residence in malarial districts.

Those who desire to make a tour of the mountains of one, two, or three months' duration, can always find in Denver, guides, teams and camp equipage; while those who wish to enjoy the benefits and pleasures of the climate in luxurious ease, can go by rail to the foot of Pike's Peak, where are the soda, and the chalybeate springs, and large and commodious hotels in the midst of most enchanting and wonderful scenery: or, to the hot soda springs of Idaho, where comfortable quarters and every facility for bathing can be had in a lovely village, encircled by cloud-wreathed mountains, and in the neighborhood of the richest and most interesting mining district of this, our modern El Dorado. All of the springs are quite celebrated for their curative effect in rheumatic affections, as also for their tonic qualities.

The second climatic division of Colorado embraces the eastern portion, which extends from the foot of the mountains to the boundary line. It is an open prairie, or plateau, which varies in altitude from 3,000 to 6,000 feet above the level of the sea. It is watered by streams rising in the mountains, which are all swift in their courses.

The soil is dry and alkaline, free from boggy and marshy places, and "blossoms as the rose," with a great variety of flowers during the spring months, but is principally covered with a short, thick herbage, called buffalo grass, which usually dries into sweet and nutritious hay during the month of August. Trees are only found along the river or creek bottoms.

This portion has a pure, rare, dry air, bracing and exhilarating in its effects, warmed and softened by the rays of a genial sun, which is seldom shaded by clouds or hidden by storms, subject to frequent changes of temperature, but nearly free from dampness at all seasons, fogs and dews being almost unknown . . . .

As dry air is a non-conductor of heat, the changes in temperature here do not affect the system readily. Many of the diseases that afflict the human race are mitigated or cured by residence in Colorado, but in this letter it is only intended to speak particularly of those affecting the air passages. The malady called Hay Asthma has never been known, and those who suffer annually from this distressing disease in other climates, may here pass over the period of its attack without feeling a symptom of it. There is probably no other part of America where persons suffering from spasmodic asthma, unconnected with structural changes in the lungs and heart, find such speedy and perfect relief. Often those who have scarcely passed a night for years without experiencing a tightness and constriction about the chest, accompanied by labored breathing, though having used almost every known remedy for tranquilizing it, on their arrival here, breathe and sleep with perfect freedom.

Those who have organic disease of the heart, or lungs, or both, improve more slowly, and a very few, usually those advanced in years, do not experience any appreciable benefit. Cases of chronic bronchitis in the great majority of instances rapidly yield to the healthful influences of the place. Having myself been a sufferer from this complaint, with copious expectoration for several years prior to making my residence in Colorado, and having experienced here perfect immunity from it for a period of seven years, I know whereof I speak.

Of the thousands of consumptives who have come to Colorado in all the stages of all of the varieties of the disease, with the hope of an immediate cure, many have sadly failed to realize their expectations, and the effect has been to bring some disrepute upon our country as a resort for this class of invalids. A careful consideration of the effect of climate upon disease and the kind of cases that improve here, will, I trust, make it one of the most popular places upon the continent. The climatic influences upon the general health is stimulating and anti-scrofulous, and its tendency upon the lungs is to correct abnormal secretion; to relieve irritability of the bronchi; to lessen local congestions and inflammations, and to calcify tuberculous or caseous deposits. The deep and full inspirations required here induce expansion of the chest and stimulate the absorptions of hepatizations.

It is my experience that a great majority of the bronchial, pneumonic and febivid forms of pulmonary consumption, readily give way to the healthful influences of the place, and that the embolic variety may be checked if the lesions are not too great and too many. To

170

syphilitic phthisis the climate can only serve as an auxiliary to a judicious medical treatment. The tubercular or scrofulous consumption is the most common as well as the most intractable and destructive type of the disease, yet I can safely say that there are hundreds who came to Colorado in the first stage of the chronic form of this complaint, who are now enjoying all that pertains to a healthful life. I can not, however, say that every one who comes thus early will recover, for hereditary taint or acquired predisposition may be so strong that the disease will go progressively through all of its stages to a fatal termination. After the second stage has been reached, a few cases are arrested, and now and then there is one in which complete recovery takes place. As, for instance, a prominent railroad man came to this country in this condition in 1867. After one year's residence in which some improvement took place, he began to cough up bloody pus and calcarous concretions, the largest of which were the size of a white bean and fully as hard as common chalk. This was soon followed by a subsidence of the cough and restoration to health, and to-day he is a strong, able-bodied man, capable of great endurance. Acute pulmonary tuberculosis is too rapid in progress to be controlled or checked by change of climate. If there is great vascular irritability and excitement in any of the above mentioned forms, even in the first stages, it has been found that the climate is too stimulating, and that a warmer and moister place like Florida, is better suited to them. I must strongly warn persons in the third stage of pulmonary consumption, or even after the breathing capacity has been diminished one-fourth, against venturing on to these elevated plains, because too great an increase of the action of the respiratory organs tends to hasten, instead of retard a fatal termination. The same cause is applicable to any forms of organic disease of the heart, excepting that induced by asthma.

The most desirable place of residence for consumptives is upon the plains, within twenty miles of the foot-hills, for this portion is protected from the dry north winds by spurs or divides from the main range; and furthermore, there is daily an interchange of currents of air between the plains and mountains, similar to the land and sea breezes upon the beach.

The mountain air is moister, and, mingling with the dry atmosphere of the plains, relieves it of any harshness it may possess.

I would advise those who have a decided predisposition to hemorrhage of the lungs, and others suffering from great debility, to avoid a too sudden transition from dense to light atmosphere, by stopping for a period of ten days at Wallace in Western Kansas.

To the young of consumptive families, Colorado offers special inducements, for here many a brilliant and useful life, that might be lost in a less salubrious climate before reaching the meridian of manhood, may be prolonged to a vigorous old age.

The wheat of Colorado is not surpassed in quality by any raised in the United States; and cattle in huge herds wander over the hills and plains, finding rich sustenance all the year round in the prairie grass; therefore, breadstuffs and beef are good, plentiful and cheap, which is an advantage to the country second only to its air, it being a known fact that in regions where abundance of good bread and beef, with all their rich, blood-making qualities, are within the reach of every family, pulmonary consumption is rarely prevalent.

Denver and many of the large towns and colonies, afford excellent educational advantages, the privileges of good society and business opportunities in addition to their sanitary advantages.

I have observed that many of the epidemic diseases that extend generally through the Western States, have reached us, but in a very mild form. I would further state that contagious diseases become mild, as a rule, after one or two transmissions, which is owning, in my opinion, to the partial drying up of the emanations and fomites, and thus rendering them less virulent.

The climate throughout the Territory is almost free from malarial poison. No better proof of the general healthfulness of the country can be given than that furnished by the last health report of the city of Denver, which shows the death ratio of the place to be only ten (10) to every one thousand (1,000) inhabitants, a fact unequalled in any other city in the Union, the next in scale being Rochester, which has fifteen to every one thousand, while New York has thirty-two, and New Orleans fifty-four to every one thousand.

172

The healthfulness of Colorado arises from its pure, dry air; its altitudes; its many bright, sunshiny days; its uniform and highly electrified atmosphere; and its brilliant and grand scenery, which produces cheerfulness and a contented frame of mind. It is impossible for me, in this letter, to enter into detail in describing the many different diseases that may, or may not be benefited by a residence here. There are, however, but a few of the curable ailments in persons possessing a sound heart, that may not be relieved or mitigated by dwelling for a few weeks or months in this climate.

I believe that any person with a fair constitution, who settles in any portion of Colorado, stands a better chance of enjoying a healthful life, and of finally attaining the full period allotted to man — three score years and ten — than in any other part of the Union.

Very respectfully, your obedient servant,

F. J. BANCROFT, M.D.

FOURTEEN: THE FIRST FIGHT FOR STATEHOOD
by Elmer Ellis

From 1861 to 1876 Colorado was a legally constituted territory of the United States. As such, the executive and judicial officers were appointed by the federal government, the people had no vote in the federal Congress and no ballots to cast in the electoral college. Throughout most of these fifteen years, a restlessness generated by the inferior territorial status was discernible within Colorado and, on several occasions, overt attempts were made to elevate the territory into statehood. The earliest of these attempts is narrated here.*

*   *   *

THE FIRST FIGHT FOR STATEHOOD

The histories of the struggles of the various Territories for admission into the Union form some of the most interesting phases of western history. When a movement of this kind succeeded it became the pride of the political group which brought it about, and went down in local history as a notable achievement. If one failed it was soon forgotten. Hence the success of Jerome B. Chaffee and Thomas M. Patterson in leading Colorado into the Union in 1876 is a familiar story, while the more interesting failure of the sixties is less well known.

Colorado was not ready for statehood in 1864. Probably few people today would claim that it was. But the Civil War had brought about chaotic conditions in national politics. The exigencies of the dominant political group at Washington led to a desire for more States from the West, and enabling acts were passed providing that Colorado, Nebraska and Nevada should hold elections to determine whether they would come into the Union under constitutions of their

------

*from Elmer Ellis, "Colorado's First Fight for Statehood, 1865-1868" in *The Colorado Magazine*, volume VIII (January, 1931), pages 23-30. Used with permission of the State Historical Society of Colorado.

own making. The act for Colorado provided that a constitutional convention should assemble on the first Monday in July, 1864, to draw up a frame of government, and that the election should be held on the second Tuesday in September.

The prospect of statehood was attractive to many Coloradoans. The vision soothed local pride; it promised home rule and a better defense of Colorado's interests at Washington. Then, too, it stimulated the interest of those to whom the territorial status had been one long fast day. "Decrepit and windbroken politicians who clamored for the support of the general government," a contemporary later complained of that political condition, "were preferred to the first class native timber to be found here in exhaustless quantities." Statehood soon had a following marshalled under the leadership of Governor John Evans and Henry M. Teller. It was advocated by the entire Colorado press, with the exception of the Daily Mining Journal of Black Hawk.

In accordance with the stipulations of the enabling act, local caucuses were held to choose delegates to the constitutional convention. The delegates met at Golden on July 4, only to adjourn to Denver for their work. Those favoring statehood were in complete control of the assembly, and proceeded at once to frame a constitution, which they probably modeled after a draft presented by Delegate William N. Byers. The result was a typical State constitution of its period, except for the salary schedule of the State officials. Sparsely populated and poor in taxable property as Colorado was, the statehood leaders correctly foresaw that the chief argument of their opponents would be the probable influence of statehood upon the annual tax bill. In anticipation of the campaign they included one of the lowest salary schedules any Colorado constitutional convention ever seriously considered. It provided such incomes as $1,000 for the Secretary of State, $400 for the Attorney General, and three dollars a day for the members of the legislature when in session. This was probably a tactical error, as it made the prospective State offices unattractive.

So confident were the advocates of statehood that they decided to hold an election for State officials at the same time that the vote was taken on statehood. A "Union Administration" party convention was held, which named a complete ticket, headed by D. T. Towne for Governor, and Colonel J. M. Chivington for Congressman.

175

Besides this slate it was understood that should statehood carry, Evans and Teller would be the party's nominees for the United States Senate before the prospective legislature. This convention handi-capped the statehood movement badly. The "Union Administration" party, as the Republicans called themselves, was easily dominant over the Democrats, and if statehood carried their nominees would in all probability be elected. Among the large numbers disappointed in the convention there was a perceptible cooling off of enthusiasm that affected the successful candidates. The nominee for Governor, who had wired his acceptance, suddenly changed his mind and with-drew when the political breeze changed its direction.

The brief campaign that followed was one "that, in bitterness, acrimony, and unscrupulousness on both sides, never was equalled in any other political contest during Colorado's Territorial period." Describing the leadership of the statehood movement, the Daily Mining Journal declared, "Old John /Evans7 works the lead, Gen. Teller on the near wheel, Col. Chivington on the off wheel, Byers is the horse 'to let, ' and Rev. King the dog under the wagon." The anti-State campaign was led by Dr. Worrall, A. A. Bradford, Judge Charles Lee Armour and Rodney French. Supporting them were the Democratic politicians — with the notable exception of that nomadic statesman, James M. Cavanaugh — who realized that statehood at this time would not give them any share in the spoils of office. To them was added the lethargy, if not always the active opposition, of many Unionists or Republican politicians who were not interested in the movement. Chaffee announced his approval of statehood so tardily that the "anti-State" convention seriously considered making him one of their candidates. The citizens of Mexican descent in the southern counties were unanimously opposed to any change that would leave them under a local government in which they were a minority. The "antis" charged that the statehood movement was merely an office seekers' scheme, and played constantly upon the unpopularity of Evans and Chivington to stimulate opposition. Statehood, they urged, would raise taxes to unreasonable heights to provide support for its institutions. Possibly with more effect, they warned that, if state-hood carried, the national government's military conscription law would apply to the new State. The statehood leaders argued, on the other hand, that the changed status would give Colorado adequate protection at Washington. With two members of the Senate and

176

electoral vote as well, such unfriendly legislation as the Pacific Railroad act, which appeared to leave Colorado off the transcontinental route, would have been prevented, and the proposed federal tax on mining profits could be fought with real weapons. They did not overlook the argument that statehood would end the terms of certain unpopular territorial officials now active against the proposed change. But their campaign was a losing fight from the beginning. In a vain attempt to save the cause, Evans announced that he would not be a candidate for the Senate in case statehood won, but the opposition never let up their attacks upon him and Chivington. When the ballots were counted, it was announced that statehood had been defeated 1,520 to 4,672, in a Territory that Senator Wade thought contained sixty thousand people.

Immediately following this election occurred one of the strangest reversals in Colorado's political history. A few days after the defeat was admitted, the <u>Rocky Mountain News</u> recorded the rumor that some of the former anti-State leaders were organizing a new statehood movement, which they expected to control. Whatever the conferences were that went on behind the scenes, the following spring a call for a constitutional convention was published on the authority of the central committees of both parties, and that of the "Anti-State" committee as well! The leaders of the defeated statehood movement gave little or no public aid to this one, and others carried it on. No authority now existed to form a State government, as the enabling act provided only for the one election. But, it was argued, possibly with some encouragement from Washington, that Congress having once agreed to it, the national government would not refuse admission because of technicalities.

The new leaders of the statehood movement, profiting by the experience of the year before, did not make the same mistakes. The convention was harmonious, chose W. A. H. Loveland chairman, and adopted resolutions favoring statehood by a vote of 43 to 6. The charter approved by it did not differ greatly from that of the year before, except that the usual salaries were attached to the State offices. Without muddying the issue by an election, the vote was to be taken on the question of statehood, complicated only by a special vote on negro suffrage. The campaign began with many more prospects of success than the one of 1864. The <u>Daily Mining Journal</u>, which had damned the former attempt with enthusiasm, now joined the rest of the press in support. The leaders of the opposition deserted and either publicly recanted or kept silent, except for Dr. Worrall, who almost alone led the vocal opposition. When the votes were counted, the statehood advocates had overturned the sentiment of the previous year in most of the northern counties. The large majorities against the change in the southern counties made the contest close, however, but after some delay it was announced that statehood had carried by 3, 025 to 2, 870, or a majority of 155. That there had been questionable practices, if not downright frauds, in some precincts was freely admitted. Negro suffrage had been overwhelmingly defeated.

Conventions were now held by the two regular parties and a temporary organization called the Sand Creek Vindication party. The Republican party was generally successful in the subsequent contest, electing its candidates for Governor and Congressman, William Gilpin and George M. Chilcott. Within the party, however, the usual harmony did not prevail. During the statehood fight the party machinery had come under the control of Jerome B. Chaffee, who directed his attention to the candidates for the legislature, with the result that most of them were friendly toward his candidacy for the Senate as well as that of Governor Evans. Chaffee's attempt to replace Teller as the Union-Administration party's candidate for the Senate was generally successful, except in Gilpin County, where the latter's friends were in a distinct majority, and the resulting split gave a local Democratic victory. When the legislature met, Evans and Chaffee were elected to the United States Senate, Chaffee defeating Teller in the Republican caucus 15 to 8. Evans, Chaffee and Chilcott now went to Washington to urge the acceptance of the new State by the federal government.

President Johnson refused to recognize the "State" of Colorado because of its failure to conform to the enabling act, and turned the matter over to Congress. When no partisan advantage was to be gained by admission, Congress, in the early spring of 1866, was not as anxious to allow it as it had been in 1864. Nevertheless, a bill to accept Colorado as a State under the government recently set up was brought in, supported chiefly by western Senators and generally opposed by Easterners. Some of the latter objected to it because of Colorado's small population, and some because of the lack of negro suffrage. Senator Ben Wade, who had supported the bill of 1864, and later supported this one, talked of rotten boroughs, and the bill was defeated 14 to 21.

Under ordinary circumstances the contest would have ended here. But 1866 was not a normal political period. The growing bitterness between President Johnson and the radical Republicans was rapidly coming to a head. Shortly after the vote on the Colorado bill, the President vetoed the Civil Rights bill. The majority of radical Republicans was large enough to pass this over his veto, but it was barely sufficient in the Senate. Anxious to increase their majority, the radical Republican leaders soon saw their error in refusing admission to a State whose Senators would add two to their majority. A reconsideration was moved by Senator Wilson of Massachusetts, and the following contest found most of the radicals now in favor of statehood, Charles Sumner being the outstanding exception. This genius of consistency wanted negro suffrage in the Constitution before he would vote for admission, and was willing to charge that "there were known and avowed arguments and there were arguments whispered in this Chamber, that these men should be admitted because we need their votes." The statehood bill now passed both houses, to the delight of its Colorado friends. President Johnson vetoed it on grounds that the population did not entitle Colorado to admission. As the bill had not received the necessary two-thirds majority on its original passage, it was useless to attempt to pass it over the veto.

As the lines between the President and his opponents were more tightly drawn, the congressional leaders made another attempt to admit Colorado the next year, and thus add Chaffee and Evans to the Senate. In order to unite more of the radicals behind statehood for Colorado, they now brought in a bill with a provision that its sponsors claimed would insure negro suffrage. Its real purpose was set forth by Senator Doolittle: "It is necessary to reenforce the majority of three-fourths in this body by the admission of the new members from the new State of Colorado and that is the reason why this is to be pressed." Nevertheless, it passed with large majorities, and again met with the presidential veto. Senator Wade now held the vetoed bill up until absences in the Senate made it a strategic moment to pass the bill over the veto. The strategy was ineffective, however, as it again failed to receive the necessary two-thirds majority.

In the meantime the fight over statehood had been revived in Colorado, if indeed it can even be said to have died down after the election. Politics in Colorado, like railroad construction and capital location, had been forming two Republican factions, which differed from each other principally over the location of control. The "Denver crowd," under Evans' and Chaffee's leadership, was the chief force behind the demand for admission and controlled the State administration, which only needed congressional approval to become the government of Colorado. The other, the "Golden crowd," now under the leadership of H. M. Teller, was in direct opposition to statehood. Their antagonism had been growing since the defeat of 1864, and, soon after the results of the election of 1865 became known, Willard, the younger brother of H. M. Teller, had written letters to friends in the House of Representatives, urging them to oppose admission. H. M. Teller and Henry C. Leach went to Washington in the spring of 1866 to lobby against the bill, and thus counter-balanced the efforts of Chaffee and Evans.

After the initial failure of the bill in Congress, public sentiment in Colorado seems to have grown steadily against statehood. If there was an actual majority for it in 1865, it is unlikely that there was in the few years following. Several attempts were made to get the territorial legislature to petition Congress for admission. Although such bills passed one house on some occasions, the only one that passed both was associated with a proposition to extend the boundaries of the proposed State north to include that part of present-day Wyoming containing the Union Pacific Railroad. Party conventions did not think it a popular move to vote an endorsement, and Teller was made chairman of the executive committee of the Republican party.

In the spring of 1868, the last attempt was made to bring Colorado into the Union under the constitution and officials of 1865. The Senate Committee on Territories held hearings at which Evans and Chaffee submitted statements. H. M. Teller went to Washington again to present the anti-State case to the committee. Arriving too late to testify, he drew up a statement in the form of a memorial to Congress. The two testimonies were summaries of the two arguments. The first represented Colorado Territory as a growing commonwealth with a population of from 75,000 to 100,000, the great majority of whom were anxious for statehood. The latter showed a population of "not exceeding thirty thousand," which was not increasing and who did not desire the burdens of statehood. So confident was Teller of the unpopularity of statehood in Colorado that he challenged Congress to allow a vote on the question. "This is all we ask. The people of Colorado feel competent to decide this question . . . ."

The publication of Teller's memorial lighted the fires of controversy again. To the "State" press it was an unpatriotic attack upon the prosperity and future of Colorado. "Let the curse of every citizen be upon him," fumed the Rocky Mountain News. "Let him be a dead man among us, so vile, so corrupt, so offensive, that the very mention of his name will excite loathing. Let the guilt of his own base acts be made to weigh so heavily upon him that he will only be too glad to escape where he cannot even hear the name of the territory he has so abused." A memorial was presented to Congress signed by a number of political workers denying the truth of Teller's statements. On the other hand, he was commended at a mass meeting in Golden, and the Colorado Transcript declared that Teller was supported by three-fourths of the people.

Late in June the new bill came up in the Senate. In the meantime Teller had been active among the Republican Senators, and had found an able champion in Roscoe Conkling, the domineering Senator from New York. Using Teller's challenge of a refernedum on the question to rally the opposition to statehood, Conkling attracted so much support that it soon became apparent that the bill could not pass without an amendment providing resubmission of the entire question to the voters in Colorado. This would have meant new elections, and possibly new Senators, if statehood carried. Confronted by these situations, the active advocates of statehood in Washington decided it was useless to push the case, and it never came to a vote. In September, Evans and Chaffee resigned "to clear the way for statehood." But that way proved to be a long one. Opposition in Congress and opposition at home were too strong to overcome, and it was not until after the rapid development of the territory in the period 1868 to 1872 that statehood became an unquestioned desire among Coloradans. And it was four years later before the national government also agreed that statehood was desirable.

FIFTEEN: ADDRESS TO THE PEOPLE OF COLORADO

*As the national election of 1876 approached, the Republican
Party, dominant in national politics since the Civil War, began to
build its offenses for the campaign. U. S. Grant would no longer
bring the magic of his name to the Republican ticket and new sources
of strength were needed. Colorado was presumed to be Republican
territory and thus, once again, it was viewed as a potentially desirable state whose three electoral votes might spell the margin of victory. Congress passed an enabling act to bring about the transforma-
tion and a constitutional convention drafted an organic charter for the
proposed state. When the convention presented its handiwork to the
people for acceptance, they attached an "Address to the People" designed to explain the document and argue its merits. The constitution
was accepted by the electorate and Colorado became a state in the
summer of 1876, in time to cast her three Republican votes for Ruther-
ford B. Hayes in the disputed election that fall.**

* * *

ADDRESS TO THE PEOPLE OF COLORADO

Your representatives, in convention assembled, under the
provisions of an act of Congress, approved March 3, A.D. 1875,
for the purpose of framing a Constitution for the State of Colorado,
have completed the work, and herewith submit the result of their
labors for your adoption or rejection. The task was an arduous one,
requiring a session of eighty-six days, during which time the Convention labored assiduously to frame a fundamental law, wise and
wholesome in itself, and which would be adapted to the general wants
of the people.

------

*from *The Constitution of the State of Colorado, Adopted in Convention, March 14,
1876; Also the Address of the Convention to the People of Colorado.* Denver,
1876, pages 54 to 65.

In a work of such magnitude, where the interests are so varied and extensive, it is to be expected that errors would creep in, and omissions pass unnoticed, but, upon the whole, we believe it contains not only all of the primitive rights guaranteed in our National Constitution, but most of those reformatory measures which the experience of the past century have proven to be wise and judicious.

The end sought to be accomplished was to secure a just and economical administration of the Departments of State, and, with this purpose in view, especial effort was made to restrict the powers of the Legislative Department, by making all laws general and of uniform operation; to establish uniformity in the Judicial Department — thereby furthering the ends of justice; to prevent the corruption of public officials; to provide for the safe keeping of all public funds, and to protect the people from unjust monopolies, and the oppression consequent upon the voting of bonds and other kinds of indebtedness to corporations.

But, believing that your interest in the instrument now submitted for your consideration, will lead you to give it personal examination, and that you may be able to form a clear and correct opinion regarding its merits, your careful attention is invited to some of the prominent features of the different articles, which we think must meet your approval.

Bill of Rights.

In this article the usual guarantees of national and civil rights have been retained, and to the end that more power should be reserved to the people, it is further declared that the General Assembly shall make no irrevocable grants of special privileges or immunities; that private property shall not be taken or damaged for public or private use without just compensation previously made to the owner thereof, or paid into court for his use; that no preference shall be given by law to religious denominations; that right and justice shall be administered without sale, denial or delay; that aliens, who are bona fide residents of the State, shall acquire, inherit, possess and enjoy property to the full extent as if native-born citizens. The Grand Jury system has been so modified as to make a grand jury consist of twelve men instead of twenty-three — any nine of whom concurring may find a bill, and the question whether it may not be abolished altogether is left to the legislature. The Petit Jury system has been so modified as to permit the organization of a jury of less than twelve men in civil cases, thereby materially reducing the expenses of our courts. The right of trial by jury in all criminal cases has been preserved, and for the purpose of protecting witnesses in criminal prosecutions, and that the accused may always meet the witnesses against him face to face, we have provided for the taking of depositions before some Judge of the Supreme, District or County Court, which can be used upon trial of the cause when the personal attendance of the witness cannot be obtained.

Executive Department.

The term of office of the Governor and other State officers, is fixed at two years, thereby giving the people frequent opportunities to correct the administration of affairs in this department.

It is made the duty of all the State officers to keep an account of all moneys received or disbursed by them, while the Treasurer is required to furnish the Governor a quarterly statement under oath, of all moneys in his hands and the place where kept or deposited, which statement is to be published for the information of the people. The Governor is required to transmit these statements to the General Assembly when called for, thus enabling the representatives of the people to expose, or by suitable laws prevent extravagance and frauds . . . .

The Governor is given the power to remove all officers by him appointed, for misconduct or malfeasance in office; he is also empowered to grant pardons, subject, however, to such regulations for the application of the same as may be provided by law . . . .

As an additional check upon ill-advised legislation, a majority of two-thirds of all the members of each House is required to pass a bill over the veto of the Governor.

The office of Lieutenant Governor is created, thereby giving the State the benefit of an officer elected by the people to fill any vacancy that might occur in the office of Governor; he is also made

184

the presiding officer in the State Senate, and has the majority vote in that body in case of a tie . . . .

Legislative Department.

The General Assembly is required to meet once in two years, and is limited to a session of forty days, after the first Legislature under the State. The term of office of the Senators is fixed at four years; that of the Representatives at two. For the first session the compensation of the members of the General Assembly is fixed at four dollars per day, and thereafter as may be provided by law. No member of the General Assembly shall, during his term of office, receive any increase of salary, or mileage, above that allowed at the time of his election.

The evils of local and special legislation being enormous, the passage of any law not general in its provisions is prohibited — thus saving the State from expenses usually incurred in passing and publishing laws secured by combinations to advance private interests, and to create dangerous monopolies.

To afford protection from hasty legislation, it is required that all bills shall be printed; that only one subject shall be embraced in each bill, which shall be clearly expressed in its title; that it shall be read on three different days in each House before being passed, and that no bill shall be introduced, except for the general expenses of the government, after the first twenty-five days of the session . . . .

To provide against extravagance we have prohibited the passing of any law giving extra compensation to any public officer, servant, agent or employé, after services rendered, without previous authority of law; nor is any officer of the State to be in any way interested in any contracts or awards by which the legislative and other departments of government are furnished with stationery, printing, paper and fuel.

It is further provided that no appropriation shall be made to any denominational, sectarian or any other institution not under the absolute control of the State . . . .

Judiciary.

Radical changes have been made in the judicial system, to meet the imperative demands of our rapidly increasing population. As at present constituted our courts are wholly inadequate to the transaction of the business brought before them. The consequence is, causes accumulate on the dockets, and are continued from term to term, both in the District Courts and in the Supreme Court, causing expensive and ruinous delays to parties litigant, and when reached for disposal sufficient time and attention cannot be devoted to their consideration to render the same satisfactory to either courts or litigants. To correct these evils an additional judicial district is provided, with an additional district judge, making four instead of three judicial districts . . . .

The district courts are invested with original jurisdiction to hear and determine all controversies in behalf of the people, concerning the rights, duties and liabilities of railroad, telegraph and toll road companies or corporations. A Supreme Court, composed of different Judges from those of the District Courts, is created. This court will have three Judges, and as constituted will obviate the objections long entertained and frequently expressed against our present system, by which the same Judge who presides over the trial of a cause in the District Court, sits in review of his own decision in the Supreme Court . . . .

Experience having shown frequent changes of the judiciary to be unwise and detrimental to the public interest, long terms are prescribed for the Judges of these courts. The Judges of the District Courts will be elected for six, and those of the Supreme Court for nine years.

. . . All judicial officers will be elected on a different day from that on which an election is held for any other purpose, thus taking judicial elections out of the arena of party politics.

Education.

By the provisions in this article the general supervision of the public schools is vested in a Board of Education.

186

The maintenance of free public schools, and the gratuitous instruction therein for all children between the ages of six and twenty-one years, is forever guaranteed.

It is declared that the public school fund shall forever remain inviolate and intact; that neither the State, nor any county, city, town or school district shall ever make any appropriation, nor pay from any public fund anything in aid of, or to help support, any school or institution of learning of any kind controlled by any church or sectarian denomination whatsoever; that no religious test shall ever be required as a condition for admission into any of the public schools, either as pupil or teacher; that no religious or sectarian dogmas shall ever be taught in any of the schools under the patronage of the State.

The General Assembly is required to pass suitable laws to husband, to the fullest extent, the several grants of land donated by the general government to this State for school purposes . . . .

Legislative Apportionment.

To guard against the undue influences to which small bodies are exposed, and in order that every portion of our extensive State, with its numerous and diversified interests, may be fairly represented, the Senate is made to consist of twenty-six, and the House of Representatives of forty-nine, members — these members not to be increased until 1890.

A State census is provided to be taken in the year 1885, and every ten years thereafter, which, with the federal census of 1880, and decennially thereafter, will enable the General Assembly to revise and correct the apportionment, on the basis of population, every five years. By these revisions the portions of the State which most rapidly increase in population will receive additional representation . . . .

Corporations.

Probably no subject has come before the Convention causing more anxiety and concern than the troublesome and vexed question pertaining to corporations. The legislatures of other States have, in most cases, been found unequal to the task of preventing abuses and protecting the people from the grasping and monopolizing tendencies of railroads and other corporations. Experience has shown that positive restrictions on the powers of the legislature in relation to these matters are necessary.

To this end we have provided for the wiping out of all dormant and sham corporations claiming special and exclusive privileges. We have denied the General Assembly the power to create corporations, or to extend or enlarge their chartered rights by special legislation, or to make such rights and privileges irrevocable; but in case it shall be found that the exercise of such rights and privileges proves injurious to the people, then the General Assembly shall have power to alter, revoke or annul such charters, when that can be done without injustice to the corporators. We have declared that railroad corporations shall be liable as common carriers, and that to avail themselves of the benefits of future legislation, they must subject themselves to all the provisions and requirements of this Constitution. We have forbidden the consolidation of parallel and competing lines, and of all unjust and unreasonable discriminations between individuals in their business with such corporations. We have carefully guarded the right of eminent domain, requiring a just compensation to be paid in cash when private property is taken, and have required all foreign corporations, as a condition of their doing business here, to have one or more known places of business, and an agent or representative within the State, upon whom the process of our courts can be served at any and all times. We have also retained the jurisdiction of our courts in case of consolidation of a corporation within the State with any foreign corporation, over that part of the corporate property within the limits of this State. We are aware that these provisions do not cover the whole ground, but it must be remembered that while some of our sister States have not gone far enough in placing restrictions on the legislative power, others have gone too far, and have had to recede. We have endeavored to take a middle ground, believing it to be more safe, and in the end that it will give more general satisfaction . . . .

Suffrage and Elections.

By this article we have given the right of suffrage to every male person over the age of twenty-one years, imposing such restrictions only as are required by the Constitution of the United States, and upon questions pertaining to schools in the several districts of the State no person is denied the right to vote on account of sex. The question of female suffrage having been strongly urged upon the Convention by petitions numerously signed and otherwise, and the Convention thinking it unwise to hazard the adoption of the Constitution upon the decision of this question, but recognizing the right of the people to express their will thereon, have required the General Assembly, at their first session, to submit the question to a direct vote of the people at the next general election thereafter. It is provided that an educational qualification for electors may be prescribed after the year of our Lord one thousand eight hundred and ninety. For the purpose of preventing frauds and of protecting the purity of the ballot-box, the system of numbering ballots has been adopted. The working of this plan has been abundantly tested, and the benefits resulting therefrom are so numerous that to have omitted it would have been to have rejected that which the experience of the older States teaches to be wise and judicious; by this plan the secrecy of the ballot is not invaded, while frauds can be easily detected and the guilty party reached, without disfranchising a whole community, as frequently results under our present system . . . .

Miscellaneous.

We have provided that all laws upon our statute books at the adoption of this Constitution, shall remain in full force and effect until altered or repealed by the legislature of the State.

We have declared that all persons who are qualified electors at the adoption of the Constitution, shall be eligible to the several State offices, to the General Assembly, and to the various county offices.

We have prohibited under very stringent provisions the importation, manufacturing and sale of all spurious or adulterated liquors. We have provided for the passing of laws, to prevent the destruction of, and to keep in good preservation the forests upon the public

domain. We have provided for the printing of this Constitution in
Spanish as well as laws passed by the General Assembly until the
year 1890, thus giving the Spanish-speaking population of the State
an equal opportunity of being fully informed of the provisions of the
fundamental law, as well as all laws passed in compliance therewith.

We have provided liberally for the amending of the Constitution,
thus giving to the people frequent opportunities of changing the organic
law when experience and public policy may require it.

In this hasty review of the several articles contained in this
Constitution, we have endeavored to call your attention to those provisions in which we presumed you would be most interested. We do
not think it necessary to enter into an elaborate argument to show why
they should meet your approval; believing that you fully appreciate the
inestimable prize secured by entering the sisterhood of States, where-
by you gain those privileges that flow only from that form of government, which is the offspring of your choice, completely free in its
principles, uniting in its powers security, happiness and prosperity
of the whole people. But it is easy to foresee that from different
causes, and from different sources, an effort will be made, and many
artifices employed, to weaken in your minds the conviction of this
truth, and we may reasonably assume that the chief objection made to
a State government will not be founded upon the character of the instrument we have framed, but upon the alleged and supposed increase
of expenses and consequent taxation. This is the old cry, and however
potent it may have been heretofore, it certainly has lost its force in
the facts of the present. We meet this objection directly, by conced-
ing that a State government will, of course, involve an increased expense over that of our present form, but we assert that this expense
will be more than balanced by the pecuniary gain alone which we will
receive by becoming a State. We will suppose that if we are not admitted now, we will not have another opportunity of admission for at
least five years. The increase in our expenses under a State government will be about $50,000 per annum, which, in five years, will
amount to $250,000. This would be saved to us, or, more properly,
be delayed in payment by remaining out of the Union five years longer.

Now, let us see what we would lose in that time: The act of
Congress granting sections sixteen and thirty-six for school purposes,

190

allows the State to select an amount of public land equal to that which has been sold out of said sections to settlers prior to survey. Under this arrangement we will be entitled to select about fifty sections of land.

The Enabling Act grants fifty other sections for public buildings, fifty sections for the penitentiary, and seventy-two sections for general purposes — making a total of two hundred and twenty-two sections, or one hundred and forty-two thousand and eighty acres of land, which, at $2.50 per acre, amounts, in value, to $385,200.

It will also be remembered that, upon becoming a State, Colorado will be entitled to five hundred thousand acres of the public land within her borders, by virtue of a grant heretofore made by Congress. This amount, if selected now, would be worth to us at least $500,000.

The enabling act also grants the State five per cent. of the proceeds from the sale of the public agricultural lands after the adoption of this Constitution. The amount to be derived from this source for the next five years would exceed one hundred thousand dollars, which, added to the value of the land above mentioned, would make a total of about $1,000,000, which is four times the estimated amount of the increased expenses of the State for this period, so that we would really gain over three-quarters of a million dollars in five years by becoming a State. More than this, the revenues from sections 16 and 36 will save the whole State, in our school taxes, from ten to twenty-five thousand dollars yearly, making a saving in five years of from fifty to one hundred thousand dollars in addition to that already estimated. Should we not be admitted, and remain in a territorial condition five years longer, most, if not all, the public agricultural and non-mineral lands in Colorado, which are worth anything, will have been sold by that time, so that there being none left for selection, we would lose all this, even if a like grant should be renewed at the end of that time. No one will doubt this statement who reflects upon the small amount of public agricultural lands now left within our Territorial limits, and considers the probable immigration for the next five years. The five per cent. alluded to would, from the same cause, like the lands granted in the enabling act, be forever lost to Colorado, and we would, therefore, at the end of that time be obliged to commence our State-hood with increased expenses, and at a dead-loss of over a million of dollars at the lowest possible estimate. In addition to these several benefits to be derived by our admission into the Union at this time, we would also call your attention to the fact that, by cutting off special legislation, we have lessened the expenses of that department almost one-half; by reducing the number of the petit and grand jurors the expenses of the judiciary department are greatly reduced, while the provisions guarding against hasty legislation at the close of the sessions of the General Assembly, will prevent great squandering of public money, and in many cases save more to the State than sufficient to pay the per diem and mileage of the members of that body.

This much for the pecuniary balance of gains and losses. Let us now look at the political and substantial advantage of Statehood as contrasted with our present condition of Territorial vassalage. By becoming a State, we elect our officers from our own people and are permitted to join in the election of the Chief Magistrate of the Nation, thus enjoying for the first time, while in Colorado, the sweets of self-government.

Our privileges will then be enlarged, we will no longer be suppliants for the rights and immunities belonging to freemen — we will have gained them. Then we will be able to assume our proper station among the States of the Union. With two Senators and a Representative in the National Congress, we will be enabled to command respect, and to secure additional appropriations for the fostering of our industries, as well as of extending our political privileges; then we will have a voice in the matter of Indian treaties, in the establishing of military posts and roads, in the location of mail routes, in the passing of laws concerning the title to mineral veins, and providing for the disposal of the mineral and pastoral lands of the State as suited to peculiar wants; also upon many other questions which at present interest us, but upon which we cannot now be heard. Who is there among you that would not rather be a citizen of an independent sovereign State, than a mere settler upon the public lands of the Territory, governed by satraps appointed and removed at pleasure, as best serves the whims and purposes of political rings and cliques — beggars, asking pittance at the gate of the nation; poor wards dependent upon the charity of political servitude? Now that the golden opportunity is afforded, shall this state of things longer exist? We confidently believe it will not. Let us cherish, then, this occasion with more than ordinary zeal,

192

actuated by the memories of the past, and inspired by the rewards for us in the future; let us arouse ourselves to the responsibilities of the hour, and, as citizens of a free republic, become, in fact, as well as in name, citizens of the American Union of Sovereign States.

SIXTEEN: JOHN W. ILIFF — CATTLEMAN

by Agnes Wright Spring

The years from 1870 to 1880 were prosperous years for Colorado. Statehood, railroads, and the removal of the Eastern Slope Indians provided solutions to old problems. Mining would soon expand from the original gold camps to exciting new silver fields. Irrigators at colony towns like Greeley were laying the foundations for the future agricultural development of the state. The decade also saw the opening of new economic empires — the cattle kingdoms ruled over by "beef barons" who converted government-owned grasslands and their own strategic holdings into one of the most colorful, romanticized epochs in the history of the West. Among the pioneer cattlemen of Colorado, none exceeded John W. Iliff as a contributor to the industry. His career is delineated here by Agnes Wright Spring, State Historian of Colorado.*

*   *   *

JOHN W. ILIFF — CATTLEMAN

John Wesley Iliff, known as the "Great Cattle King of the Western Plains," whose name was "famous from Texas to Lake Superior, and from the Atlantic to the Pacific," made such an outstanding success of his western range cattle business in northeastern Colorado and southeastern Wyoming that he was acclaimed for many years by writers for newspapers, magazines and books, both in this country and abroad.

------

*from Agnes Wright Spring, " 'A Genius for Handling Cattle': John W. Iliff," part three of *When Grass Was King: Contributions to the Western Range Cattle Industry Study* by Maurice Frink, W. Turrentine Jackson, and Agnes Wright Spring, Boulder, 1956, pages 335-429 *passim*. Used with permission of the author and The University of Colorado Press.

194

Such acclamation, especially during the late 1870's and early 1880's, undoubtedly had far-reaching effect on those considering investment in the range livestock business. Even though many cattlemen eventually owned more cattle and horses and actually controlled greater grazing acreages than did Iliff, writers continued through the years to refer to him, as did one at the time of his death, as the "most extensive cattle breeder and cattle raiser of the Far West." . . .

John Wesley Iliff grew up with cattle, studied the cattle business and engaged in buying and selling cattle most of his life. Born December 18, 1831, in McLuney, Perry County, Ohio, he was the son of Thomas Iliff, a well-to-do farmer who specialized in the raising of fine stock near Zanesville, Ohio. His early youth was spent in the Ohio Valley region from which cattle had been trailed across the Alleghenies to market for more than forty-five years. It is reasonable to assume that some of Thomas Iliff's cattle may have been included in a few of those drives.

When John W. Iliff was eighteen years old the big gold rush to California was on, and by the time Argonauts began to return to their Ohio homes with tales of the West, young Iliff was attending Ohio Wesleyan University at Delaware, Ohio.

By 1856, when young Iliff left college, the ruts of the Oregon and California Trails and the old Santa Fe Trail already were worn deep by the tread of thousands of oxen, mules, horses and men. Popular reading of the day included Parkman's California and the Oregon Trail (1849), Irving's Adventures of Captain Bonneville (1837) and John Charles Fremont's journals of his western explorations.

Thomas Iliff offered his son a $7,500 interest in a good Ohio farm if he would settle on the place and farm it. But "stimulated by the accounts of Western enterprise and Western fortunes, /he/ declined this offer, saying: 'No; give me the $500 and let me go West.'"

It is probable that he went west with friends from Ohio or joined Buckeye acquaintances in Kansas, for he soon helped to organize Ohio City Town Company, which laid out Ohio City /now Princeton/ in April, 1857 . . . . The "first store was erected by J. W. Iliff, the money being raised by popular subscription . . . ."

At the time Ohio City was laid out, the Territories of Colorado and Wyoming were yet unborn; the Territories of Kansas and Nebraska were only two years old. Council Grove, a small village, about fifty-six miles to the west, was the farthest western settlement on the Santa Fe Trail in Kansas Territory, except Allison's ranch at the mouth of Walnut Creek, five miles west of the Big Bend, and Bent's /New/ Fort on the upper Arkansas, where Fort Wise was afterward built . . . .

Iliff, a large, fine looking young man, who had been named for the religious leader, John Wesley, at once began to acquire land, on which he may have done some farming . . . .

To this area in Kansas came the news of the first gold discoveries near Pikes Peak . . . .

Many of the settlers immediately began to make plans to leave for the "promised land" as early as possible . . . .

Meantime, John W. Iliff had been adding steadily to his income through his mercantile business, and possibly through his farm lands, until he had accumulated two or three thousand dollars. Early in 1859, he disposed of his Ohio City store and invested in a small ox-train of provisions to open a store on Cherry Creek in the Pikes Peak area . . . .

Just when Mr. Iliff arrived at the junction of Cherry Creek and the South Platte River is not of available record. Although William N. Byers, editor of the Rocky Mountain News, was attempting to print the names of all new arrivals, Iliff's name did not appear in the news-paper. It could be that he arrived in Denver City before the first issue of the Rocky Mountain News was printed on April 19, or there may not have been room in the newspaper to list all comers . . . .

By August, 1859, John Wesley Iliff owned two lots in Denver City. An advertisement appearing in The Denver City and Auraria Directory, 1859 . . . read:

Fenton, Auld & Iliff
Merchants on Blake St.
A. Fenton, Rushford, Mo.
D. Auld, Atchison, K.T.
J. W. Iliff, Ohio City, K.T.
Groceries, provision and Clothing
Larimer between F and G

. . . "Business was good and there was no difficulty in dispos-
ing of their merchandise at good prices." Later in the autumn, Iliff
traded a "stock of groceries" to P. G. Lowe for twenty-four mules
and a wagon . . . .

This trade with Lowe may have marked the end of Iliff's mercantile business, though it is generally stated that he continued in
that business a little less than a year and a half after reaching Cherry
Creek, before entering the livestock business.

Launching a Cattle Career

. . . On February 28, 1861, President Buchanan signed the bill
creating the Territory of Colorado. This gave to the area a feeling of
permanency and recognition which its substantial citizens desired.
News of this action in Washington reached Denver on March 4, and
immediately stimulated business. Creation of the territory may have
been the factor which caused John W. Iliff to sell out his store and to
invest all that he had in a small herd of cattle. Henceforth he devoted
his efforts to dealing in cattle exclusively.

When the Territory was organized, a large majority of its population was in the town of Denver, and in the Clear Creek, the Boulder
and the South Park mining districts. What is now northeastern Colorado was a vast hunting ground of the Arapahoes and Cheyennes. It
was all included in old Weld County. J. W. Iliff decided to cast his lot
in that county, and he used the north bank of the South Platte River as
his base line. He established a cow camp on Crow Creek near its
junction with the South Platte River.

One of Iliff's neighbors was Elbridge Gerry, an early-day fur
trader, who had married twin daughters of Swift Bird, a chief of the
Oglalas. And because of his friendliness with the Indians and his
wives' relationship to them, "Little Gerry" was able to warn the
white men of impending attacks. To the west of Iliff's grazing grounds,
in the beginning, were friendly Arapahoe Indians, led by Left Hand and
Chief Friday.

When Iliff launched his range cattle business in 1861, beef on
the hoof was 8¢ per pound and was retailing at 12¢. His operating

197

expenses were comparatively small, comprising salaries of a few cowboys at from $35 to $40 a month, corrals constructed from adobe or pointed poles which could be obtained along the creeks, and a cow camp near water. He did not then have the expense of running a chuck-wagon as his herdsmen carried their provisions on horseback, enough to last a week. Through close supervision, Iliff was able to hold his range losses during the winter to 5 per cent when other cattlemen lost as high as 35 per cent. Whenever he sold a few cattle, he "put the money back into the business to acquire land and to buy more cattle."

No detailed records are available of Mr. Iliff's financial operations during the period 1862-1864, but it is certain that he was in a most advantageous location to accumulate cattle and to make considerable money through the sale of those which he "reconditioned" on the native grasses at little cost. It was estimated that as much as 20 per cent to 25 per cent gain in weight would come in a few months on such grasses . . . .

With the Civil War increasing in intensity at this time, Colorado troops were needed far and wide, and the Indians began sporadic forays in the least protected areas. As the numbers of canvas-topped wagons and rumbling stagecoaches increased, and as the white men pushed deeper and deeper into the Indians' buffalo hunting grounds, the red men went on a rampage. Horses were stolen from ranches, cattle were killed and white men were scalped.

Iliff's cowboys and camps escaped these early depredations but had plenty of trouble with the Indians in later years . . . .

. . . "After a season or two, he (Iliff) began buying breeding bulls regularly in Illinois and Iowa. He used only choice Shorthorn bulls and paid from $60 to $80 each for them."

Although the summer of 1863 was one of severe drouth and the South Platte "went dry," there were many small streams running through the grazing lands. Iliff established a cow camp at Fremont's Orchard, about forty-eight miles east of present-day Greeley. At or near that point sixteen small streams united with the South Platte. Between all of those streams were ridges of rolling prairie land, covered at all times with nutritious grasses . . . .

The year 1865 was known as "The Bloody Year on the Plains," because of the Indian troubles. At this time, Iliff went to the Chero-kee Nation. There he and Fenton bought a herd of 1,300 head of cattle and drove it to Fort Union, New Mexico, on a government contract.

To drive cattle from the Cherokee Strip to New Mexico at that time was extremely hazardous because of the danger from attacks by the Comanches, Cheyennes and Kiowas. Too, waterless stretches of country had to be crossed. But Iliff took the herd through in safety. It is possible that the presence of Kit Carson's troops on the Santa Fe Trail at that time helped make the trip successful . . . .

Big Contracts in Beef

By 1866, John W. Iliff had become established in the livestock business and was listed in a Denver directory as a "Stock Dealer." . . . He not only was busy handling his own cattle, but . . . was at that time acting as . . . /a/ Denver agent to sell Texas longhorns.

In 1866 Oliver Loving and Charles Goodnight, Texas drovers, joined herds twenty-five miles south of Belknap, Texas, and, with eighteen armed men, started a drive of 2,000 head of mixed cattle to Colorado. They decided to go through New Mexico along the old Butter-field Trail to avoid the danger from Indians along the route through Indian Territory. The route they took swung down to the southwest, then turned up the Pecos to the Rockies. This route later became known as the Goodnight-Loving Trail.

After selling the steers for $12,000 at Fort Sumner, N. M., Goodnight started back to Texas for more cattle. Loving continued north with from 700 to 800 cows and calves which he sold to J. W. Iliff "in the vicinity of Denver." The price Iliff paid for these cattle is not known. It probably was less than the 8¢ a pound on foot which the two- and three-year-old steers had brought at Fort Sumner.

Although Congress had provided for the building of a Missouri railway as early as 1862, the actual surveys and construction work had been retarded by the Civil War. Now, however, the Union Pacific

was making good progress in construction across the prairies of
Nebraska Territory. Denver citizens hoped that the railway would
cross the Continental Divide over Berthoud Pass. When, on November 23, 1866, General Grenville M. Dodge, Chief Engineer of the
Union Pacific Railroad, made a report recommending that the trans-
Missouri railway be built through southern Wyoming, Denver looked
upon his decision as little less than ruinous. Leading business firms
began moving their goods to Cheyenne.

As soon as the railway route was determined upon by the railway company, John W. Iliff began to plan for the sale of some of his
cattle to the Union Pacific construction gangs and to troops that would
be guarding them. He made a deal . . . to supply beef to . . . Union
Pacific construction crews, "agreeing to drive the cattle as far as 100
miles," if necessary.

Soon after General Dodge, in the summer of 1867, selected a
site for the railway construction camp to be called Cheyenne, Iliff
established a cow camp about five miles down Crow Creek from the
new townsite . . . .

By the time most of Julesburg, Colorado, reached Cheyenne on
flat cars in November, 1867, and was unloaded at the "end of track,"
John Iliff was planning to purchase a large herd of Texas longhorns
which Charles Goodnight was trailing to southern Colorado . . . .

Early in 1868, Iliff and Fenton, who had long been associated
in business, visited Goodnight's Apishapa ranch and bought $40,000
worth of cattle to be delivered at Cheyenne. This was Iliff's largest
cattle transaction of record, up to that time. Goodnight trailed the
cattle north by a route which passed just east of Pueblo and Denver
and hit the Platte at Crow Creek near where Greeley later was located.
Goodnight swam the herd there, recalling later that "those old Texas
steers, with only a portion of their heads and horns above water,
looked like a million floating rocking chairs." . . .

This herd which Goodnight delivered to Iliff at his camp near
Cheyenne in February, 1868, was the second trail herd of Texas
cattle to come up through Colorado into Wyoming. Iliff sold some of
the animals as beef to local butchers. Some he shipped at the rate

of from one to two carloads daily to Chicago dealers. This beef, slaughtered on Crow Creek south of Cheyenne, shipped in quarters in iced cars, created a great deal of interest and caused one Wyoming editor to predict that this was "destined to become an important trade with the eastern cities and towns."

With the arrival of the Goodnight herd at the Crow Creek camp, Iliff transferred his residence from Denver to Cheyenne . . . .

. . . /The_/ move . . . was successful from the beginning. His business grew at a tremendous rate. In June, 1868, he made a trip to Pueblo and other parts of southern Colorado, where he purchased $45,000 worth of cattle . . . .

Displaying his usual sound judgment, J. W. Iliff selected in 1868, as his manager and bookkeeper, Colonel Edward F. Bishop, whose experience and ability were in a great measure instrumental in building up the immense business that Mr. Iliff later enjoyed. Employed at a large salary, Colonel Bishop was entrusted with the running of an average of forty thousand head of cattle and the supplying of large government contracts for beef, both for soldiers at the army posts and the Indian department, besides shipping thousands of beeves to the eastern markets . . . .

Profits Rather Than Pleasure

With the Union Pacific Railroad in full operation, Dr. H. Latham, Union Pacific Surgeon, was making every effort possible to induce settlers to come to Colorado and Wyoming in order to increase the company's business. He wrote numerous articles and included in them letters from many of the successful livestock men of the Colorado-Wyoming area.

On August 3, 1870, the Rocky Mountain News published an article entitled "Stock Growing." "The raising of horses, cattle and sheep," said the editor, "must ever be one of the chief industries of the Great Plains. People of the eastern and middle states cannot understand and are slow to believe that stock lives and thrives the year round upon the natural grasses of the prairies all the way up to fifty degrees of north latitude . . . . From a great number of letters in

201

proof of his (Dr. Latham's) argument we select extracts from the following. The first is from Mr. J. W. Iliff, who is well known to almost every business man in Colorado. He writes:

" 'I have been engaged in the stock business in Colorado and Wyoming for the past eight years. During all that time I have grazed stock in nearly all the valleys of these territories, both summer and winter. The cost of both summering and wintering is simply the cost of herding, as no feeding or sheltering is required. I consider the summer cured grasses of these plains and the valleys as superior to hay. My cattle have not only kept in good order on the grass through all of the eight winters, but many of them, thin in the fall, have become fine beef by spring. During this time I have owned twenty thousand head of cattle. The per cent of loss in wintering here is much less than in the states, where cattle are stabled and fed on corn and hay. The cost of raising cattle here can be shown from the fact that I should be glad to contract to furnish any quantity of beef from heavy fat cattle in Chicago at seven cents, net weight . . . .' "

. . . In commenting on the range cattle business in Wyoming, Governor Campbell said: "These cattle literally raised themselves for market. They have been out on the range during the entire winter without shelter and without feed from the stack, and have been prepared for slaughter almost without cost, save the expense of gathering and shipping them. A herd of 1,000 could be handled at a cost of $1.75 per head. If an owner wished to run 5,000, he could reduce the cost to $1.40, and a herd of 10,000 would bring the cost down to $1.00 each. It is also reliably stated that such stock growers as J. W. Iliff, who grazes 25,000, can figure the expense as low as 65¢ to 75¢ per head."

For a good many years Iliff bought from 10,000 to 15,000 Texas cattle each season. They weighed from 600 to 800 pounds and cost him from $10 to $15 per head. After he had fattened them on grass for a year or two and they had reached 1,000 pounds he sold them from $30 to $37 a head, or even as high as $50.

He had from 6,000 to 7,000 breeding cows of his own and sold his own steers, weighing about 1,100 pounds each, at from $38 to $50 a head. He used about 200 horses in his ranch operations and bought most of them from Goodnight and other Texas drovers. Goodnight continued his trail drives until about 1876. He delivered from twenty-five to thirty thousand head of cattle at Iliff's headquarters, "in the northeastern corner of Colorado, at the cottonwood grove known as Fremont's orchard."

Iliff is said to have claimed his yearly expenses on 25,000 head of Texas longhorns ranging on the plains was only 62¢ to 75¢ per head. He imported many fine bulls to improve the breed of his cattle. On one ranch alone he kept 80 choice Durham and Hereford bulls.

About forty men were employed on the ranches or at the cow camps during the summer and about a dozen remained for the year around. Wages varied from $25 to $30 per month for the herds-men . . . .

Weather was always something to be reckoned with in the western range country and one hard winter was expected about every seven years . . . .

About the middle of November, 1871, a blizzard struck north-eastern Colorado. Eugene Williams of Weld County, who was living with his family on a new little ranch about thirty miles west of Gree-ley, wrote that "The storm continued for several hours and the whole country was covered with a foot or more of snow. Then it turned very cold and the snow froze. Every week or so there was more snow, until the ground was covered with from one to three feet of it. The cattle could not get at the grass and thousands of them died of starvation and lack of water, as all streams were frozen over, ex-cept a few places in the river, where the current was too swift to allow it to freeze . . . ."

. . . Iliff spent a good part of the winter at Cole's ranch and at Fremont's Orchard. He sanded the ice on the South Platte river and put his cattle across to the south side of the river in bunches . . . . "In spite of all he could do, less than half of them were recovered, and these had strayed in springtime into two different states and four different territories. More than $20,000 was expended in efforts to find them." . . . "Yet /read a report/ the Cattle King, and many

203

cattle princes beside him, make money from cattle-raising on the plains, for they learn much by experience, and the demand is great enough to warrant all their risks." . . .

Where the Cattle Grazed

"It was an axiom of the 'cow country' that water controlled the range. Cattle were able to travel many miles to water, but water they must have, and he who had title to the land upon which there was water was not likely to be troubled by outsiders crowding in on the contiguous range."

The inventory of lands made after the death of John W. Iliff, in 1878, showed that he owned 105 "parcels" of range land, aggregating 15,558 acres in fifty-four different sections. In no one 640-acre section did he own more than 360 acres. Of the 105 "parcels," forty-four were 40-acre tracts; twenty-seven were 80-acre tracts; fifteen were 160-acre tracts; and some pieces contained as few as fourteen acres. Almost every piece of this land was contiguous to or accessible to water.

Some of these tracts were located along the South Platte River where various smaller streams flowed into it. Some were along Crow Creek and Little Crow Creek or important tributaries including Porter, Geary and Simpson Creeks. Also there were holdings on Horsetail Creek, at the mouths of Wild Cat Creek and Pawnee Creek. Other pieces were near small, unnamed lakes.

. . . in acquiring pasture lands, "it was customary to file on or purchase quarter sections of land fronting on water courses, so that actual ownership might extend only a fourth of a mile, which would be sufficient to control the backland, because the grass was useless without water . . . . Once having acquired considerable water frontage, the adjacent open range could be appropriated without formality of law, but with the sanction of custom and tacit consent of the community, which found in cattle or sheep raising its chief industrial asset." . . .

Iliff's lands were scattered across the range for 100 miles or more from the eastern boundary of Colorado and for more than sixty miles north and south . . . .

Visitors to the West in the 1870's were amazed at the immensity of the Iliff ranching operations . . . . Henry T. Williams, on his transcontinental tour, said:

". . . With a range 150 miles long, Iliff has the 'boss ranche' of this western country. It begins at Julesburg, on the Union Pacific Railroad, and extends to Greeley . . . . Its southern boundary is the South Platte River; its northern, the divide, rocky and bluffy, just south of the Lodge Pole Creek . . . . The chief ranche is nearly south of Sidney and 40 miles from Julesburg. At this ranche there are houses, sheds, stables and corrals and more than two sections of land fenced in . . . . Here are his private stock yards, with corrals, chutes and pens and all necessary conveniences for handling cattle. It is near the river, and has fine watering facilities, while from the adjoining bottomlands plenty of hay may be cut for the use of the horses employed in herding. He cuts no hay for his cattle; they live the entire year on the rich native grasses on his range, and with the exception of a severe winter, now and then, the percentage of loss is not very great." . . .

The End of the Trail

John W. Iliff had seen the range country change from a grassland grazed only by buffalo, antelope and deer to a much sought after pastureland for the great herds that were pushing in from Texas, Oregon, Montana and Nebraska.

During the years that a depression had blanketed the United States' economic structure since the "panic" of 1873, the livestock business of the western range country had come through with unbelievably good profits. It was not strange that newcomers were pointing their herds toward Colorado and her neighboring territories.

John W. Iliff evidently could see that the free open range grazing grounds would soon be hedged in by these recent arrivals, by the advancement of general agriculture and by the increase of native born cattle. For some time he had been investing part of his cattle profits in Denver real estate, in stock in the German National Bank and the

City National Bank of Denver and in shares of stock in the Union Stock Yards in Chicago.

His cattle dealings were based on sound contracts which carried a forfeiture for failure to deliver. But shrewd as he was in business matters, he did not guard his own health.

On December 10, 1877, he was stricken with what the doctors pronounced "obstructive jaundice" . . . . About noon /on February 9, 187_8_/ he quietly passed away . . . .

John W. Iliff was deserving of the homage and recognition accorded him. The inventory of his estate proved that he had made an outstanding success of the western range cattle business. He accumulated the bulk of his wealth when the world of free grass was his for the taking. He was an economic trail-blazer. His range was clean, untrammeled, free of disease, of overcrowding and of overspeculation. He was far in advance of most of the men whose names have been widely publicized by writers, in connection with the "boom days" of the western range cattle industry.

John Iliff was buying range cattle and spotting water holes the very year that the dashing Weld County cattleman, Captain the Honorable Lyulph Gilchrist Stanley Ogilvy, son of the Earl of Airlie, was born. He had accumulated a fortune and had passed over the Great Divide before such "cattle barons" as Sir Horace Plunkett, Moreton and Richard Frewen, the Oelrich brothers and Teschemacher and Debillier had stepped foot in the Rocky Mountain Region. He died three years before Jim Bridger passed on.

Iliff did not live to know the Wyoming Stock Growers Association, as that name was not adopted until 1879. He died fourteen years before the Johnson County War. His herds did not feel the restriction of wire fences. Iliff did not experience the "attractive proposition of cow punching as seen from the veranda of the Cheyenne Club," — there was no Cheyenne Club in his day. In Iliff's time, men in Cheyenne congregated at Tim Dyer's or at the Railroad House.

John W. Iliff found and used the free grass of the range just as the trapper took the free beaver and otter from the mountain streams.

He did not push anyone out of his way — he was the first "comer." He broke trail in northern Colorado's range cattle business.

Iliff tasted the grime and dust of trail herds. His nostrils knew the acrid odor of hair and hide touched with a hot iron. But most of all he knew the meaning of dollars and cents. He operated on sound business principles. He paid as he went. He bought bulls and herds of cattle with carefully detailed contracts — fair both to the drover and the buyer. His herds of cattle never were "tossed about in a reckless manner over a dram of Scotch in a club house" or sold on book count. He neither bought nor sold calves as mavericks at a roundup. The laws governing mavericks were passed after he had gone.

John W. Iliff laid such a solid foundation in his livestock business that his widow and her associates, J. S. Brown and D. H. and J. W. Snyder, were able to carry on and to settle his estate with highly satisfactory financial results.

Had Iliff lived to be engulfed by the great cattle boom of the 1880's would he have retrenched? Cut down his herds? Sold out and invested in real estate? Or would he have bought more cattle and perhaps ventured into the mining business, as did so many other cattlemen, had he lived through the 1880's and 1890's?

It is likely that he would have read the warnings aright. He probably would have adopted changed methods and would have accepted conditions as they arose, as facts inevitable and unavoidable, and would have tried to conquer them. All of which, however, is conjecture. What we do know is that he was a real pioneer cattleman. His range was beset by the prickly pear of the plains, not by the tumbleweed of the nester.

We join George Cross of Wyoming in saying: "The free open, unlimited range and with it the big-hearted cowman, whose latch was ever open to friend and stranger, and the fearless, hard-working, generous cowboy are gone forever. The pioneer sheds tears for his lost Eden."

SEVENTEEN: THE SILVER MINES OF LEADVILLE

by Stephen F. Smart

Gold had brought to the Pike's Peak region its first sizeable white population; silver provided the now maturing frontier of Colorado with a second treasure-hunt, spinning its economic spiral to dizzy heights in the late 1870s and early 1880s. Silver was mined in the state as early as 1864 at Georgetown, but it was the Leadville boom, high in the Rockies beyond the earlier horizons, that captured the interest of much of America as it experienced its bonanza years, combining in a wild and reckless way some of the good and much of the evil of a "second generation" mining camp. The following description of young Leadville in its second year (along with helpful hints for silver seekers), is from a pamphlet published by the Kansas Pacific Railway, designed to augment passenger traffic on its lines to Colorado.*

*   *   *

THE SILVER MINES OF LEADVILLE

Imagine two great snow-capped ranges of mountains having a general northern and southern extension, whose sharply accented crests, rising here and there into towering peaks, range parallel to each other and inclose a beautiful valley about ten miles in width, and green already with vernal tints. Meandering through the valley mid-way, perhaps, from either range is a little stream which gleams

------

*from Stephen F. Smart, *Leadville, Ten Mile, Eagle River, Elk Mountain, Tin Cup and all other noted Colorado Mining Camps, Illustrated, with accurate map of the Leadville District, and Kansas and Colorado, Together with U. S. and State Mining Laws, and Rules of the National Land Department.* Kansas City, 1879, pages 3-4, 6-9, 17-20.

in the moonlight like a thread of molten silver. From the foot-hills
to timber-line extend forests of spruce, above which the mountains
are bald and uncompromising in their solitary, stately grandeur.
The range to the west is the SAGUACHE — the backbone of the Cor-
dilleras de la Sierra Madres — the Continental Divide, down whose
eastern slope, trickles the melting snow which feeds the mighty
rivers of the Mississippi Valley, while the accumulations upon the
other side, find their way across arid deserts and through gigantic
cañons to the Pacific Ocean. The eastern range is the Mosquito, or
Mesquite of more ancient geographers — which forms the western
boundary of SOUTH PARK. The silvery stream which flows without
turbulence through the valley, is the Arkansas. Upon the occidental
slope of the Mosquito Range, nearly opposite and but fourteen miles
from Fairplay through MOSQUITO PASS, is the famous city of

Leadville

which, perhaps, came nearer being "built in a day," than any other
city of the world. The region around Leadville attained great notori-
ety many years ago, and the valley once boasted of a population of
not less than 10,000 people. This was in 1859 and the four succeeding years. Gold had been discovered in California and other gulches
in 1859, and Mongolian and Caucasian mingled in the eager fray for
the precious metal. It is thought that from $5,000,000 to $7,000,000
were washed from the placers, which seemed to exhaust the deposit,
and the miners left for more profitable fields of labor. At that time,
the existence of the carbonates was known, but supposing them to
carry lead only, the miners cast them aside as worthless.

In 1874, the "float" attracted the attention of a miner named
Wood while working in California gulch, and he and his partner,
Stevens, followed the indications until, in 1875, the "MIKE LODE"
was opened and the value of the carbonates, in a measure, determined. The following year the ROCK, STONE, LIME, BULL'S EYE,
IRON and IRON HAT were discovered, and in the fall of the same
year, 1876, the GALLAGHER BROTHERS opened the CAMP BIRD.
During the summer of 1877, the rich deposit known as the CARBON-
ATE MINE was struck, and early in 1878 the mineral was found in
large quantities on what is known as FREYER HILL, about a mile
north-east of the city of Leadville. The LITTLE PITTSBURG, NEW

DISCOVERY, WINNEMUC, CARONIFEROUS, LITTLE CHIEF, DIVES, CHRYSOLITE, VULTURE and many other mines of great value speedily followed. In June, 1878, there were probably from twenty-five to thirty discoveries of mineral on IRON MOUNTAIN, FREYER HILL and IOWA GULCH of which, perhaps, fifteen showed valuable ore, and were paying properties. A great many other discoveries of mineral had been made, but in most instances only low grade ore had been reached and it was not worth working. Up to that time, there had been a few discoveries in Stray Horse Gulch, while the territory lying between the LITTLE and BIG EVANS GULCHES had not been disturbed.

It is to the discovery of this carbonate of lead, that Leadville owes its name and fame, and it is upon the extent of the mineral that it depends for its prosperity and future history. There are two kinds of carbonate ore: the hard carbonate in which the iron and lead are but slightly oxidized and carbonated, requiring force of powder to remove it, while, in the soft carbonate which is removed and taken out with pick and shovel, the iron and lead show a greater degree of oxidization and carbonization, and it appears to the ordinary observer, like a coarse yellow sand. Of the characteristics of these ores and causes which led to the deposit, little can be said. They are found under the "grass roots" near the timber-line and in well-defined veins high above it, as well as heavily deposited in the gulches and on the ridges which divide them . . . .

The City of Leadville

Leadville is finely situated on the left bank of California Gulch, on a broad and gentle slope near the foot of the Mosquito Range. The streets lying parallel to the general direction of the mountains, are comparatively level, while those leading from the valley have an easy grade. In all Colorado I doubt if there is another location possessed of grander external attractions. From the corporate limits eastward, the hills, famous for their deposits of carbonate ore, slope upward into the Mosquito Range, which overlooks the city at an altitude varying from 12,000 to 13,500 feet above tide. To the west, stretches far away to the north and south the snow-enshrouded crest of the Saguache, and intermediate is the charming valley of the Arkansas. Twelve miles south of Leadville are the famous Twin Lakes. Within easy reach, to

210

the northwest, is the Mountain of the Holy Cross, and nearly north, Mount Lincoln rears its hoary head 14,500 feet above the sea, forming a series of remarkable attractions for tourists.

The growth of Leadville is unprecedented. In January, 1878, the camp consisted of twenty or twenty-five log cabins. Four months later, the number of buildings had increased to 400, and to-day there are not less than 20,000 people living within the city limits of Leadville, occupying, probably, 1,800 buildings. The streets are laid out with commendable regularity, Chestnut street and Harrison avenue (running at right angles) being the principal thoroughfares, where the business of the city is chiefly done. The commercial houses are, with three or four exceptions, constructed of wood, sometimes with an attempt at architectural beauty, but more frequently exhibiting that degree of haste which always characterizes a new mining camp. But the stores are not confined, by any means, to the principal streets. All the way from Malta to the foot of the carbonate hills, one finds stores, shops, real-estate offices, laundries and boarding houses in profusion, and it is difficult to determine, from any visible token, the limits of the city. The city probably covers an area of three miles long by one and a half wide, and it is safe to say that wherever there is no house, one is either in process of erection or in contemplation. Outside of the main streets, building is going on everywhere, and the sound of the ax and hammer and saw is constant. Log houses predominate, but a log house in this land of silver is preferable to the finest architectural creation in a land of mortgages and debt.

Approaching Leadville from Malta, one finds a blockade of four, six and eight mule teams ladened with ore or merchandise, through which he must engineer his way. Everybody is good-natured; even the mules seem in good humor, and the activity and dead earnestness which pervade everybody and everything are in striking contrast to the silence above the timber line. Reaching the limits of the city, the scene is beyond description. Eighteen months ago a wilderness! To-day a thronging, eager, determined populace of not less than twenty thousand! The streets are lined with people, or rather filled with them; for sidewalks would not hold the dense mass of humanity which crowds into the principal streets of Leadville. The hotels, stores, doorways, crosswalks, saloons, offices — all are crowded, and the first feeling is one of oppression. It reminds one of a perpetual

211

Fourth of July or a circus day. Few idlers are observed, and you classify them at once. They were born tired, and scorn to do an honest day's work. The large majority of the people are busy. You catch the welcome sound of "Millions," and feel better for it. You hear of "prospects," "high grade," "low grade," "out-put," "lode," "out-crop," "pocket," "tunnel," "drift," at every hand. You see men exhibiting the results of a recent discovery. The clicking of billiard balls and checks; the well known cry of " 'Ere's your evening pa-a-per;" the importunities of "Shine-'em-ups;" the appearance of well dressed women, children of various ages, cripples, itinerant "doctors," peripatetic orange and apple vendors, combine to excite a lively curiosity on the part of a newcomer. Night closes in quickly, and then the city is aglow with enthusiasm. Off on the outlying hills bright lights are seen. They each mark the location of a mine where men are delving for the precious ore. You step into one of the gambling places (and you can't miss them) and see hundreds of men hard at work swapping their wealth for a few minutes' excitement. Gamblers are not in Leadville for "fun." They mean business, and no one suspects them of playing a square game. There is less drinking done than one would expect; but much more of it than is necessary.

Every branch of business is represented at Leadville, from the wholesale house seeking its trade from the numerous settlements which have sprung up throughout this marvelously rich country, to the hand-wagon of the itinerant tradesman. The following summary of the different business houses will give a tolerably correct idea of the commercial importance of the city.

According to a late enumeration, there are now in Leadville ten hay and grain stores, ten lumber yards, twelve blacksmith shops, four banks, over twenty hotels, three theaters, one opera house, eight smelting works, twelve dry-good stores, eight hardware stores, eight clothing stores, thirty groceries, thirteen boot and shoe shops, fifteen livery stables, twenty-five bakeries and confectioneries, fourteen saw mills, twenty meat markets, seven drug stores, two soda-water makers, twenty-five cigar stands, thirty-eight restaurants, over 100 saloons and dance-houses; doctors, lawyers, milliners and persons who live on the misfortunes of others are all well and largely represented. There are five churches, Young Men's Christian and Temperance Organizations, besides Masonic and Odd Fellow's Lodges.

Leadville has three excellent newspapers — the Reveille, Eclipse and Chronicle, which have telegraphic dispatches from various associations and individuals. Water works are being erected and a gas company has been incorporated; both will soon be in full operation. Rents are high. Eligible building lots on Harrison Avenue and Chestnut Street range from $1,000 to $8,000, which six months ago could have been bought from $50 to $100. Residence lots range all the way from $100 to several hundred dollars. A good store, one story 25 x 40 and thereabouts, rents from $200 to $300 a month. Offices rent from $30 to $100 a month. Probably there are at this time a thousand or more houses of various descriptions in process of erection. The city already extends almost from Malta to the foot of Freyer Hill, and is receiving an accession of from 200 to 250 a day.

Board in private families costs from $7 to $15 per week; Hotels demand from $2 to $4 per day. Single meals can be gotten at restaurants from 25 cents upward; and a man can live in Leadville about as cheaply as anywhere else . . . .

The City has good water works, an excellent police department, a fair fire department, and is putting in a fire alarm and gas works. All this and much more has been accomplished in eighteen months.

Health

Much has been written regarding the health of the people sojourning at Leadville, and many false impressions have gone abroad. The fact is that unacclimated people have to become acclimated before they feel perfectly well. If they unduly expose themselves, they are quite as apt to get sick at Leadville as any where else; but from all I could learn, there has not been an excessive mortality at Leadville, and the reports to that effect may be regarded as colored either through ignorance or design. The cause of the sickness at Leadville is more largely attributable to debauchery than to any climatic influence. Everyday there arrive in the city from 200 to 250 people. Such of these as are insufficiently clad, poorly fed, drink, lie around rum and gambling hells, spend their substance in riotous living, and neglect the precautions necessary to health, are apt to become diseased and the same effect would obtain anywhere; but persons who take care of themselves, abstain from intoxicating drinks, keep away from the gambling dens and keep from the nymphes du pave who infest Leadville, as well as Paris, will have as much immunity from disease at Leadville, as at any other point in the Mountains . . . .

Prospecting

Prospecting is simply hunting for mineral, and in cases where the mineral lies in fissure veins deeply imbedded in granite, gneissoid, or rock of like density, the work not only requires muscle, courage and patience, but a considerable knowledge of geology and mineralogy. The prospector must have some idea of the external indication of the presence of veins which may be hundreds of feet below, and thousands of feet distant from the point where the "blossom" is found.

First the prospector seeks the "blossom" which indicates the presence of the mineral, and then he next tries to find out where it comes from. He examines carefully the topography of the country, turns over loose stones, peers into and along beds of streams, and is perhaps, at last, rewarded by finding the "blossom" rock. He carefully turns it over. If its edges are sharp and defined, and the fracture evidently of recent date, he is satisfied the vein is near at hand. If on the contrary, the corners are rounded and the fracture of remote date, he is satisfied it must have traveled a considerable distance. In either case, he must hunt patiently, and often for a long time, before he strikes the prize.

But prospecting at Leadville is quite another affair. The carbonate mineral instead of being found in verticle veins, held in the strong embrace of the solid rock which must be drilled and blasted and tunneled before the mineral is reached, occupies a more nearly

horizontal position,

varying with the dip of the surface. Up to the present time, there are no certain superficial evidences of the existence of the mineral. From the day the first carbonate mine was struck, down to the present time, the prospector has worked in the dark, until his spade stuck the ore. Proximity to a known body of ore, is perhaps the only "guide." If a person gets a claim near a mine in which mineral is known to exist, he

214

has reasonable assurance of a valuable claim. And it being a determined fact that carbonate ore exists in large and paying quantities not only at Leadville, but in various directions for FIFTY miles around, the prospector who starts in to-day, has every advantage over those whose luck alone brought to light the first carbonate ore in the Leadville district.

Pay ore is found at Leadville on Freyer, Carbonate and Iron Hills, in all the gulches, above timber line, across the valley of the Arkansas, at Oro, Malta, near the grass roots and hundreds of feet below the surface. The same condition at Ten-Mile, Eagle River, on Elk Mountains, at Twin Lakes, beyond the Saguache, in the Gunnison Country, at Chalk Mountain, Tin Cup — shafts being sunk and new paying mines being constantly found. If these facts mean anything, they mean that inasmuch as the prospector who goes in now has the benefit of all who have gone in before and a knowledge of the great extent of the carbonate deposit to guide him to the best location, he stands

a better chance

of speedy and sure success than he would have stood a year ago. The pioneers have "blazed" the way, and it is an easy matter for any man with provisions for a few months, a level head and vigorous muscle to follow a path already marked out. In prospecting, three men should go together. They need each a pick, costing $1.50, a shovel, $1.50; they are then fully equipped so far as tools are concerned for commencing a shaft, which should be about four feet by six. After going down a few feet, a bucket costing $5; windlass and rope at say $25; drills and hammers, fuse and blasting powder at $10 making a total cost for out-fit of $49. If working some distance from town, a burro will be needed and can be obtained from $15 to $30. Provisions for a party of three, would not cost above $30 a month, and a temporary shanty can be built in a short time, at no cost save labor. Thus a prospecting tour of two months can be made at a total expenditure of less than ONE HUNDRED DOLLARS — many of the most valuable mines were discovered on a less expenditure than that, and what has been done will be repeated hundreds of times before the summer is over. There remains after getting the out-fit, nothing to do but "dig."

Grub Stakes.

A grub stake is a prospecting out-fit furnished by men of wealth, i.e. those who can command a hundred dollars or so, to impecunious miners. For instance, A and B desire to prospect and not having the means to procure the necessary out-fit; or perhaps, they have sunk a shaft until their means are exhausted, C comes along and gives them a "grub stake" for an interest in whatever they may find. In other words he "mines by proxy." A grub stake of less than fifty dollars got Gov. Tabor one-half of the Little Pittsburg and made him a millionaire, and GRUB STAKES properly placed and followed up are to-day, as good investments as any man ought to wish.

Locating a Mine.

The process of coming into possession of a mine is this: A man stakes out his claim — 300 by 1,500 feet. To do this he sets up a stake three inches in diameter, square at the top, and, if his name be John Smith, written in pencil upon the four sides, "John Smith's lode, corner No. 1." He steps off the distance, and sets up such a stake on each corner. Then he begins to sink his shaft. Two men work the windlass and one digs, and the three take turns in digging. Sometimes a fourth man cuts the timber to be used in "timbering" the shaft — that is, walling it up to prevent its caving in. Good saplings, adapted for that purpose, grow on the mountain side, and it takes all the trees on fifteen acres to timber the average shaft. Thus it happens that the original owners of a claim often number four men, and almost always number three. The shaft is usually four feet wide and six feet long. Three men working at such a shaft can go down through the first fifty feet at the rate of from three to five feet per day, timbering as they go; and through the next fifty feet two and a half to three and a half feet per day; that will probably bring them to rock, through which they must blast, and they cannot go faster than two feet per day, and even that is good work. On a contract the first fifty feet will cost $3.50 per foot, the next fifty $5.50 per foot, and after that it will cost from $8 to $15 per foot to go down, according to the hardness and depth of the rock. The contract price for sinking a shaft averages $4 to $6 per foot, including curbing.

Thus the diggers go down through the wash and the porphyry,

216

and the rock and the iron, if they find the last two, until they come to the contact. The depth which they will have to go varies, as I have said. In the Adelaide mines, mineral is in some places but four feet under the surface; in the Morning Star it is 250 feet. On an average it is 100 feet down. Even the most experienced miner cannot tell by looking at what is before him, whether the stuff has mineral in it or not. So he has it assayed. This costs from $1.50 to $5 and takes from two hours to a day. If he finds he has mineral, he goes for a United States surveyor, and has his claim surveyed and recorded, and he writes on his four stakes the date when the survey was made. He now owns the claim. It is his without having to pay the government anything, as the latter gives the claim to the man who finds the mineral. It is a disputed point whether iron is "mineral" in the sense contemplated by the law, but the custom here is to have surveys made on finds of iron.

In staking out his claim, the owner is not compelled to run his survey over the claim that he first staked out. He can shift his lines in any direction that he chooses, determining that by the pitch and direction of his own vein or deposit. It will often happen that he will thus take in the shaft which is being sunk by another man near him — will "survey him in," as it is called — and that other man has no recourse.

Suppose several men have claims staked out near his and have shafts started. As soon as the first man strikes mineral, the others feel that their chances for striking it are good, and they all go to work with might and main to be the next to strike it, for that man is the lucky one, since he has the next choice of land. Additional "shifts" of men are put on, the work goes forward night and day, a horse is used to turn the windlass if it can be so arranged, and the race is as if for dear life. When the next man finds mineral he makes a break for a surveyor, and if two strike it at the same time they race like mad for one, for the claim first surveyed is the one that holds the land.

It often happens that this mineral is found having such a direction that a survey has to be made over a claim already surveyed. In that case the new survey can hold the land within its claim and outside the other claim, but that part lying within the first claim remains to

217

the owners of the first claim. However, if the second claim is a rich one, the overlapping portions have enough mineral in them to satisfy any man; but in any case the new claimant yields with good grace. Surveys are always made one hundred and fifty feet each way to the side lines from the discovery shaft; they cannot be made two hundred feet one way and one hundred feet the other, nor be divided up unevenly; therefore it happens often that a man cannot get a "full claim" — that is, one three hundred feet wide — but has to be content with what he can get.

"Bonding a Mine"

is a process needing explanation. After a set of men have found mineral, it frequently happens that they bond it to some one to sell — that is, they execute an instrument setting forth that, in consideration of the bonder putting up so much of a forfeit, he shall have a certain number of days, thirty, sixty or ninety, within which he may sell the mine at whatever he can get for it, with the understanding that if the sale is made the owners of the mine are to receive a stipulated price. For example, the Little Giant had a half interest bonded for $110,000. The bonder was at liberty to sell that half interest for as much more as he could get for it within the time agreed upon. If he failed to sell it within that time he lost his forfeit — forfeits range from $1,000 to $5,000 — and the control of the mine reverted to the owners.

EIGHTEEN: WATER CONFLICTS AND CONTROLS

by Robert G. Dunbar

*While the mineral wealth of Colorado dominated the economic life
of the state during the nineteenth century, the agricultural foundations
then being laid would provide the base for the major economic activity
of the twentieth century. The area that had earlier been termed "The
Great American Desert" proved full of obstacles to ordinary farming
as practiced in more humid regions of the country. But irrigation and
dry farming techniques would contribute, in time, to reduce the "desert"
to profitable farms. Not only were the practical techniques of farming
different from those of other regions; the legal structure needed radical
modification too. Professor Robert G. Dunbar here traces the story of
how some of the early changes in the law of water rights were brought
about.* *

*   *   *

WATER CONFLICTS AND CONTROLS

The agriculture of the arid West has its own peculiar problems.
Since the annual rainfall averages less than 20 inches, the supply of
water is insufficient for agriculture as it is practiced in the eastern
part of the United States. Consequently, farmers of the Great Plains
and the Rocky Mountain region farm very differently from those in
the humid East. Whereas those of the humid East are often concerned
about a surplus of water, those of the arid West are generally concerned about a deficiency of it. They must either add it to the land by

------

*from Robert G. Dunbar, "Water Conflicts and Controls in Colorado" in *Agricultural
History*, volume XXII (July, 1948), pages 180-186. Used with permission of the
author and the publisher.

irrigation or conserve it in the soil by dry-farming techniques. Of necessity the farmers of the arid West have developed not only different agricultural techniques but also different laws and institutions for the control of water which have no counterpart in eastern agriculture.

These new irrigation techniques and institutions were developed with great difficulty. Most of the men who developed them came from the humid areas where they had no acquaintance with the methods necessary for farming in a dry country. They might have learned something from the Spanish-speaking people of the Southwest, but either they did not settle among them or they scorned the different culture. Those who settled in California and Colorado received some help from the miners, but in general these early Anglo-American irrigators dug their first ditches without pattern or previous experience. Their early ditches were dug in the bottom lands near the streams. They were short and small. Oftentimes they worked badly and sometimes crops failed for want of water, but the irrigators learned from each experience. Within a decade or so, they were building larger and larger canals out onto the benchlands.

More difficult than the construction of the ditches, dams, and laterals — the physical plant of an irrigation society — was the invention of institutions for social control. The pioneer irrigators were individualists. They were antagonistic to laws and institutions which would control their lives and property. Yet human experience dating back to predynastic Egypt had demonstrated that irrigation required some subordination of the individual to group control. The result was a conflict between the needs of an irrigation society and frontier individualism. Presumably, this conflict occurred in each of the Rocky Mountain States, but in Colorado it led to the formulation of a system of public control of water which had a wide influence. It is to this conflict that we now direct our attention.

Utah and California were already thriving communities based on irrigation when the gold rush of 1859 peopled the mountain gulches of central Colorado with miners and the broad valleys of the South Platte and its tributaries with farmers intent upon supplying the mining camps with wild hay and agricultural produce at high prices. These fifty-niner farmers inaugurated what has been called "the third

220

germinal point" in the development of western irrigation institutions.

According to the records, David K. Wall was the first of their number to irrigate. With experience gained from raising potatoes by irrigation in California, Wall diverted water from Clear Creek onto the site of present-day Golden, Colorado, and in the summer of 1859 irrigated two thousand dollars worth of produce. That fall, the fall of the organization of Jefferson Territory, other pioneer irrigators started to dig ditches to take water from Boulder Creek and Bear Creek, north and south of Clear Creek. The next year diversions were made from Saint Vrain Creek and the Cache la Poudre River, and in 1861, from the Big Thompson River, with the result that within three years after the initial gold rush, one or more irrigation ditches had been taken out of nearly all the principal streams of the upper South Platte Valley.

As long as the ditches were confined to the river bottoms, the streams supplied an abundance of water for all users, and the question of who could use the water did not arise. It was after the streams became overappropriated by the construction of larger ditches extending to the benchlands, that the question of property rights in water arose. Then the stream flow became insufficient to supply all of the ditches, and, especially in time of drought, water users were faced with a scarcity of water. Scarcity precipitated conflicts, and these conflicts highlighted the need for a definition of water rights and for the creation of institutions for the public control of the streams. One of the most consequential of these conflicts occurred in the Cache la Poudre Valley in the summer of 1874.

Four years previously Nathan C. Meeker and his Union Colony associates had founded the community of Greeley on the banks of the Cache la Poudre River near its junction with the South Platte. This event was one of the most important in the early agricultural development of the State. The colony members came principally from New England and the North Central States. They were men and women of more than average education and learning. Consequently, they brought to the solution of agricultural problems more than average insight.

The colony was a cooperative undertaking. Each member subscribed $155, and the trustees of the colony furnished the land and

221

constructed the irrigation ditches. Two ditches were taken out of the Cache la Poudre — Colony Canal No. 3 and Colony Canal No. 2. Canal No. 3 was taken out of the south bank of the river to supply the town lots, and Canal No. 2, a much larger ditch, was a diversion from the north bank of the river to irrigate the farms on the benchland north of Greeley. In fact, Colony Canal No. 2 was by far the largest diversion yet made from the Poudre. It was begun in the fall of 1870 for use during the 1871 growing season, but its construction was so faulty that it failed to provide sufficient water. As a result, the farmers who depended on it experienced a crop failure. Although the colony nearly foundered in the resulting crisis, the ditch was repaired and enlarged, and was operated successfully in 1872.

Apparently encouraged by the success of this crop season, several members of the colony, headed by its first vice president, General R. A. Cameron, organized a business venture known as the Agricultural Colony, which they located 25 miles up the Cache la Poudre River at Fort Collins, near the place where the river emerges from the mountains. Here in 1872 and 1873, two more canals, Larimer County Canal No. 2 and the Lake Canal, were taken out of the river. These two canals had a capacity roughly equal to that of the two Union Colony canals. Thus the stage was set for the historic conflict of 1874.

The early summer of 1874 was unusually dry. There was no rain, and the days were very warm. Forest fires raged in the mountains, and grasshoppers appeared on the plains. The Poudre was extremely low, the lowest, according to the Fort Collins Standard, since 1863. At Greeley there was not enough water in the river to supply both ditches of the colony, and early in July the trustees of the colony ordered the headgates of Canal No. 2 to be closed two days a week so that some water could be supplied to Canal No. 3.

This situation alarmed the Union Colony. Its leaders knew that water was scarce, but they were also aware of the two big ditches 25 miles up the river which the Fort Collins people had dug the year before. It made no difference that the Greeley ditches antedated those at Fort Collins by two years. The water came to Fort Collins first, so that the upstream farmers were able to deprive the downstream users of all water if they so desired. Who had the better right to the use of the waters of a stream, the early comers or the late comers?

This was a question that had not arisen in the frontier settlement of the humid East. "Who shall have the preference when water becomes scarce?" asked the editor of the Fort Collins Standard. What will be the law of waters in the arid West? The Greeley leaders felt that upon a definite answer to these questions depended the future of their community.

Nathan C. Meeker, as founder of the colony and editor of the Greeley Tribune, formulated their demands. First, he demanded the recognition of the principle that the early comers have a better right to the waters of a stream than the late comers, that priority of appropriation gives a prior right to the use of the water. This legal doctrine had already been partially formulated by the miners of California and Colorado and had been mentioned in a territorial law of 1864. Meeker felt that the property and investment of the Union Colony would not be secure until it was recognized that the colony's canals by virtue of prior appropriation had a right to the water of the Cache la Poudre River prior to that of the canals constructed later by the Fort Collins irrigators. Second, Meeker proposed the control of the river by a superintendent and the equitable division of the water by that official. He wrote in the Tribune for July 8, 1874:

> It looks to us as though it would be much better to
> consolidate the interests of every ditch owner, and
> to make the river an irrigation canal, subject to such
> superintendence as is established on our Number Two;
> for by this means everyone would have his rights, the
> supply of water would be constant, and all would know
> what to depend upon.

This proposal foreshadowed the historic legislation of 1879. Third, Meeker proposed that the flood waters of the Poudre be caught and conserved in a mountain reservoir. "It is expected," he wrote, "that a large amount of water can be saved during the spring and summer floods by having a strong dam made in the mountains, and that in this way all can have what they need." Here he foreshadowed the later reservoir development of the Cache la Poudre Valley. Fourth, he proposed that "every project for taking out more water shall be knocked in the head," that further diversion of the Poudre be prohibited.

223

With such a program in mind, Meeker and two other men went to Fort Collins on July 9 to investigate the situation. They returned and reported that the two Fort Collins canals were full of water and that much more water than could be used was running in Larmier County Canal No. 2. The next step was to apply for a perpetual injunction against the officers of each canal. When this decision became known in Fort Collins, General R. A. Cameron and the owners of the Lake Canal went to Greeley and suggested a conference of the ditch owners of the two communities in order to settle the controversy out of court. It was agreed that the conference would be held at a schoolhouse, midway between the two towns on July 15, 1874.

The convention met on the date designated. About forty men, representing about twenty ditches, attended. The Greeley delegation, in accordance with Meeker's program, demanded recognition of their prior rights and the appointment of a river commission to divide the water equitably. On the other hand, the Fort Collins delegation refused to recognize the prior rights of the Greeley canals but favored the appointment of one person to divide the water according to need during that summer. The debate was lively. Meeker wanted a continuation of the injunction proceedings in order to produce a test case and to secure a definition of property rights in water from the courts. Finally, in return for a suspension of the injunction, the Fort Collins farmers agreed to permit more water to flow down the river, and the conference broke up without any of the issues being settled.

On the basis of a figure of speech in David Boyd's A History: Greeley and the Union Colony of Colorado, it has sometimes been supposed that this meeting was stormy and that it broke up with threats of violence. The contemporary accounts make it clear that this supposition is erroneous. The Colorado Sun, which was published at Greeley, reported: "There were no indications of a quarrel during the conference. Indeed, with the exception, in one instance, of heated remarks, the best of feeling prevailed throughout the convention." On the other hand, it is also clear that Boyd did lose his temper and "that one of the Greeley gentlemen was forced to his feet to utter a disclaimer for the Hibernian warrior."

Accounts differ as to the amount of water which the Fort Collins owners let down the river, but it is evident that Meeker believed the

224

agreement was not honored. Happily, the drought was broken on July 20 when "sufficient rain fell to soak the ground to the depth of five inches." Other rains followed, and the controversy was not renewed. But the Greeley people did not forget. Wrote Boyd, "from this day forth we had set our hearts on having some regulations looking towards a distribution of the waters of the state in harmony with the principle of prior appropriation."

Less than two years later, the constitutional convention decided the question of prior rights in favor of the Greeley position. It met on December 20, 1875 and created among its committees a committee on irrigation, agriculture and manufactures, consisting of nine members. To it were appointed two representatives from Weld County, of which Greeley is the county seat, but none were appointed from the Fort Collins area. S. J. Plumb of Weld County was made chairman. On February 11, 1876, this committee presented a report which contained a section on prior rights. This section was somewhat revised by the convention and adopted as part of the Constitution of Colorado in these words:

> The right to divert the unappropriated waters of any
> natural stream to beneficial uses shall never be denied.
> Priority of appropriation shall give the better right as
> between those using the water for the same purpose; but
> when the waters of any natural stream are not sufficient
> for the service of all those desiring the use of the same,
> those using the water for domestic purposes shall have
> the preference over those claiming for any other purpose,
> and those using the water for agricultural purposes shall
> have preference over those using the same for manufac-
> turing purposes.

Nathan C. Meeker expressed his approval in the columns of the Greeley Tribune. However, still undetermined was a method of ascertaining priorities.

The constitutional convention also laid the basis for the public control of the waters of the State by declaring that "the water of every natural stream . . . within the State of Colorado is hereby declared to be the property of the public, and the same is dedicated to the use of the people of the State, " but it did not create nor suggest any machinery of control aside from a method of fixing "maximum rates to be charged for the use of water." Nor did the first State legislature. Rather, it was the second and the third legislatures that finally enacted into law the desires of the Greeley farmers.

As has been said, the Greeley farmers did not forget the experiences of 1874. Consequently, in the spring of 1878, they were concerned when Benjamin H. Eaton, who later became a governor of Colorado, began the construction of a canal larger than any yet taken out of the Cache la Poudre. It was to be 70 miles long with a capacity sufficient to irrigate 70,000 acres. Not only did the Greeley farmers become concerned, but also the Fort Collins farmers, who now saw their water rights threatened by the big new ditch. Likewise, farther south on Saint Vrain Creek, pioneer farmers such as L. C. Mead and C. A. Pound became alarmed about their water supply. To these irrigators legislation to protect their water rights seemed necessary.

The Greeley people again assumed the initiative. Shortly after the elections to the second general assembly, in which J. L. Brush of Greeley and L. C. Mead were elected to the House and Judge Silas B. A. Haynes of Greeley was elected to the Senate, J. L. Brush and Judge Haynes called a meeting of Weld County farmers to discuss the need for legislation on irrigation matters. The meeting was held at Greeley on October 19, 1878. It was not very well attended, but there were several from the Saint Vrain, including L. C. Mead, who was elected chairman. In a few hours those in attendance decided that legislation was needed to provide some method of determining prior rights, to provide for the measurement of the streams, and to create stream districts with a public official in each one to superintend the distribution of the water. Consequently, they agreed to call a state-wide meeting to be held in Denver during the first week in December and authorized J. S. Stanger, editor of the Colorado Farmer, to make the necessary arrangements.

The Denver convention lasted three days, December 5-7, 1878. It was attended by at least fifty-one men, mostly farmers, representing twenty-nine ditch companies or agricultural communities located in the South Platte Valley. The Greeley district was represented by J. Max Clark, B. S. LaGrange, J. D. Buckley, and David Boyd. The

Upper Poudre, where many were now convinced of the need for control, sent R. Q. Tenney, J. S. McCelland, J. G. Coy, A. L. Emigh, I. L. Bailey, and John C. Abbott. The Saint Vrain, Big Thompson, and Boulder valleys were also well represented.

The meeting was quickly organized, and L. C. Mead, as chairman, appointed a committee on business, headed by David Boyd, to prepare the agenda. The committee was not agreed as to the necessity for legislation, but the majority reported three proposals for discussion. Two of the proposals, the measurement of the streams and the division of the State into irrigation districts, had been discussed at the previous meeting in Greeley, but the proposal to appoint a State commissioner of irrigation was new and foreshadowed the creation later of the office known as State Engineer. The convention discussed each proposal. Some, like G. W. Harriman of Bear Creek, opposed any legislation as unnecessary and expensive. "If the people of the Cache la Poudre want legislation," he is reported to have said, "let them have a district law and pay for it themselves." The proposal to measure the water in the streams provoked the most debate. J. Max Clark supported the proposal by a reference to the successful measurement of streams in northern Italy, but "Mr. Devinney said it was absolutely impossible to measure the water in the streams so as to be of any use to the farmer." David Barnes of the Big Thompson thought that the streams fluctuated too much for measurement and that it would be more feasible to measure the snow in the mountains. On the third day the members of the convention summarized their agreements in a memorial to the legislature, appointed a committee of five to draft a bill, and adjourned.

The memorial proposed a set of institutions for the control of irrigation waters new to Anglo-American experience. Such institutions had not been necessary east of the 98th meridian, and west of it they had not developed beyond the regulation of individual ditches. The memorial urged the application of the idea of regulation to entire streams and to the entire State. In this the South Platte farmers had no precedents, only their needs to guide them. Their proposals grew out of their frontier experience in an arid country and formed another attempt to adapt themselves to a new environment.

The memorial proposed, first, that the president of the State

227

board of agriculture serve as a commissioner of irrigation, although his duties in this capacity were left undefined. This arrangement was a compromise with the original proposal in order to reduce the operational expenses of the new organization and to make it as economical as possible. Second, the memorial proposed "that measures should be taken for ascertaining and perpetuating the priority of the right of ditches, individuals and farms to the use of water in each irrigation district." Third, the memorial proposed "that the State should be divided into irrigation districts, according to the natural courses of the streams and that commissioners be appointed for the several districts." If carried out the State would have a new administrative system with districts conforming to the watersheds of the streams rather than to the artificial counties and a new set of public officials called commissioners. It was proposed that these stream commissioners be appointed by the county commissioners and that their duties consist of dividing the water in their districts among the users in accordance with their prior rights and of recording in the county clerk's offices data concerning the size of the ditches, time of construction, and similar information. These proposals were a development of Meeker's idea that the river should be made "an irrigation canal subject to . . . superintendence." Fourth, the farmer's memorial to the second general assembly proposed not only that the streams be measured but also that "there should be some uniform method adopted for measuring water entering the different ditches." In addition, the memorial included several other proposals on reservoirs, pollutions of the streams, and the police powers of the stream commissioners.

This memorial served as a guide to the committee of five which spent a week in the preparation of a bill which was introduced into the legislature as House Bill No. 22 by L. C. Mead. The committee had the most difficulty devising a method of ascertaining priorities. As it turned out, this part of the bill was completely rewritten in the committee on irrigation by Judge H. P. H. Bromwell, a lawyer who was sympathetic to the efforts of the farmers. In general, the legal profession was opposed to the proposed institutions, but Judge Bromwell was "strongly impressed with the necessity of legislation on this subject."

Opposition of the bill developed mostly in the Senate. A study published in 1912 gives the impression that the cattlemen opposed legislation of this nature, but I have found no evidence to support this view in the case of House Bill No. 22. Although the Rocky Mountain News reported that "there are nineteen stockraisers on the floor of the house," few objections were raised when it was presented for debate, and it passed the House 34 to 4, with 11 absent or not voting. In the Senate, however, the bill was stubbornly opposed, not by the cattlemen, but by Senator L. R. Rhodes supported by the senators from the Spanish-speaking communities in the southern part of the State. Rhodes was a young lawyer from Fort Collins who shared the antipathy of many members of his profession to the proposed legislation. He was also a member of the Democratic Party, and in this chamber House Bill No. 22 became a political issue. Most of the Democrats voted against it, whereas the Republicans supported it. Whatever his motives, Rhodes' opposition was determined. Three times he attempted to kill the bill. On February 7, 1879, he moved to strike out all of the bill after the enacting clause.

> He said the passage of the bill would be detrimental
> to all the best farming interests in the State. Want
> of time prevented him from pointing out all the object-
> tionable features of the bill. He saw no use of any
> legislation on the subject of irrigation. The decisions
> of the Supreme Courts of California and Nevada have
> settled all the questions of prior rights, and these
> precedents are all the law that is needed. The bill
> should be entitled a bill to increase the practice of
> attorneys in the rural districts.

When the final vote was taken in the Senate a few hours before adjournment on February 9, 16 voted in the affirmative, and 8 voted with Senator Rhodes in the negative.

The irrigation law which the legislature enacted on February 9, 1879 was the first of several which created the present system in Colorado for the administration of its streams. It formed 10 water districts, 9 of them in the South Platte Valley. Most of them comprised an entire watershed. The valley of the Cache la Poudre, for instance, became Water District No. 3 as it remains to this day. New districts have been added until today /1947/ they number 70 and include every valley in the State. In each district, the law provided

229

for a water commissioner to divide the stream waters of his district among the ditches according to their prior rights. In Colorado today there are 62 such officials. In addition, the law provided that priorities were to be determined by the district courts which were to appoint referees to take testimony and gather proof as to the time the ditches were constructed, together with their original capacities. The law, however, omitted any mention of a State commissioner of irrigation or the measurement of the streams.

The first referee, as well as the first water commissioners, was appointed in 1879. H. N. Haynes, the son of Judge Haynes, was appointed for the Cache la Poudre, but when he had taken his testimony and had his evidence ready for court action, the lawyers found the method of ascertaining priorities unsatisfactory. Action was therefore delayed until the next legislature could remedy the deficiency. The third general assembly which met in 1881 not only corrected this deficiency but also completed the original program of the Denver convention. It created the office of State Engineer and assigned to this official the duty of measuring the streams of the State in cubic feet per second. In addition, it created three water divisions, administrative units larger than the water districts and comprising entire drainage basins. The South Platte drainage basin became Water Division No. 1 and the Arkansas Valley became Water Division No. 2. Six years later each of these divisions, which now number seven, was provided with a superintendent. In this manner, Colorado became "the first State to enact a code of laws for the public administration of streams . . . ."

Significant as these events are for Colorado, they have an equal significance beyond the boundaries of the State. The legislation of 1879 and 1881 immediately attracted attention in California, Utah, and Wyoming. Eventually, each of the eleven Western States — with the exception of Montana — in some measure patterned its system for the public control and administration of water after that of Colorado. The farmers of Greeley evolved an administrative system not only for the State of Colorado but also, with modifications, for most of the arid West.

NINETEEN: THE MEEKER MASSACRE

by Forbes Parkhill

The Ute Indians were hunting and warring in the high mountains
of Colorado when the Spanish first penetrated the region. They were
still in possession of most of their tribal lands when the Eastern Slope
Indians were escorted to reservations outside Colorado. Inevitably,
however, the day approached when the Ute lands were coveted by the
white settlers and pressures were generated for removal of the tribe.
A sensational climax exploded in September, 1879, when the Meeker
Massacre touched off the last chorus of the long refrain "The Utes
Must Go!" The massacre at the White River Agency, and the battle at
Milk Creek, are narrated here by Forbes Parkhill. *

*   *   *

THE MEEKER MASSACRE

The Meeker Massacre and the Thornburgh Battle in north-
western Colorado in September, 1879, have formed the subject
matter of a vast amount of published fact and fiction, and unfor-
tunately, of a great deal of fiction parading as fact. Fiction and
history cannot be judged by the same set of standards. In seeking the causes of the Meeker Massacre and the Thornburgh Battle
— causes which have been the subject of endless controversy —
let's make certain we know what is historical fact and what is fiction. This . . . is an attempt to sift fiction from fact, so far as
that is possible.

------

*from Forbes Parkhill, "The Meeker Massacre and Thornburgh Battle: Fact and
Fiction" in *1945 Brand Book*, Denver, 1946, pages 91-110. Copyright 1946 by
The Westerners, Denver Posse. Used with permission of the Denver Westerners.

The Utes were mountain Indians, occupying at the time of the Civil War, most of the mountainous western half of Colorado and a part of eastern Utah. In 1863, Territorial Governor John Evans, representing the federal government, made a treaty with the Tabeguache Utes by which the Indians agreed to leave that portion of their "perpetual" reservation known as the San Luis Valley.

In 1868 Governor Alexander Hunt negotiated a treaty providing that the confederated Utes, embracing all bands under the leadership of Chief Ouray, were to occupy "forever" a reservation including all of Colorado west of the 107th meridian and south of a line 15 miles north of the 40th parallel. Draw a line through Pagosa Springs, Gunnison and Yampa, and you have the eastern boundary. A line directly west of Yampa would approximate the northern boundary.

The so-called Southern Utes occupied the southern part of this huge reservation; the Uncompahgre Utes the central portion, and the White River Utes, with whom we are particularly concerned, the northern portion.

Immediately rich ore deposits were discovered in the San Juan country, and the white man began to covet that area. In 1872 a government commission tried, unsuccessfully, to induce the Utes to give up this rich region. Another commission under Felix Brunot was more successful the following year. In 1874 the Brunot treaty was ratified by the United States Senate.

Under the Brunot treaty Chief Ouray was to receive $1,000 a year for life. Article 3 of the treaty provided "$25,000 annually for the benefit of the Ute Indians, annually forever, disbursed or invested as the president may direct." The payment was in consideration of the relinquishment by the Utes of the rich San Juan mining region.

Up to the time of the Meeker Massacre, five years after the ratification of this solemn national obligation by the United States Senate, only a small portion of this payment had ever reached the Utes. Payment customarily was made to the Indians in the form of supplies and annuity goods, rather than in cash. By '79 a backlog of $65,000, appropriated by Congress to meet this obligation to the

Utes, had been withheld by the Indian Bureau.

At a Congressional investigation following the Meeker Massacre, William M. Leeds, former chief clerk of the Indian Office, testified that the president had not directed that the payments be withheld or invested, but that the Bureau had nullified the solemn obligation of the nation under the treaty, merely because "The Bureau feared trouble — the Indians might buy firearms." Such was the power of what today would be called Bureaucracy to substitute its opinion for a solemn national treaty obligation ratified by the United States Senate.

However, some supplies and annuity goods had been shipped to the White River Utes in '76. Owing to the failure of a freighter to meet his obligation to transport the supplies from Rawlins, Wyo., to the agency, the supplies remained in the Union Pacific railroad warehouse at Rawlins for two years, piling up storage charges.

The Utes, bewildered by government red tape, found what they believed was a simple solution — if the Great White Father couldn't get the supplies from the warehouse to the agency, what was simpler than for the Indians to go to the warehouse? A band went to Rawlins to get their supplies and annuity goods but, except for some temporary rations, red tape prevented the release of the supplies. In '78 some annuity goods were sent to the agency, but the railroad kept a sufficient supply of flour and oats to protect its storage bill. Finally it was found that most of these supplies had spoiled, and their value was not worth the storage charges. They were not redeemed by the government and the railroad was left literally "holding the bags."

Meanwhile settlers were swarming to the West by the tens of thousands, many following Horace Greeley's popular, though not original, advice to "Go West, young man." Among Greeley's proteges was Nathaniel C. Meeker, a poet and a special writer on agricultural subjects for the New York Tribune.

Meeker was a disciple of Fourier, the French socialist, who advocated the organization of society into self-sufficient phalanxes. Meeker promoted such a phalanx, based upon communal principles, in an eastern state, but it ended in failure. In 1870, supported by Greeley, he organized the Union Colony at Greeley, which he described in the Greeley Tribune as "a system of cooperation within limited bounds." Through the 'seventies and 'eighties, some thirty-five colonization schemes based to some degree on a communal system had been established in Colorado.

Meeker was a deeply religious, obstinate, earnest reformer, so eager to develop the brotherhood of man that he was willing to use force, if necessary, to do good to his fellow man. His followers in the Union Colony called him "Father" Meeker, and worshiped him with what amounted almost to religious fervor. His enemies opposed him bitterly, and he continuously was complaining about "lack of cooperation" on the part of colonists and outsiders alike. His opponents charged that what Meeker meant by "cooperation" was unquestioning obedience to his orders. They said that when all did not go well with the Union Colony, and many colonists withdrew, Meeker saw "lack of cooperation" as the reason for his two failures. He earnestly felt that "forcible cooperation" would being success, and saw in the then vacant post of Indian agent at the White River Ute agency the opportunity to achieve the brotherhood of man through cooperation enforced by the might of the United States Government. Whether this is fact or fiction remains undetermined.

Through the influence of Greeley, he was appointed Indian agent in the spring of '78, and took to the agency with him his wife, his daughter Josephine, and a group of workers from the Union Colony. In an era when the Indian Bureau was notorious for corruption among its employees, no enemy ever charged Meeker with dishonesty. He was so scrupulously honest that he refused to accept gifts from his Indian wards for fear he might be accused of accepting bribes. Apparently he was not opposed to nepotism, for his son Ralph had been his secretary at the Union Colony, and his 20-year-old daughter Josie, employed as a teacher, drew a salary larger than any employee at the agency except Meeker himself — although at no time did she have more than three pupils in her school.

Governor Pitkin said, "A purer and better man than Meeker was never appointed to an Indian agency," but added that he did not understand Indians sufficiently.

Perhaps the best key to Meeker's character is found in his letter to Senator Teller, in which he wrote, "I shall propose to cut every Indian down to the bare starvation point if he will not work." He proposed to civilize the Utes overnight, if he had to starve them to do it. He once reported, "The most hopeful thing is that there are several families complaining bitterly of cold, and they want houses."

Meeker entered into his plan to create a Utopia overnight with all the fervor of a religious zealot. The agency at that time was located in a narrow canon of the White River, some ten miles upstream from the present town of Meeker. Snows were deep in the winter, and the canon was too narrow for the farms Meeker envisioned. He decided to move the agency to Powell's Bottom, a broad valley some four miles below the present town of Meeker. But the Utes had other ideas.

The proposed site was the most convenient expanse of grassland for the grazing of their ponies. If it were plowed up and converted into farming land, little grass would be left. Meeker untactfully suggested that if there was not sufficient grass they could kill part of their ponies. An Indian's wealth being measured by the number of his ponies, this suggestion was received with anything but enthusiasm. Yet, from Meeker's standpoint, it was quite logical. As long as the Indians possessed ponies and firearms, they would remain nomads, hunters of wild game. Deprive them of their ponies and their guns, and they would be forced to become farmers.

The government had recognized Douglas, a 60-year-old factional leader, as chief of the White River Utes. The leader who controlled by far the largest following, however, was Jack, 38 years old, also known as Captain Jack, Ute Jack and Ute John. Jack had been reared by a Mormon family, had served as a scout leader under General Crook in the Sioux campaign, and consequently spoke reasonably good English. The third tribal leader of consequence was Johnson, who was a medicine man rather than a chief. Johnson owned an excellent Henry rifle, was a crack shot, an inveterate gambler, and a racer of ponies.

Despite the objections of the Indians, Meeker moved the agency buildings to the new site. He laid out a model community homesite, and offered to give every Indian a homesite. Strangely enough, the

Utes couldn't understand how he had the power to give them land that, under the Brunot treaty, they considered already theirs. Meeker built a cabin for Johnson and his two wives, in the belief that others would be led by Johnson's example into ways of civilization. One of Johnson's wives, Susan, was a sister of Chief Ouray.

By tribal custom the male Indian provided game sufficient to feed his family, and his squaw performed all the work around the house. Except for squaws, manual labor was regarded as degrading. To demand that a male Indian labor in the fields was as humiliating as if some dictator told . . . /men today7 that hereafter they and their male children would be required to cook the meals, dry the dishes, wash the diapers and to perform other household duties we regard as in woman's sphere. They met Meeker's suggestion just about as you would meet the suggestion that you abandon your businesses and professions and take up housework.

Meeker had one field plowed and planted, but the labor was performed by the white agency employees, with the help of a few squaws. Meanwhile Meeker was making every effort to cut red tape and get the annuity goods and supplies delivered, and had succeeded so well that the government's failure to deliver these goods cannot be considered as one of the principal cuases of the Meeker Massacre.

There was no trading post at the agency, but there were four just outside the limits of the reservation. These stores sold arms, ammunition and whiskey to the Indians, and Meeker complained officially that one was operated as a house of prostitution staffed by Indian girls. Meeker made every effort to prevent the sale of arms and ammunition and whiskey to his wards at these stores, but without success. At the Union Colony he had crusaded against the use of intoxicants, had prohibited in its charter the sale of liquor in Greeley, and had written in the Tribune, "Having known how to strangle the the demon of rum for two years, we have learned how to strangle it for all time to come."

Most western Indian agents, recognizing the fact that the Indian was by nature a nomad and a huntsman, and that he could not be turned into a farmer overnight, permitted the sale of firearms and ammunition by the post trader, where it could be controlled.

236

The White River Utes, with little or no annuity goods for two years, would have starved if they had not killed wild game. And to get arms and ammunition for this purpose they were forced to leave the reservation. They would, however, have left the reservation under any circumstances. They never regarded the reservation boundary as anything but a fence to keep the white man away. They ranged as far east as the plains north of Denver before the buffalo was exterminated, as far north as central Wyoming, and west as far as the Uintah Reservation in Utah. Frequently Meeker would never see his wards except when they returned to the agency, usually in the Fall, for the distribution of annuity goods.

Sometimes they set fire to the range, "so the grass would grow better next year" — a method of fertilizing still practiced by the white man. But now, as these ranges were filling with settlers, a grass fire frequently would wipe out a farmer's house and haystacks. To the Utes, this was the farmer's hard luck, and they did not see why it should be necessary to abandon a practice of generations' standing.

Likewise they sometimes set fire to the forests to drive game into the open where it could be killed more easily, and "because it provided dry firewood for next season's hunting trip." Naturally this practice did not set well with the settlers. Feeling against the Utes became bitter among the Colorado whites. Congressman Belford . . . introduced a bill providing for their removal to Indian Territory.

Discovery of the rich San Juan mining area led to the belief that more riches could be found on the vast reservation of the consolidated Utes. The movement to get rid of the Indians, to get this vast section of the state on the tax rolls, to exploit the resources of the immense reservation, gained momentum steadily. Most Colorado whites of the period were convinced that "the only good Indian was a dead Indian."

Meeker did his best to keep his charges on the reservation. But he had no police force, and he feared to follow the example of other Indian agents who had created a force of Indian police, because he feared and distrusted the brown breathren he was so determined to civilize. Naturally he was without authority outside the reservation boundaries.

When numerous complaints were received from white settlers of the damage caused by the Utes, he wrote to Major T. T. Thornburgh, in command of the army post at Fort Steele, near Rawlins, Wyoming, asking for his assistance in keeping the Utes on the reservation. Thornburgh, as disclosed by subsequent investigations, reported that the ranchmen had no complaint to make other than that the Indians killed too much game, and supported this statement by letters from a number of cattlemen and settlers. How could it be possible that on the one hand the Utes were being charged with the wanton destruction of the lives and property of the whites, and Thornburgh reported there was no trouble with the Indians? Which was fact, which was fiction?

It should be understood that Fort Steele was in the army Department of the Platte, under General George Crook, and that the jurisdiction of this department extended only to the Colorado line. Colorado was in the Department of the Missouri under General John Pope. It is significant that the letters accompanying Thornburgh's report were from Wyoming ranchmen. Apparently he was reluctant to go beyond his own territorial jurisdiction in his investigation, for fear of casting a reflection upon the commanding general of the adjoining department.

Again, how was it possible that the white residents of Wyoming and Utah, where the Utes ranged widely, had no complaints to make against the Indians, while the residents of Colorado held them to be murderous, wantonly destructive savages? Did an Indian who was peaceable and harmless in Utah and Wyoming become a murderer and a firebug when he crossed the state line into Colorado?

The answer is found in the fact that it was the Colorado whites who had everything to gain by ejecting the Indians from their state and exploiting the reservation resources. Residents of Utah and Wyoming had no interest in placing the reservation resources on the Colorado tax rolls. Keep this in mind in sifting fact from fiction concerning the reports of Ute outrages in Colorado. There are such instances — Jack himself admitted one such charge against two of his men — but it likewise is probable that every theft of horses, every forest fire caused by lightning, every unsolved killing was likely to be charged to the Indians.

The government owned a herd of cattle on the reservation for the

238

use of the Utes. Under the conditions of the open range as they then existed, these cattle mingled with herds owned by neighboring cattlemen, and it is not strange that many calves of the Indian herd were picked up as mavericks by unscrupulous cattlemen. Uncle Sam was considered fair game. So were the Indians.

The agency herd bore the I.D. — Indian Department — brand. This brand is most easily blotched, and Meeker officially charged that a neighboring cattleman registered the "Double Box" brand because the two strokes of a running iron changed the I.D. into the cattleman's brand.

As the tension between whites and Indians grew, General Pope dispatched a company of cavalry — they were not called "troops" of cavalry until later — into Middle Park. These were Negro soldiers, called "buffalo" soldiers by the Indians, who detested Negroes, and were commanded by Captain Dodge.

In the summer of '79 two Utes, Bennett and Chinaman, were charged with burning the home of a settler in Middle Park, and the sheriff of Grand County went to the agency with a warrant for their arrest. Meeker still further incurred the enmity of the Utes when he tried to give them up to the law, but the two fugitives refused to surrender and the sheriff was without authority to make an arrest on the reservation.

Meeker decided to fence and plow another field alongside the agency buildings, but met bitter opposition because the field would have destroyed the Indian pony race track, and because plowed fields meant farming and farming meant work and they had no intention of working. When Meeker ordered a white farmhand to plow the field regardless of objections, a bullet fired by the son of the medicine man, Johnson, whistled past his head, and the project was abandoned. Johnson quarreled with Meeker, dragged him from the agency, pushed him backward over a hitching rail and injured his back.

Meeker immediately sent letters to Governor Pitkin and to the military authorities asking for help. Pitkin wired to Washington, and Major Thornburgh was ordered to the agency, in command of a company of cavalry and a company of infantry from Fort Steele, and two companies of cavalry from Fort D. A. Russell at Cheyenne. The company of infantry was left at Little Bear Creek to guard the expedition's supplies.

Meanwhile Jack had just returned from Denver, where he had asked Governor Pitkin's help in getting Meeker removed from the agency. Chief Ouray already had asked the removal of Meeker. Pitkin, who believed Meeker a "pure and noble soul" had given Jack an evasive answer. Jack and several other Utes met Thornburgh as the expedition neared the reservation, and warned him if the soldiers entered the reservation the Utes would regard it as an act of war and would fight.

Jack suggested that the expedition halt and that Thornburgh send five men, along with five Indians, to the agency to remove Meeker. Thornburgh agreed tentatively to the plan to send five men to the agency, and communicated the proposal to Meeker by courier. Had Jack's suggestion been followed, the investigating commission later reported, the massacre and battle would have been averted.

Meanwhile Thornburgh moved his troops to within a mile of the reservation boundary, on Milk Creek, some twenty-five miles from the agency. That night, according to testimony at subsequent hearings, he held a staff meeting and changed his mind, deciding to move on into the reservation and to establish a camp within some twelve miles of the agency before sending his five emissaries forward. This decision was based on the belief that the troops must be within easy striking distance if hostilities developed. It undoubtedly was one of the immediate causes of the subsequent Thornburgh battle, as when, on the morning of September 29, the troops began to move across the reservation boundary, the waiting Utes regarded it as a breach of faith.

Jack had deployed his warriors on both sides of the main road passing through Red Canyon. Thornburgh, however, recognizing the danger of an ambush in the canon, sent his men forward on a trail that cut across the adjoining ridge. He sent his adjutant, Lieutenant Cherry, ahead with an advance guard, and left one company at the Milk Creek bivouac to guard the supplies.

Lieutenant Cherry later testified that he saw from 300 to 400 Utes deployed along the ridge ahead. Jack insisted that no more than 50 or 60 Utes took part in the battle against Thornburgh's force of some 175 men. Josie later said the warriors in the tribe numbered from 150 to 175. Cherry ordered his men to deploy in skirmish line, and waved his hat in what he said was a signal of friendship to the Indians.

Cavalry commands often are given by means of arm signals. Jack later said the Utes took the waved hat to be a signal to charge. Captain Payne, deploying on Cherry's left, testified he took the signal to mean, "we have sighted the enemy." Thornburgh was under orders not to fire unless attacked.

Cherry said the Indians fired the first shot, wounding a soldier at his side. The Indians claimed the soldiers fired first. Cherry then heard an outburst of shooting on his left, and the battle was on.

Because the troops had taken the trail instead of the road, a group of Utes on the far side of the road were enabled to swing in behind the advance guard, and almost cut them off. Thornburgh sent back word to the bivouac to arrange the wagons in a circle to withstand a siege. He was killed a few minutes later. Two soldiers were killed and several wounded before the advance guard succeeded in retreating to the hastily formed stockade.

Captain Payne, the ranking officer, ordered forty horses killed by the soldiers to form a temporary barricade. Thirty more horses were stampeded and captured by the Utes, who charged once, were repelled, and settled down to a siege. The Utes set fire to the grass and the besieged soldiers barely escaped being burned out by the fire, which spread in succeeding days some twenty miles back into the Danforth Hills.

During the night the soldiers dug trenches. They were equipped with Springfield carbines, which recently had replaced the Civil War needle guns. These carbines were not very accurate, and their range was not great.

The Indians were equipped with a variety of weapons, including several excellent Spencer, Henry and Sharps hunting rifles, and a number of late model Winchesters that they had bought the preceding week at the off-reservation trading posts.

One Ute, later identified as the marksman Johnson, established himself in the willows just beyond the range of the cavalry carbines, and began methodically picking off the horses and mules in the stockade, so that only four remained at the end of the siege.

That night three couriers were sent for help, including Scout John Rankin, a civilian, and a soldier. Rankin's 150-mile ride to Rawlins has been the subject of considerable controversy. Some newspaper accounts had it that he ran the entire distance afoot. Some reported that he had ridden the 150 miles in 24 hours. The army reported that he made the ride in 48 hours. But the most reliable accounts agree that, with two changes of horses at local ranches, he made the ride in 17 1/2 hours . . . . Lieutenant Paddok's published account credits Private Murphy with making the ride.

The other two couriers felt their work accomplished when they warned ranchers in the Bear River Valley, from which there immediately began an exodus of ranchmen and their families. A written message was left impaled on a sagebrush branch on the trail from Middle Park.

Meanwhile Captain Dodge with his Negro soldiers from Middle Park had received orders, issued before the battle, to join Thornburgh. Proceeding at a leisurely pace, he found the message on the sagebrush clump, and immediately headed for the scene of the battle. His pack train was left with Thornburgh's supply company which had camped on the Bear. He reached the besieged soldiers on the morning of the third day after the beginning of the battle, but instead of being of assistance to them, his presence proved merely an additional drain on the food supplies, as his horses were quickly picked off by the Ute marksman.

Immediately upon the outbreak of the battle at the edge of the reservation, an Indian courier was sent to the twenty remaining Utes, under Chief Douglas, at the agency. Shortly after lunch, while the womenfolk were washing the dishes, the Indians stole the firearms in the employees' sleeping quarters, and opened fire on Meeker and his

242

men. Three of the employees were shot as they were spreading dirt on the roof of one of the new buildings.

No survivor witnessed the actual killing of Meeker. He was last seen passing the kitchen door on his way to lock the room from which the employees' guns had been stolen. Many accounts say Meeker was dragged from his room by a log chain around his neck, and that a barrel stave (some say an iron stake) was driven through his mouth into the ground. This is more probably fiction than fact, for Mrs. Meeker testified that when his body was last seen that evening, he was laid out on the ground as if for burial, stripped of all clothing except a shirt, and with a bullet wound through the forehead. Neither Mrs. Meeker nor daughter Josephine mentioned the log chain, nor the stake. Meeker probably was shot in his own room by the son of Johnson, who was killed a few minutes later by one of the agency employees. Every white man at the agency, except for the one who had been sent out as a courier, was murdered.

The women — Mrs. Meeker, 68 years old and lame; Josie Meeker, 20; Mrs. Price, the housekeeper and wife of the agency blacksmith — with the two small Price children and an agency employee, Dresser, took refuge in the agency milk house, because it was built of green cottonwood logs and would be difficult to burn.

In the evening they made a break for liberty across the plowed field north of the agency, hoping to lose themselves in the tall sagebrush beyond. The Utes saw them and opened fire. Dresser gained the sagebrush, wounded, reached a coal mine twelve miles from the agency, lay down to rest and bled to death from his wounds. His body was found in the mine days later.

Mrs. Meeker was wounded in the thigh, and was captured along with the other two women and the two children, and the five were taken to different Indian camps.

Meanwhile Colonel Wesley Merritt had set out at the head of a rescue expedition, and reached the besieged soldiers on the morning of the fifth day. At the same time a white courier from Chief Ouray brought orders to the Utes to cease fighting. The Indians immediately melted away, and fled south to various refuges in the Uncompahgre country. Merritt established camp on the present site of the town of Meeker.

He was intent upon pressing south to rescue the kidnapped women and children, but orders from Washington forbade this course, stating it probably meant death for the captives, and that a civilian commission was meeting with Chief Ouray at the Los Pinos Ute Agency, with the hope that Ouray would order his tribesmen to surrender the captives.

Merritt built permanent log buildings, which he occupied the ensuing winter . . . .

When the temporary military post was abandoned, the log buildings constituted a ready-made town for whoever might care to move in. The buildings were occupied gradually by white settlers. Thus the present town of Meeker originated . . . .

A joint delegation of whites and Ouray's Indians set out for the camp on Plateau Creek, northwest of Gunnison, where the captives were being held. The poem, "Chipeta's Ride," telling of how Ouray's squaw sped on her trusty pony to rescue the white women single-handed is 100 per cent fiction, for Chipeta was not a member of the rescue party. The prisoners were surrendered, and upon their arrival at the Los Pinos agency, and during their return through Denver to their home in Greeley, they were interviewed repeatedly and their story became a nation-wide sensation. They had been held captive 23 days.

Meanwhile a joint civilian and military commission was appointed to investigate the massacre and battle and to bring the guilty persons to justice. The women captives and many Indians were examined, and at the conclusion of its hearings the commission fastened the responsibility upon twelve ringleaders, and demanded that Ouray produce them for trial. Ouray promised to do so if given enough time to find them. He never produced them. Jack surrendered voluntarily and was held at Fort Leavenworth for a time and then was released. No individual was ever punished for his part in the massacre or the battle. War Department records show the investigation of the committee caused much bitterness in military circles, because the commission apparently sought to fix responsibility only for the massacre, and made no effort to seek out and punish those responsible for the killing of soldiers in the Thornburgh battle.

Throughout the many newspaper interviews, all three women insisted that they had not been criminally attacked while being held captive. However, during the first investigation, upon receiving the pledge of the commission that their testimony would be kept secret, each testified that she had been outraged. The secrecy pledge of the commission was broken when the proceedings of the commission were published the following year.

There is considerable reason to believe that the testimony concerning the outraging of the women is more fiction than fact. When it is considered that many months had passed without the arrest of the killers of Meeker, Mrs. Price's husband and other agency employees, it is only natural that these women should feel most bitter, and should do everything in their power to spur the authorities to action. Nothing presumably could accomplish this end better than to change their original story and to insist that they had been outraged. Mrs. Meeker at the time was 68 years old, lame, and suffering from a bullet wound in her thigh. Chief Ouray scoffed at the stories of the outraging, insisting that it was impossible because the squaws of the Utes named by the white women "would never have permitted such a thing."

In the second investigation, conducted in Washington in 1880 under congressional authority, no mention of the alleged outrages was made by Josie Meeker, the only one of the three women to testify. Josie later became secretary to Senator Teller, lectured on the subject of the massacre, and died a few years later of a pulmonary ailment . . . .

The upshot of the whole affair was that no person was punished for his part in the affair, but the Utes were removed from their reservation to the present Ute reservation, which is much smaller, in southwestern Colorado, and the huge reservation of the late seventies was opened to exploitation and occupancy by the white man.

The army reported 25 whites killed, including 11 civilians; 41 wounded, and 39 Indians killed. Jack testified that only 19 Indians were killed, and 7 were missing.

Clinton B. Fisk, a member of the Board of Indian Commissioners, testified:

> (Meeker) was as unfit as a man could possibly be; destitute of tact and knowledge of Indian character; too old; unhappily constituted in his mental organization; his whole agency and administration almost a failure. His management of the Utes and his threats to bring soldiers in, had very much to do with the massacre.

Most of the Indian witnesses said Meeker had told them that Thornburgh was bringing a wagonload of chains and manacles to shackle them. Their chief complaint was based on Meeker's effort to make them into farmers. They also charged he spoke with a "forked tongue, " telling them one thing one day, and another the next. Jack complained that he had promised him a new red wagon, but when the wagons arrived he kept them and gave Jack an old, used wagon, which he forced him to return after thirty days.

In Josie's school the Utes saw a design to enslave them. They reasoned: if their children were educated, they would become carpenters; as carpenters, they would have to build houses; having built houses, they would have to live in them; living in houses, they could hunt no longer, but would have to become farmers; farmers must work, and to a buck Indian, work was degrading . . . .

In summary, the causes of the massacre and battle were:

1 — Broadly, the attitude of the white residents of Colorado, who wanted to get rid of the Utes and open the huge reservation to exploitation.

2 — The incredible stupidity of a corrupt and inefficient Indian Bureau.

3 — The unfortunate personality of Indian Agent Meeker, who was temperamentally and emotionally unfit for such a post.

4 — Errors in judgment on the part of leaders of the Thorn-burgh expedition.

5 — Least of all, . . . the reactions of the Indians themselves, who were thoroughly bewildered by the white man's efforts to civilize them overnight, rightfully resentful over the white man's repeatedly broken promises, and who used the only means they knew to fight for what they considered their rights.

TWENTY: THE UNCOMPAHGRE UTE "GOES WEST"
by Walker D. Wyman

The answer of Coloradans to the Indian depredations and murders at White River was an ever louder volume to the cry "The Utes Must Go." And go they did, reluctantly but surely, to the Utah Territory. This "final solution" to Colorado's Indian "problem" is described by Professor Walker D. Wyman.*

*   *   *

THE UNCOMPAHGRE UTE "GOES WEST"

. . . The history of the settlement of the "West" is prefaced throughout by the removal of the Indian. The first white settlers in any frontier community were pulled to that particular area in search of the "better" life which the physical and social environment were supposed to afford. This was often done without considering the consequences of trespassing upon Indian land; hence open hostilities with the original owners became a part of the history of westward expansion. A far-away federal government, stimulated into activity by western senators and military imperialists, constantly shifted its policy to meet the exigencies arising when the red and white frontiers clashed. To control and direct the flow of population into the West was a difficult task, an impossible task. So they purchased the Indian titles, gave generous annuities in exchange for possession of the land, and tried to interest the red man in agriculture so as to make him "take root" in his allotted reservations.

------

*from Walker D. Wyman, "A Preface to the Settlement of Grand Junction: The Uncompahgre Ute 'Goes West'" in *The Colorado Magazine*, volume X (January, 1933), pages 22-27. Used with permission of the State Historical Society of Colorado.

The Ute Indians were the "first families" of Colorado, so far as the white emigrants were concerned. But these first families were not so fortunate as the first white families of Virginia. For instead of amassing fortunes and becoming political and social leaders in the fabric of society, they sold their heritage for a mess of pottage and were pushed over into the Uintah Basin in Utah. There they live today, those who remain, in the fashion characteristic of many of our first families who happened to have the wrong pigment in their epidermis.

Beginning in 1863 negotiations paved the way for the ultimate removal of the Utes from the Rocky Mountain region. By 1880 they had been pushed to the western slope, and located in three different agencies — in southern Colorado, in the Uncompahgre area, and on the White River. There were some 2,900 of them, most of whom were successfully resisting the new policy of making them agricultural and "civilized." It was quite well agreed on the part of the clergy-agents located among the Utes that in "weaning them from their migratory or roving habits and inducing them to permanently locate /sic7 homes for themselves and families, lies the solution of the problem of Ute civilization . . . . Like children, the Utes need kindly but firm and honest treatment for their successful government."

However, by the latter part of the 1870s, even if peace did reign on the western slope of the Rockies, there was a growing sentiment that the Utes must go. As early as 1878 a bill had been drafted for Congress expressing that feeling. Homeseekers had begun to turn their eager eyes toward this new El Dorado. The vibrating frontier town of Gunnison, located in the Gunnison River valley, was famous by 1879 as an outfitting center for the newly developed mining regions. It looked wistfully toward the "Grand" valley, and with a speculative eye, for there lay a potent supply of vegetables and grain for hungry miners and burrows.

But it was the "Meeker Massacre" at the White River Agency which gave the dramatic touch to the Ute land desire, set fire to the tinder of emotional intensity, and aroused the final outburst of resentment which rang throughout the mountain area in the four pregnant words — "The Ute must go."

Troops were moved to this western frontier to quell a probable

249

uprising in 1880. Pioneers "flooded the Governor of Colorado with telegrams offering their services for war. Multitudes in and about Denver — old soldiers, gray-haired frontiersmen, and tenderfeet — were ready to go." In the treaty of that year, the Uncompahgre Utes relinquished all their former reservation in that mountain area, and were to be allotted forty-acre farms in the Grand valley, "if sufficient quantity of agricultural land shall be there; if not, then upon such other unoccupied lands as may be found in that vicinity and in the Territory of Utah." The residue of the land, in case they located there, was to be open to settlement. The San Juan tributaries were to remain the home of the Southern Utes.

The White River bands, who had behaved in such an unorthodox manner in the "Meeker Massacre" (and who had been invoked to do so by the lack of tact and patience on the part of their agent, Nathan P. Meeker), agreed to go. They were to be removed by the Department of War to the Uintah Basin — ever toward the west and the setting of their sun.

The committee appointed "to secure the ratification of the agreement /an Act of Congress, June, 1880, providing for relinquishment of the existing claims/ and to execute the provisions of same," set about the business of removing the Uncompahgre Utes to the Colorado (or Grand) valley near the junction of the Gunnison. Surveyors had already begun the task of laying off the forty-acre farms for them. Probably seeing that eventually the Indian would have to give way to the white man (for ere long the D. & R. G. Railroad from Ogden, Utah, to Denver, Colorado, would run through here bringing in its wake a wave of population), the committee really stretched the treaty provisions and found it convenient to believe that the Utes would be happier on the agricultural lands in the Uintah Basin. There was dissension in the committee, but the Secretary of the Interior upheld those who would wind up the Ute problem once and for all. He probably feared border warfare. And, after all, he must have reasoned, what does it matter to a Ute whether he is in this or that state, in a valley or a basin? It did not, he concluded.

Thus it was decreed that the Utes must go, in a fine interpretation which could have been done only by those with power and authority. Perhaps destiny itself had a hand in the matter. "Horses, wagons,

250

agricultural implements and stock cattle sufficient for their reasonable wants and also saw mills and grist mills as may be necessary . . ." were to be furnished. The removal was to be made as soon as possible. The year of 1881 must not be filled with border tragedy.

Accordingly Commissioner Otto Mears went to the new reservation one hundred and seventy-five miles southeast of Salt Lake. After contracting for the buildings and seeing the new agency become a physical reality, he left to see the removal of the Utes. He left behind him there on the Green River not far from old Fort Bridger, a warehouse, blacksmith shop, agency building, carpenter shop, medical house, doctor's residence, employee's houses, and corrals — all built or in the stage of construction. Everything was ready for the grand reception of the red man — everything but the red man himself.

In the spring of 1881 Colonel R. S. Mackenzie, "a splendid officer and a gentleman and he was never known to question an order given him," had nine companies of infantry and six companies of cavalry assembled in the Uncompahgre region. Brigadier-General John Pope started for the region himself, but was forced to abandon the trip because of the Apache outbreak in Arizona.

The Utes idled away the summer because "of the fact that removal was anticipated early . . . , and it was the expressed desire of the department /of Interior/ that no seed should be planted . . ." However, the twenty farmers of the band did plant a small amount of corn, potatoes, and squash. This unsettled condition brought considerable gambling, horse-racing and other light forms of amusement.

Still the Indians "demurred, desiring they might be located in the Uncompahgre valley . . . ." They hesitated to leave the land of their fathers. They asked leave of time for the fall hunt, and for more time to gather in the stock. On August 22, 1881, their agent, W. H. Berry, called them to council, telling them to make ready for the exodus within the next three days. Three weeks' provisions were promised them; the agency and certain property would be removed to their new home at once; and those who had made improvements were to be compensated for them upon their arrival in the Uintah Basin.

251

Still the Utes dallied. They demanded payment for improvements before leaving. Some said they had heard that stock could
not live around the Green River. The agent gave them another
twenty-four hours to consider. But the next day they refused to
make the westward trek. Then Colonel Mackenzie was placed in
full charge of them. On the twenty-third day of August the Colonel
reported to his superior officer that the Utes had refused to comply
with the agent's orders to move. Brigadier-General Pope wired
these instructions:

"You will use no military force against the Utes unless called
upon in writing to do so by the commissioners or the agent, stating
that they cannot move the Indians without military force. If such
application is made, you will assume charge of the matter yourself,
giving such orders and taking such action as you yourself will consider best, being careful to use no more force than is necessary to
accomplish the object . . . ."

Acting upon these orders Colonel Mackenzie had a pow-wow
with the chiefs at his cantonment. The agent reported that after
learning that they were under his (Mackenzie's) charge, and hearing
from him good and friendly advice as to their peaceable compliance
with their agreement, they concluded at once to remove, "thus showing that they had no serious objection to moving." Furthermore,
since "certain unprincipled whites . . . had poisoned the minds of
the Indians against removing by representing in every way possible
the action of the department and their agent, it is not to be wondered
that the Indian, naturally suspicious as he is, should endeavor to
remain in the valley or country to which they were so fondly attached."

But the Colonel's report to headquarters differs. According to
that, he gave his orders to the Ute chiefs and punctuated them with
the threat of force if necessary, and "would take from them every gun
and pony they possessed," if the move was not immediately made. He
gave them one day to palaver and decide. Observation posts were set
up on the gentle hills which rose along the side of the Uncompahgre
River near the present day Olathe. Bloodshed was expected for many
Indians were armed — a good gun had long been worth a good pony,
and it is said that upon one instance cartridges sold for one dollar
each. Soldiers, eager for action and tired of "fooling" with the

dilatory redskins, made ready to wheel into action on the morning of August 27. Mackenzie had turned the control of them back to the agent on the day before. Three weeks' rations were issued. Boats had been placed at the Grand and Green Rivers. Two hours were granted for the procession to start.

And thus the long drawn-out caravan began the thirteen-day march along the old Indian trail — all "apparently cheerful and happy" reported the sympathetic agent — amid a profusion of autumn color and genuine Indian beauty. Slowly and sullenly they filed along the Uncompahgre, down the Gunnison to the Colorado, and then westward on that sprawled-out river toward their new lands and home. Fourteen hundred fifty-eight homeless Indians, including squaws, bucks, braves, and children, driving ahead of them over 10,000 sheep and goats, riding, leading, or herding 8,000 small ponies, made their way down the historic river, indifferently drinking in the beauties of the late summer sun playing on the mountains. Chief Colorow, famous for his profound stubborness and resistance to this removal, was the last to leave the valley — a dull prosaic dash of copper at the end of a long Indian sentence.

On the morning of September 7, 1881, the last of the Utes were past the junction of the Colorado and Gunnison Rivers. Cottonwoods were left smouldering by those revengeful to the very last. But the tepees were packed on the backs of the ponies for the last time, the goats and sheep were ahead for their last grazing in Grand valley. If one had stood on Pinon Mesa, what a march of a retreating civilization he could have seen! Here was the last defeat of the red man. Here the frontiers of white man met, crushing the Utes in its mighty embrace. What a sight to see the vanquished shift from the last scene of action. Probably restless children with hair disheveled, following the drifting sheep. Yelping dogs, scenting the trail, eyeing suspiciously the river banks, occasionally chasing fruitlessly a bounding rabbit or a chattering prairie dog. Bucks mounted on ponies, scouting for enemies and game. Old men, who had forsaken the chase, obediently falling in line on their horses to lead the squaw of their households, who in spite of a century of riding perhaps appeared ungraceful in the saddle.

253

TWENTY-ONE: TROUBLE IN CRIPPLE CREEK

by Stewart H. Holbrook

The year 1890 forms a convenient dividing date in the history of Colorado. The previous decade had been a time of enthusiastic and prosperous exploitation of mineral and agricultural lands. After 1890 the state, and the nation, found themselves in a decade of depression and disorder. One of the few bright omens during the dark days was the new gold camp at Cripple Creek. While the silver mines and all related industries declined, the gold fields at Cripple Creek prospered. Then troubles came to Cripple Creek too. The first of what proved to be a protracted series of conflicts between mine workers and mine own- ers threatened to destroy the uniquely flourishing camp. This is the story of industrial warfare in Cripple Creek in the year 1894.*

*   *   *

TROUBLE IN CRIPPLE CREEK

Like most mining camps, Cripple Creek was set in a somewhat appalling region. It lay in the first range of the Rockies twenty miles west of Colorado Springs and eighty-five miles south and a little west of Denver. The altitude ranged from nine to twelve thousand feet. The miners who worked in the Buena Vista lived in "the highest in- corporated town in North America." This was Altman, 10, 620 feet above the sea.

Volcanoes had piled up the hills. Steaming hot waters from deep in the earth percolated to the surface, bearing gold telluride in solution, with quartz. The whole area presented a rough, gaunt as- pect of barren rocky ridges, almost arid, with sudden valleys marked by scrub trees and in season with a wealth of alpine flowers. These

------

*from *The Rocky Mountain Revolution* by Stewart H. Holbrook. Copyright (c) 1956 by Stewart Holbrook. Reprinted by permission of Holt, Rinehart and Winston, Inc.

brief patches of brilliance, however, did little to soften the feeling that here one was in a grim and bitter country. It was not, as one observer remarked, a place to invite human habitation . . . .

. . . There had been no mining or much of any other activity in the area until 1891. In that year Bob Womack, a cowhand on the Bennett & Myers ranch along the Creek, was spending his spare time prospecting for silver. Among other efforts he dug a hole forty feet deep into the side of Mount Pisgah, a small volcanic cone west of Pikes Peak, and came up with some likely-looking ore. He toted a sack of it to an assayer in Colorado Springs. It panned out at around a hundred and forty dollars a ton, in gold. Whereupon Womack performed in the manner expected of lucky prospectors. He got good and drunk, and on recovery found he had sold his claim outright for five hundred dollars.

A rush got under way immediately, and in it was Winfield Scott Stratton, a kindly, sad-eyed carpenter who so much preferred prospecting to his trade that when he left home this time, to head for Cripple Creek, his wife divorced him for nonsupport. Mrs. Stratton's action, though understandable, was for her tragically premature. Stratton staked out a couple of claims near Womack's discovery. When he died ten years later he left a fortune of twenty million dollars, which lawyers had to defend against the claims of an even dozen women, all of whom said they were Stratton's widow. Incidentally, Stratton was only one of the twenty-eight authentic millionaires of the Cripple Creek mining district.

Less than two years after the original strike, Cripple Creek city had a population of five thousand. The adjacent towns of Victor, Altman, Independence, Anaconda, Goldfield, Arequa, and Elkton were coming or already had come into being. One hundred and fifty actual mines were being worked. Another five hundred or so had their substance as lithographs on handsomely printed stock certificates. The Colorado & Midland railroad was building a line in from Divide on the north. The Florence & Cripple Creek was coming in from the south. In their first full year of operating, these roads carried out more than six million dollars' of gold-bearing ore, little more than a sample of what was to come.

255

Then came the nationwide money panic of 1893. The price of silver sagged, closing mines all over the West. Banks and factories closed too. There were wage cuts, and strikes. Bread lines appeared in most cities. Not so in Cripple Creek, whose gold mines continued to run full blast.

In 1894 there were violent strikes at Pullman, Illinois, and in the Eastern coal fields. State and federal troops were called, and a Socialist, Eugene Debs, was put in jail for "fomenting a revolution." Meanwhile, the news got around that the Cripple Creek district was booming. Plenty of jobs. Good pay. No strikes. The backwash of foot-loose men began to flood prosperous Cripple Creek. Every freight brought the jobless and the destitute. They had either to be fed at public expense, or run out of town. Several hundred of them soon took off to join the "Commonwealth Army" organized by "General" Jacob Coxey, a Populist, to march on Washington and to demand that the government do something to "relieve social distress." But many others remained in Cripple Creek. To some of the astute mine operators it seemed a propitious time to get more work for the same pay.

Presently all the mines in the district posted notice that on February 1, 1894, the working shift would be ten instead of the usual eight or nine hours. The daily wage was not raised. The workday was merely lengthened. The miners were understandingly alarmed but not surprised. They had expected something of the sort, and the more intelligent of them had already taken steps. At Altman they organized Free Coinage Union No. 19 and affiliated with the brand-new Western Federation of Miners, with headquarters in Butte, Montana. Other unions in the Cripple Creek district were formed at Cripple Creek city, Victor, and Anaconda. These were included in the Altman charter from the Federation.

Elected president of the Cripple Creek union district was John Calderwood, a Scot born at Kilmarnock, who had gone to work in the coal mines at nine, come to the United States at seventeen, and attended the McKeesport School of Mines, from which he was graduated in 1876. Before coming to Cripple Creek, he had headed the local miners' union at Aspen. He was a grave, cool, and courteous man. He also was convinced that miners' unions were an absolute necessity. A week after the mine operators posted their notice, Free Coinage

Union issued a demand that the working shift of all mines in the district be made eight hours. The lines were set.

One who knew the Cripple Creek miners of this era observed that they were not the mining population familiar to the Eastern coal fields. Few were foreign-born. They were "neither ignorant nor easily cowed," but were "of the characteristic frontiersman type." They had come to Cripple Creek "not so much to find work as to seek fortune." They were rough, ready, used to shifting for themselves. They were reckless, ready to cast everything on a single die. And they had "small respect for authority."

The same observer said the mine operators were as much frontiersmen as the working stiffs. Most of them had played in luck and knew it.

With such forces arrayed against each other, it was not astonishing that nothing came of the few attempts made in January to find a basis for settlement. On February 1 the mines went to the ten-hour shift. On the seventh parties of union men circulated throughout the district, calling out the men. By noon every mine was closed save the Portland, Pikes Peak, Gold Dollar, and a few smaller outfits, all of which had promptly agreed to the demand for an eight-hour shift.

Now there followed an uneasy quiet. All union miners working were assessed fifteen dollars a month for a strikers' relief fund. The Butte union sent eight hundred dollars, and seven hundred dollars came from miners in the San Juan district. In Cripple Creek city the Green Bee grocery offered credit to the strikers. Soup kitchens were set up in all the towns.

By the end of February all smelters in Colorado were either closed or running part time. In early March the operators' front crumbled some more when the Gold King and Granite mines resumed work on an eight-hour shift. On March 14 the ten-hour operators got the district court to enjoin miners against interfering with operation of the Cripple Creek ten-hour mines. Sheriff Frank Bowers went around posting the injunction notices. Though his training for the job had been mostly as bouncer in a saloon, with a brief term as a night town marshal, he was a bighearted fellow with a yearning to be loved by everybody. Being sheriff of El Paso County in 1894 was no occupation for him.

A few of the mines attempted to open with ten-hour shifts. But the nonunion help was "quickly discouraged." Then Charles Keith, superintendent of the Victor, phoned Sheriff Bowers to say that a gang of Altman miners were coming to destroy his mine. Bowers sent six deputies. As soon as they reached Altman they were seized by Altman town officers and a posse of miners claiming to be the Altman police force, who turned the invaders around and ordered them to leave. They did.

Sheriff Bowers phoned Governor Davis H. Waite, possibly enlarging somewhat on conditions and making out that Cripple Creek was virtually in chaos. In 1892 Waite had been the Populist candidate for governor of Colorado and was elected by a good majority. He was sixty-seven years old, and has been described as a Moses with a flowing white beard and a voice like Rocky Mountain thunder. He had not long since horrified all conservatives by declaiming publicly that, rather than see "the money power" gain the upper hand, it were infinitely better "that blood should flow to the horses' bridles." Otherwise, said he, "our national liberties would be destroyed."

The Governor ordered out the militia to the number of three hundred soldiers, who went by train to Midland, then made an all-night march overland to arrive at Cripple Creek in the morning. After conferring with Sheriff Bowers, the militia commander refused to take his men up the hill to Altman. President Calderwood had assured the militia officer that neither he nor any member of the union would resist arrest. The soldiers were recalled at once.

Bowers now went ahead to arrest Calderwood, Mayor Dean and Town Marshal Daly of Altman, and eighteen miners, who were taken to Colorado Springs, tried on various charges, and acquitted. Except with the mining interests, President Calderwood and union members were gaining sympathy throughout the state. Their discipline had been perfect. But the excitements during March had advertised the strike widely through newspapers and attracted the usual crew of hoodlums and professional criminals. It is significant that a local commentator wrote that "a particularly turbulent element" came into the

258

district from the Coeur d'Alene country of Idaho.

What had been an uneasy peace during much of April was dented by bits of violence. Stores and warehouses were broken into and arms and ammunition stolen. Several nonunion men were beaten up. A deputy sheriff was wounded. At a secret meeting in Colorado Springs of the mine operators, Sheriff Bowers was called into consultation: Could he furnish protection for a large force of strikebreakers? No, said he, he couldn't. The county was financially unable to engage and equip the army that such a move would require. The operators said that they would pay the bill. Bowers then agreed to muster the required army of deputies.

Though the operators had meant their meeting to be secret, news of it leaked, and the officers of Free Coinage Union at Altman prepared for the worst. President Calderwood had been asked by the Western Federation of Miners to tour Colorado's other mining camps on behalf of the Cripple Creek strike. Before leaving he asked an old friend, Junius J. Johnson, to take charge of union affairs. A former West Pointer, Johnson set about establishing a military camp and headquarters on Bull Hill, the high steep bluff that commanded the town of Altman.

Johnson was a calm and excellent commander. The camp quickly took form, and men were drilled and detailed to certain duties or responsibilities. A breastworks went up. A commissary was stocked. The first order of the day, any day, was strict discipline.

Commander Johnson's chief troubles stemmed from a gang of toughs who had mistakenly been admitted to union membership. Several of these were of that "turbulent" Coeur d'Alene element. Others were ex-convicts. Their leader was "General" Jack Smith whom, to keep peace, Johnson had to accept as his lieutenant. Smith's first act was to capture a couple of alleged spies of the mine operators and beat them nigh to death.

One evening late in May Commander Johnson received word that a small army of gunmen were on their way to the Cripple Creek district. Though they were officially described as "El Paso County deputy sheriffs," they were really ex-policemen and ex-firemen, all from

259

Denver, who were being paid by the mine operators as agreed upon with Sheriff Bowers. A second message to Johnson reported that the first objective of the coming army was to be the strikers' camp on Bull Hill. Commander Johnson told his men that these mercenaries from Denver must not be permitted on Bull Hill; then he sent out details to make certain arrangements he believed might deter the gunmen without a formal battle.

At about nine o'clock on the morning of May 25 — it was still 1894 — two flatcars loaded with a hundred and twenty-five of the Denver gunmen rolled along the Florence & Cripple Creek railroad in full view of Bull Hill. The train stopped; the deputies got off and started to establish their base camp before marching up to attack the strikers at Altman. Just then, said a witness, "the whole sky over and around Victor town seemed to explode," and the shaft house at the Strong mine was wafted three hundred feet into the air, then disintegrated, by a blast that was felt even on Bull Hill, where wild cheering blended with the echoes.

A moment later a second blast ripped the Strong's steam boiler loose and sent it skyward; and down came a shower of timbers, hunks of iron, pieces of cable, and iron wheels of assorted sizes. The deputies, tough men though they might be, were appalled at such a welcome. They clambered back on the flatcars and the train backed out of sight of Bull Hill.

While the dismayed deputies reconsidered matters, the whole Cripple Creek area seemed to explode with excitement. Yelling mobs broke into liquor warehouses and emerged with cases, jugs, and kegs of whisky, and whole barrels of the same. This just happened to be also the day that the F. & C.C. railroad paid off its grading crew of two hundred men. Almost automatically they headed for the nearest saloons. By early afternoon the half-dozen towns in the Cripple Creek district were so many bedlams of drunken men.

This was the kind of chaos much appreciated by "the Coeur d'Alene element." That night a mob of union men loaded a flatcar with capped dynamite, then started it coasting downgrade in the hope it would collide with another car still on the track near the Denver gunmen's camp. Instead, it left the rails on a curve and exploded,

260

killing a cow.

"General" Jack Smith collected his crew of drunken hoodlums and loaded two wagons with dynamite. He was, he said, going to blow up every mine shaft and every mine superintendent's house in the district. Commander Johnson prevented this worse than idiotic expedition from leaving camp. He ordered Smith to sober up, and then, if he felt like doing something for the cause, to take his gang and chase the retreating Denver army out of the district.

Smith sobered up — a little — then led his mob to Victor town. There, about midnight, they stole a work train, fired up the locomotive, then tore out of town southward with a miner at the throttle. Somewhere in the night out of Victor they caught up with the Denver gang and fought a bloody battle among the boulders. One deputy was killed, and one striker. Five more miners were captured by the Denverites. /author's note: In retaliation, says David Lavender, the union incarcerated three officials of the Strong mine who were caught in the shaft-house explosion; and "eventually all eight captives were released through a formal prisoner-of-war exchange unprecedented in United States labor strife." See his The Big Divide./

During the night Union President Calderwood returned from his organizing tour and moved quickly to prevent further bloodshed. He locked up "General" Jack Smith and asked saloonkeepers to close their doors. Quiet was restored, briefly, while more violence was being prepared. At a so-called Law and Order meeting in Colorado Springs, the mine operators' stronghold, Sheriff Bowers was authorized to engage twelve hundred additional deputies. They were recruited in all parts of the state, then sent to a camp established on the Colorado & Midland railroad at Divide. Governor Waite issued a doubleheaded proclamation: He called on the strikers to desist from their unlawful assembly on Bull Hill. He declared the big force of deputies to be illegal and ordered it to be disbanded. Then he ordered the militia to be alerted.

Neither the Bull Hill army nor Bowers's mob of deputies made any attempt to disband. Each remained in camp while an honest effort of arbitration was made by President Calderwood, mineowners Dave Moffat and J. J. Hagerman, various civic leaders, and Governor

261

Waite himself. The meeting was held in a hall on Colorado College campus. It was forced to break up when a vast mob of howling citizens gathered at the college. They were bent on lynching Calderwood and Governor Waite, both of whom were blamed for the Cripple Creek disorders. /author's note: See Benjamin McKie Rastall's account in Bulletin of the University of Wisconsin, No. 198 (Feb., 1908)._7 Judge Horace Gray Lunt stepped out on the porch to address the mob and hold their attention, and the governor of Colorado and John Calderwood slipped out a rear door, got into a cab that was waiting for them, and were taken to board the Governor's special train, and so to Denver. The incident is an illuminating commentary on the state of law and order in the Colorado Athens of 1894.

The determined arbitrators resumed their conference in Denver. Two days later the mineowners and the Free Coinage Union signed an agreement: eight hours' work for three dollars; no discrimination against union or nonunion men. It was a notable victory for the union.

But the business was far from finished. The army of deputies was still in camp at Divide. Bull Hill was still in the possession of the Free Coinage Union army. Governor Waite now turned out the Colorado militia and sent them to Cripple Creek. The Governor, whose support of the union never wavered, meant that the militia should prevent Sheriff Bowers's deputies from attacking the union stronghold. If calm could be maintained, then all would be well. Union miners were ready to return to work; the mine operators were anxious to have them.

But nothing even approaching calm could be maintained. By the time the militia arrived, in command of General E. J. Brooks, the army of deputies had broken up, cut telephone and telegraph wires, held newspaper reporters under guard, and advanced toward Bull Hill. At daybreak they ran into pickets. There was some shooting, though nobody was hit. The deputies paused to hold a council of war.

At this juncture the militia arrived. While the troops were unloading, General Brooks conferred with Sheriff Bowers and County Commissioner W. S. Boynton. Friction quickly developed as to which of the two armies should have command of the situation. Nor did it help to clarify matters that Bowers did not want the deputies to attack

262

Bull Hill, while Boynton was determined they should. The bickering went on. Meanwhile, the Bull Hill army was busy with additional defensive measures.

Under West Pointer Junius Johnson, men had mined the hill with dynamite charges connected with electric wires to explode at press of a button. Every miner had a rifle and a cartridge belt. Every miner had in a vest pocket five dynamite cartridges the size of pencils, fitted with percussion caps. The Free Coinage Union artillery was a possibly unique combination of medieval and modern arms: a tremendous bow gun capable of throwing missiles a quarter of a mile with fine accuracy; the missiles were beer bottles filled with explosive and capped to go off on impact. These things, plus a grade steeper than that which faced the British troops at Bunker Hill, presented obvious hazards to any head-on attack.

The efficient and resolute preparations on Bull Hill were in contrast to the muddled complications that had stalled the Colorado militia and the army of deputies. Exactly who ordered whom to do what was never clear; but after a while the twelve hundred deputies started to move on the enemy. The enemy was ready. Just as the deputies began to march, the whistle at the Victor mine let go a long wail of warning. The hillside immediately took on the look of an anthill; from far below the deputies could see hundreds of men swarming to their posts.

General Brooks decided he must act. Bugles sounded and the militia went forward at the double-quick. They intercepted the deputies before a shot was fired. In the name of the State of Colorado, General Brooks ordered them back to their camp, then led his own troops up the hill. The miners offered no resistance, but permitted the militia to occupy their fort and Altman town.

The army of deputies, however, was bound to have some action. Instead of dispersing, they marched into Cripple Creek town, where they arrested many persons, clubbed a few more, and made themselves fairly objectionable. General Brooks speedily moved militia into the town and took charge. The deputies were put aboard a train for Colorado Springs.

The mines of the Cripple Creek district resumed work with an eight-hour shift. John Calderwood and some three hundred miners peacefully submitted to arrest on various charges ranging from disorderly conduct to attempted homicide. Only four were convicted, and all were pardoned long before expiration of their sentences.

Free Coinage Union No. 19, Western Federation of Miners, gained enormous prestige in labor circles in the United States, and with many people who had no connection with unions. By winning the strike it also gave a powerful impetus to the new and still weak federation just when it was needed.

The new sense of power prompted federation officials to send organizers to Leadville where the silver-poor mine operators were content to pay workers two and a half dollars a day. A union was formed and demanded a three-dollar wage. The operators brought in strikebreakers, many of whom were beaten up and run out of town by the union "regulators." Whereupon the owners of the Coronado and Emmet mines built a high board fence around their surface workings. One night soon the Coronado fence was dynamited, buildings set afire, and one town fireman shot and killed when trying to stem the fire. Then the union regulators attacked in force, to be met with gunfire from strikebreakers within the stockade. Three union men died. The attackers moved up a homemade cannon contrived from a length of steam pipe. It worked pretty well, too. One round served to blow a wide hole through the fence. In went the attackers, only to lose still another man. That ended the battle, but not the trouble. Militia were called in, and for a long period Leadville was virtually under military rule. The strikers eventually returned to work at the operators' terms.

A little later the federation won a partial victory at Telluride, where strikers closed the Smuggler-Union mine and ambushed an armed night shift of strikebreakers, killing three, wounding five more. They then chased the scabs into their stockade and besieged them. When their ammunition gave out, the scabs surrendered on condition they not be molested. The strikers agreed, then brutally beat their enemies. One died. Next, they marched the strikebreakers out of camp and over thirteen-thousand-foot Imogene Pass, and ordered them to keep moving.

A settlement was reached later by which the federation won its demands. So-called settlements often leave a few matters not quite settled. A year after settlement of the Telluride strike, an unknown gunman shot and killed Arthur Collins, manager of the Smuggler-Union mine, as he sat reading at his fireside. At Cripple Creek, more than three years after settlement of that strike, the homes of four men were invaded by thugs and the victims mercilessly beaten. At Altman, "General" Jack Smith was shot to death. Truces could be signed. They could not wipe out bitter memories.

One defeat, two victories. The Western Federation of Miners could feel it had done pretty well in Colorado. Except for the Coeur d'Alenes, it had made good progress elsewhere. When it staged the first Cripple Creek strike in 1894, the federation was hardly more than a name. By 1903, more than two hundred active unions were enrolled under its banner.

TWENTY-TWO: GOVERNOR WAITE AND HIS SILVER PANACEA
by Leon W. Fuller

*Many of Colorado's difficulties during the 1890s fit the general
pattern of national problems, as the Panic of 1893 ushered in a period
of depression. But to Coloradans, and other westerners, the economic
collapse was compounded when the federal government repealed its
silver coinage legislation, bringing a complete collapse to the silver
mines and related industries. While those intimately associated with
the production of silver saw their salvation in a return to unlimited
purchase of silver by the federal government, others were interested
in the same idea as an inflationary device to alleviate the depression.
The question of a return to a bi-metallic standard soon became a political issue, with the newly formed People's Party, or Populists, finding
excitement and votes in their championing of "free silver." In Colorado,
in 1892, the Populists elected Davis Waite governor of the state. His
attempts to cope with the problems of the day are related here.**

* * *

GOVERNOR WAITE AND HIS SILVER PANACEA

. . . Long before the "battle of the standards" of 1896, Colorado, as the premier mining commonwealth of the mountain region,
was beginning to experience the effects of mounting production costs
and declining prices. Even the Silver Purchase Act of 1890 had failed
to give relief, and demand for free and unlimited coinage was becoming universal in the West.

The importance of silver in the economy of the state at that time
can scarcely be exaggerated. The bonanza fields at Aspen, Leadville
and Creede had attained a record output by 1892, the total for the

------

*from Leon W. Fuller, "Governor Waite and His Silver Panacea" in *The Colorado
Magazine*, volume X (March, 1933), pages 41-47. Used with permission of the
State Historical Society of Colorado.

266

state representing double the amount for 1887 and one-half the total production of the United States. Denver and other industrial centers, the railroads, and farmers, merchants and laborers alike were all to a degree dependent upon silver for their prosperity. A crisis was imminent, as world over-production had diminished the value of silver reckoned in gold. Production in Colorado had been excessively stimulated by the speculative mania of the eighties and a flood of eastern capital seeking quick and fabulous returns. The rapid expansion of the railway network had opened and over-developed new mineral districts. But the point of diminishing returns was being reached as high labor, reduction and transportation costs cut deeply into profits. A fall in price below a dollar per ounce would endanger profitable operation in many fields. A drop below eighty cents would be a catastrophe.

The crusade for free coinage of silver to restore the mint price of $1.29 had been carried on with unabated zeal for a decade. Coloradans were convinced that the precious metals had played a major role in the evolution of civilization; the principal catastrophes of history were attributed to periodic shortages of specie. Divine sanction for silver was invoked by reference to scripture, and the Bible was quoted: "Yea, the Almighty shall be thy defense and thou shalt have plenty of silver"; "And Abraham weighed to Ephra . . . 400 shekels of silver, current money with the merchant." It was generally believed that the demonetization of the metal in 1873 was the outcome of a conspiracy to contract the currency in behalf of creditors and demand was insistent that Congress restore the "money of the Bible and the Constitution."

Westerners resented the accusation so often levelled at the "silver barons" of the West that they were willing to debauch the national currency to advance selfish and sectional interests. Free coinage was desirable, it was argued, "not because Colorado had silver to sell . . . but because the nation needs more money." Thus the abuses of the "dishonest" gold dollar with its unfair burden upon western debtors would be ended. Silver coinage would produce a needed expansion of the currency and restore the just value of money. Only then, declared the Colorado Silver Convention of 1889, will prosperity return "to every farm and workshop in the land."

267

The early nineties was a period of increasing economic stress for Colorado. The grievances of farmers and laborers, in particular, combined with the general resentment at the apathy of the old parties in the matter of silver paved the way for new political alignments. An Independent party (a coalition of dissentient groups) had polled 5,000 votes in 1890. A year later, the People's Party was in the field, with silver occupying an important place in its program. By 1893, non-partisan silver clubs were being organized in every section of the state, pledged to support only silver men for office. Their activities were coordinated by the Colorado Silver League, whose membership by July numbered over 40,000. It denounced the "unscrupulous money-changers" of the East and besought national assistance in a crusade for the restoration of silver.

By summer the political pot was boiling, and when Harrison and Cleveland were again declared the nominees of the major parties there were wholesale desertions from the ranks in Colorado. The People's Party profited by the existing chaos and attracted the support of many old-party adherents who were aggrieved because of the injustice done to silver. Davis H. Waite of Aspen was nominated for governor, and his choice was ratified by the state Silver League. Moreover, the silver Democrats obtained control of their party organization and threw its support to the Populist ticket, both state and national.

And while Waite emphasized the silver issue in his campaign, it was for him a symbol of revolt against corporate power and the oppressions of a financial oligarchy entrenched in the old parties. If elected, he proposed "to change the present system of government by which there was class discrimination so that the principles, 'equal rights to all and special privileges to none' . . . would be established and maintained." Populists were fully convinced that the general stagnation of all productive processes was due to "a system of finance which is sweating the blood, contracting the energies and dampening the joys of life among our people everywhere."

Republicans resented the implication that they were hostile to silver or in alliance with eastern and foreign monopolists. Populism represented, not silver, but fiat money. Paper mills, not silver mines, would be stimulated to activity by a Populist victory. Moreover, it would injure the credit of the state and drive out capital.

268

Populism, declared a Republican jurist, "means the paralysis of trade . . . the destruction of social order." The silver issue was only a screen under cover of which the People's Party intended to foist upon the state its untried program of socialistic panaceas.

Waite and his associates were swept into office by the rising tide of dissent. He attributed his victory to silver: "That was the issue upon which the battle was fought and won." But he was also irrevocably committed to a program of social reform and a philosophy of government which were anathema to the ruling interests of the state. As chief executive in a time of exceptional difficulty and unsettlement, he was faced with almost insurmountable obstacles to the realization of his pledges.

As the panic of 1893 swept over the nation, Colorado witnessed the complete collapse of her prosperity. As a debtor commonwealth, developed on the almost exclusive basis of credit, she felt the situation keenly. Failures and foreclosures multiplied alarmingly and virtually all silver mines and smelters closed in June as the price of the metal fell to 62 cents. Business was at a standstill. "The movement of . . . commodities from the western sections has completely stopped," declared a Union Pacific official at Omaha. Unemployment rose to 45,000 by the end of the summer, a startling total for a state of half a million population. A relief camp was set up in Denver and by the end of the year more than 20,000 men, it was estimated, had left the state.

The collapse of silver united all classes momentarily in the common interest. Although silver had been struck down by the operation of economic law, to the inflamed minds of Coloradoans the deed appeared to have been the willful act of the moneyed interests of the East, another step in their program for the economic enslavement of the West. The financiers of Wall Street seemed to have joined hands with the money lords of Europe in a war of extermination against the popular metal and an attempt to universalize the gold standard. Waite was convinced that the whole affair was a "bankers' panic" intentionally created in order to contract the currency and achieve a more complete subjugation of the exploited classes.

Meetings were held in all parts of the state and fiery addresses

269

and resolutions denounced the "conspiracy" against silver and insisted upon Colorado's right of self-preservation. Threats of secession were even voiced. E. R. Holden, a prominent mining magnate, sent a telegram to a New York paper declaring that half a million people were on the verge of starvation. "We will repudiate all our bonds and obligations," he warned, and predicted "a new Declaration of Independence and the establishment of a Western empire."

The climax of protest was a great mass meeting held at the Denver Coliseum on July 11, representing thirty-nine counties of the state. Rash sentiments were expressed in the hysteria of resentment then sweeping the commonwealth. "The pioneers of Colorado have had their contract violated," declared President Merrick of the Silver League. A powerful Appeal to the Country, drafted by T. M. Patterson of the Rocky Mountain News, hinted at a union of West and South against the common aggressor.

The high point of the occasion was the famous speech of Governor Waite. Wrought up to a high pitch of indignation by the crisis which seemed to have confirmed his most direful predictions, his mood was keyed to the exigencies of the hour. If America, in its economic and governmental policy, had become "only a province of European monarchies," he asserted, "then we need another revolution — another appeal to arms and to the God of hosts." The war had begun, the "eternal warfare of monarchy and monopoly against the right of the people to self-government . . . . Our weapons are argument and the ballot — 'a free ballot and a fair count.' And if the money power shall attempt to sustain its usurpations by 'the strong hand,' we shall meet that issue when it is forced upon us, for it is better, infinitely better, that blood should flow to the horses' bridles than our national liberties should be destroyed."

Waite's address was endorsed by the convention by a vote of 324 to 63, amid a frenzy of enthusiasm. Populists hailed it as a bold and uncompromising challenge to the eastern money power. But Senator Teller criticised the "rabid frothings" of the Governor as pernicious and unrepresentative of sober opinion in the state. The Republican press condemned the "criminal folly" of this and similar utterances. Eastern opinion ridiculed the "rabid utterances of the silverites at Denver"; they will "cost the cause they are championing many friends," warned an editor. "Bloody Bridles" Waite became a national celebrity and a symbol of western Populism.

When Congress, convened in special session, repealed the purchase clause of the Sherman Silver Act, Colorado's cup of woe seemed overflowing. "I see no hope for us . . . it means the utter ruin of Colorado," commented Waite. Even Senator Teller declared that repeal would make the people "serfs of the men who hold the pursestrings of the world." And the conservative Denver Republican insisted: "At present the country is governed by the East. . . . The South and West are subject to the East and, as in the case of all provinces, their interests are sacrificed for those of the governing section."

It had been suggested that a special session of the state legislature be called for enacting a program of relief. Waite was at first opposed to the idea, but when it became evident that Congress was about to repeal the Sherman law, he gave the proposal serious consideration. "If repeal carries," he declared in August, "I think I shall summon the legislature together and see if there is not some way to save part of the state from going to utter ruin, if the nation will not save it all."

Numerous projects were being discussed, including modification of the trust deed and attachment laws and other relief for debtors. Of particular interest was a plan for a state silver bullion depository, certificates of deposit to be accepted as currency throughout the state. Thus, declared the Attorney General, silver could "be made a rampart behind which we may be safe from the money changers." A more daring proposal, made notorious through its espousal by Governor Waite, was the scheme to ship Colorado silver to Mexico, there to be coined into Mexican dollars which would then be made legal tender by the state of Colorado. Waite was favorably impressed with the plan. "I am anxious to know," he wrote to President Diaz, "Upon what terms the mints of Mexico would receive and coin for us our bullion silver," and asserted his intention to secure "a legal status to the Mexican dollar in the . . . states of the American Union." Diaz responded sympathetically and Waite proceeded with his plans for legislative action. Although bitterly opposed by the business interests of the state, he convoked the assembly in extraordinary session in January, 1894.

271

Governor Waite's message delivered on this occasion represents the climax of radical Populist theory in Colorado. He excoriated the "corrupt money power that has wrested the public laws from their proper purposes to grant special privileges to monopoly." War had been made upon the state's chief industry; legislation was the one remaining recourse for the suffering people. An elaborate program of remedial proposals was outlined but emphasis was placed upon his plan for the restoration of silver. He boldly advocated that the state of Colorado declare foreign gold and silver coins (of requisite fineness) a legal tender within the state. Such a power, he insisted, had never been delegated to Congress and hence was reserved to the states. The latter might declare gold and silver coins legal tender. Since the Federal Government refused to coin silver, as contemplated in the Constitution, Colorado might make good the deficiency by ruling that foreign silver coins (Mexican dollars coined from Colorado silver) were legal tender within her boundaries. Other states, he hoped, would follow her example, silver would be restored to its old coinage value and an abundance of money would soon be in circulation.

Waite's "fandango dollar" scheme was promptly repudiated by the legislature as of dubious constitutionality and calculated to bring discredit upon the state. It was widely ridiculed throughout the nation and regarded as further evidence of the aberrations of western Populism. However resentful Coloradans might be at what they deemed the injustice done to silver, sober opinion was inclined to discountenance extremist panaceas or threats of sectional revolt. The best results could be achieved, it was believed, by "keeping step to the music of the union."

Although it came to nothing, Colorado's silver revolt deserves a niche in the record of American sectionalism. The nation grew as a federation of sections, each one an economic empire in its own right. National policy has generally been a compromise, the resultant of conflicting interests and forces. Aggrieved groups or localities have almost invariably resorted to the doctrine of states' rights in self-defense. We have only to recall the protest of the Virginia and Kentucky Resolutions, the action of New England at the Hartford Convention, or the tariff nullificationists of South Carolina. Waite and his associates were acting in accordance with an established American tradition in reverting to states' rights in defense of sectional

272

interest. As in the case of most of their predecessors, such action proved futile. Colorado's salvation lay not in revolt or secession, but in a wise and patient adjustment to the necessities imposed by cooperative living in that broader American community of which she formed a part.

TWENTY-THREE: HARD ROCK DRILLING CONTESTS IN COLORADO

by Victor I. Noxon and Forest Crossen

Out of the mining camps of the American West, in a rather natural progression, came a contest of skill and endurance that lasted until the mining frontier itself had gone. Hard rock drilling contests provided spectators at fairs and expositions an exciting opportunity to wager, watch and cheer their champions. Some of the "drillers" and their skills are described here by a man who saw "the best" of them. *

*   *   *

HARD ROCK DRILLING CONTESTS

I have taken a deep interest in hand rock-drilling contests for over fifty years. I have seen most of the best drillers — both single and double-hand — that Colorado has produced. My most intimate acquaintance was with the men of Clear Creek, Gilpin and Boulder counties who won honors in the early days at this highly colored and truly representative test of mining skill. All this, of course, before the days of pneumatic drills.

Rock-drilling matches began among the miners of individual mines. Then mining camps picked their favorites to appear against the best men of a rival camp. Counties picked their champions by a process of elimination, usually held during the latter part of the summer. The Fourth of July contests were for local interest only. The county competitors met at the annual Carnival of Mountain and Plain, held in Denver each October. It was these state contests that really put rock-drilling on a clean business-like basis.

— — — — — —

*from "Hard Rock Drilling Contests in Colorado" as told by Victor I. Noxon to Forest Crossen, in *The Colorado Magazine*, volume XI (May, 1934), pages 81-85. Used with permission of the State Historical Society of Colorado.

William Libby and Charles Rowe of Idaho Springs were supreme among the local drillers for a number of years. They held
state honors, too. They were Cornish miners, and they had a tremendous following among their countrymen. This was during the
'80s.

Rowe and Libby were small men, weighing about 135 pounds.
They were particularly skillful, more than making up for their lack
in weight in the hammer blows. They came down with the double-
jack directly on the head of the drill, thus making a good clean cutting stroke. The manner in which the drill is turned and held makes
a great deal of difference. These two men forced the other miners,
larger man than they were, to follow their practices before they
went down to defeat before superior muscles and weight.

The Cornishmen in general were much smaller than the Nova
Scotians, who were numerous in Boulder, Clear Creek and Gilpin
counties in those days, or the Swedes and Irish of a later period.
Mullis of Central City was a big Cousinjack and a hard man to defeat
in a drilling contest.

Clear Creek County developed Edward Chamberlain, who won
the championship for the western states two or three times. Henry
Tarr, who won state honors, was also from this county. Sullivan
Tarr, his younger brother, developed into a mighty hammerman and
won the world's championship.

Boulder County had "Bud" Shaw, Jim Pittman and Thurman Collins. Pittman and Collins made a very powerful team. They acquitted
themselves very well in contests. Shaw carried off the honors in
many local and county contests.

So far I have been talking about double-hand drilling. There
were also single-hand contests. Al Yockey of Central City was unbeaten for several years during the '90s. His supremacy was superseded by Charles Wahlstrom of Boulder. Fred Dopp of Jimtown,
Boulder County, is the present /1934?/ unbeaten champion.

Although single-hand drilling contests were mighty feats of skill
and endurance, they never attracted the attention that the double-hand

commanded.

Definite rules and practices were laid down and rigorously followed. Drillers would go into training two weeks or longer before a contest, coming out of the mines in order to get their wind in shape to stand the 15-minute contests. It was not until about 1900 that ten minutes became the accepted time of the contests. A six-to-eight pound hammer was used in the double-hand drilling, and a four-pound hammer for the single-hand contests. The single-hand drillers used three-quarter inch drills; the double-hand men seven-eighths inch steel.

A timer with a stop-watch called the minutes, thus giving the drillers an opportunity to change off from their positions as hammermen or drill turners. During the last four or five minutes the timer called time at each half minute. Two judges watched each team of contestants and measured the hole to fractions of an inch.

The blows that a hammerman struck to the minute was usually known by his trainers. The usual speed was 67 or 68. Some drillers could average 75 or 76. This, of course, was very fast. Regularity in speed minute after minute was sought after by every man who went into training.

The sharpening of drills became a fine art. The men who could put an edge on tools that would hold up through the terrific pounding of a fifteen-minute contest were few. They became specialists, fitting up steel for drillers all over this western mining country. Sometimes the sharpener worked directly with the champions, learning to temper the steel to fit the demands that the individuals put on it. This process frequently took months. John Lind of Idaho Springs was one of the best tool sharpeners of the early days. He sharpened drill steel for many champions.

Seldom if ever did the drillers sharpen their own steel. However, one of the members of a famous Leadville team was an expert tool sharpener. He was a blacksmith by trade, and his partner was a miner. Sometimes there was grumbling about this blacksmith taking part in a sport essentially for miners . . . .

Extreme care was taken in the selection of the stone for these drilling contests. Silver Plume granite was widely used in Clear Creek and Gilpin counties. It was shipped to other parts of the state for most of the important drilling contests. It was a very hard, uniform stone. Drillers from the three northern hard rock counties could usually drill from two to three inches deeper in the stone used in the Leadville contest in the allotted fifteen minutes than they could in the Silver Plume granite.

The prizes offered in these contests were not to be talked of lightly. Five hundred to one thousand dollars was common for first honors in the county double-hand drills. There were second and third prizes. Singlehanded drilling usually netted the champion from $300 to $500, with perhaps a third that amount for the second man. The state prizes ranged from $4,000 to $5,000 for the first in the double-hand, and $1,500 for the single-hand championship.

Each champion had his supporters, who backed him with every dollar that they could lay their hands on. Feeling ran high at some of the contests. During the latter '80s Rory McGillivray of Idaho Springs and his partner drilled against Mullis and his teammate of Central City. The Cornish of Central were backing Mullis to their last dollars, and the affair nearly ended in a riot. It took firm tact and a forceful move on the part of the police to avert trouble.

The story of the Tarr brothers, Henry and Sullivan, and Edward Chamberlain of Idaho Springs, has an unusual interest. All three were miners. Henry Tarr and Chamberlain teamed up together for drilling contests and were successful. They won local and state honors, them competed for the championship of the West, at El Paso, Texas, during the '90s. They won it.

Sullivan Tarr was younger than his brother by about three years. He began practicing and became a very good driller. He was a fast hammerman, striking terrific blows directly on the head of the drill. In action he was a stirring looking figure. Stripped to the waist, his mighty muscles stood out in his arms and shoulders, rippling beneath his white skin.

A big drilling match was held at Cripple Creek. Sullivan Tarr had been away in another part of the country but had returned a short time before. He heard about the match and went down to Cripple Creek. He had no partner, and he did not want to drill single-hand; the prize for team drilling was several thousand dollars. Hurriedly he looked around and found a man who would turn the drill for him, himself a good driller. Sullivan mounted the platform and pounded that drill fifteen minutes without a let-up! He sank that hole three inches deeper than the nearest contestants!

After that he could make a team. He carried off big money with his brother, Chamberlain, and other men. In this respect he was something like Rory McGillivray, who could take nearly any common driller and make a winning team.

Cripple Creek once sent a challenge to Idaho Springs to put up a man who would pound the drill all the way through the contest, 10 minutes, with another man to turn it against a similar team of theirs. The men who sent that challenge knew that Rory McGillivray was out of the state. Sullivan Tarr too was absent.

We had to do some fast thinking. We telegraphed McGillivray, who was working in Butte, Montana, to come home immediately. When he arrived, we secured him a job in the Shafter Mine. When the time for the drilling contest arrived, he had been working at the mine over a month. We had to do this, because there were rules that required a man to be a miner in his own community for a trial like this one. We cautioned everyone to say nothing about his return.

The day of the drilling contest came. The crowd that accompanied the challenging team from Cripple Creek was a large one. It was flushed with the assurance of victory; a good many thousands of dollars changed hands in bets that day. They put their champion hammerman up on the platform with his drill turner. The man stood there in the sun, big, brawny, with mighty muscles that were stirring to see.

Suddenly our crowd parted. A man sprang to the platform, a man stripped to his waist. He straightened up, and the crowd from Cripple Creek actually groaned its surprise. There was McGillivray, the giant Nova Scotian, the last man in the world whom they wanted to

278

see. They protested that he had not been in the camp, that we had brought him in from the outside. But we could show that he had been employed for the required month.

The contest began. McGillivray beat the team from Cripple Creek by three inches.

We had a man in Idaho Springs who was especially skillful in turning the drill. His name was Avery Johnson. He was not much of a hammerman, but he had a trick in handling the drill that I have never seen duplicated. He could lift the drill up eight or ten inches when he turned it, doing this between hammer blows, and plunge it down, thereby getting another cutting stroke. It was beautifully done, almost too fast for the eye to follow. The team that he drilled on won several matches before the judges learned what he was doing. Finally the rules were modified because of his practice, thereby putting a stop to his skill.

A great deal depends on the drill turner in one of these matches. If care is not taken the hole will have "fitchers" in it, that is, it gets three-sided. Then it takes a very skillful man to cut these out and get the hole uniform again, doing this without losing time.

The days are past when two men can drill from 32 to 35 inches in hard Silver Plume granite in 15 minutes. This unique contest of skill, so representative of the adventurous, high-strung miners of the early days, will forever live in the folk-tales of the Old West.

TWENTY-FOUR: THE PROGRESSIVE PARTY IN 1914

The structure of Colorado politics from 1890 to 1920 constantly changed. The rise and fall of the Populists, the interjection of the silver issue into partisan campaigns, and the numerous "fusion" movements joining silverites with segments of the traditional Republican and Democratic parties characterized the early years. Then, in 1912, the Colorado Progressives entered the field as a "third force," dedicated to the principles proclaimed by their national leader, Theodore Roosevelt. In 1914 the Progressives wrote a militantly liberal platform, delineating their position on a series of questions involving social, political, and economic reform and bitterly assailing both the Democratic and Republican parties for their past sins. In the election that autumn, the Progressives were defeated. Their candidate for governor, Edward P. Costigan, hastened to describe the causes of failure in a letter printed here following the party platform. *

* * *

PLATFORM OF PROGRESSIVE PARTY — 1914

Conceived in high purpose, and born of a desire to serve mankind, the Progressive party in Colorado alone of all political organizations in the state, has the freedom from entanglements and has the firm courage to proclaim and establish the principles of justice and equality under government through law.

The Progressive party of Colorado at its first election two years ago, received approximately 70,000 votes as a result of the advanced progressive and humanitarian principles approved by the Progressive

------

*from *Papers of Edward P. Costigan Relating to the Progressive Movement in Colorado 1902-1917*, edited by Colin B. Goodykoontz, Boulder, 1941, pages 292 to 304. Used with permission of the University of Colorado Press.

280

party in state and nation. The past two years of industrial strife and wanton destruction of life and property have not only justified but emphasized the necessity of the enactment into law and the enforcement of those principles. We, the Progressive party, therefore indorse the state and national platforms of the party of 1912 and pledge ourselves to their fulfillment without fear or favor.

We indorse the candidacy of Theodore Roosevelt for the Progressive nomination for president in 1916.

The issue in Colorado in 1914 is the same issue that existed in 1912 and in previous campaigns for many years back, to-wit: Shall the government of Colorado be conducted by special privilege for the few, or shall it be conducted by the people on behalf of the people?

For years the bosses have ruled this state, first under one party, then under another. In 1914, as in previous campaigns, both old parties are controlled entirely by and for special interests. The Democratic party is being largely financed by the liquor interests and by those interests that hope to profit through the destruction of federal conservation; the Republican party has been and is now the party of special privilege in Colorado and is drawing its campaign sustenance from the great corporate and public utility interests of this state.

The Progressive party alone stands free from any alliance or control of any nature whatsoever. It has placed before the people of Colorado a ticket composed of men and women who declare it to be their purpose, if elected, to enter upon a program of development of the immense resources of Colorado in favor, not of a few, but of all the people.

In the past two years civil war has existed in the coal fields, and the first requirement of the state today is the establishment of an effective government. The sovereign power of the state represented by an overwhelming Democratic majority in executive, legislative and judicial branches, has not only been helpless to remedy conditions, but has been compelled in order to avert further bloodshed to call upon the military arm of the federal government.

The Progressive party and its candidates stand for law, order and justice. We hold it to be a prime duty of the state to enforce law and order impartially at all times and under all circumstances. We yield to no party in our devotion to and insistence upon orderly government and the settlement of all disputes without destruction of life or property.

We unreservedly condemn private warfare and we pledge ourselves to prevent contestants on any side from arming or preparing to arm for such purposes.

We also hold that there can be no permanent orderly government, under law without justice; that is, justice to all, to labor, to capital and to the public alike.

After 30 years of warning, neither the Democratic party nor the Republican party in Colorado, controlled as they have been by special interests, have been able or willing even to enter upon a solution of our difficulties. The sole result of the great industrial conflicts of 1884, 1894, 1904 and 1914, each fiercer and more disastrous than the preceding one, is a tremendous war debt to be borne by ourselves and our children, culminating in the war debt of 1904 and the war debt of 1914, each approximately $1,000,000, and still unpaid.

In order that the industrial warfare that has continued for years under both old parties may be settled equitably, the Progressive party declares itself in favor of the enactment of an arbitration act along the lines of the Canadian arbitration act, providing compulsory investigation of all labor disputes before a strike or lockout is declared, and under which all the facts are made public by a disinterested body and arbitration of the points in issue is sought. Since its enactment in 1907, numerous labor strikes in Canada have been settled, involving over 150,000 workers, without the loss of life or property.

We believe workers should be permitted to organize and to deal as an organization with their employers. The right of men working for wages to bargain collectively should always be recognized.

Coal is a public necessity, and we believe that the constitution should be amended, making coal mining a public utility. This accomplished, then within constitutional limitations proper and adequate legislation could be enacted, not only governing sanitary working conditions in mines, but regulating the price of coal to the consumer, if need be, in public crises as we fix reasonable freight rates with reference to the railroads and control the hours and conditions of the men working thereon. And we believe that the state should be permitted, in case of necessity, to purchase, develop and condemn coal lands, now privately owned, allowing, of course, just compensation.

With reference to the many thousands of acres of leased school coal lands, from which the state now receives a mere pittance of a royalty of 10 cents per ton, and upon which some of the largest mines are located, we insist that all future leases or renewals by the state shall contain provisions giving to the state the power of supervision over sanitary and other working conditions in the mines and the regulation of the prices at which the coal shall be sold to the consumer, allowing a reasonable profit to the operator; and providing for a forfeiture of the lease in case of a violation of its terms.

We regard it as nothing less than a shame that Colorado's minimum wage law for women and minors should have remained on the statute books for two years without any attempt having been made to enforce its provisions, and we pledge ourselves to secure the appointment of a commission that will immediately see to the protection of women and minor workers under this law.

We pledge ourselves to the enactment of an effective workingmen's compensation law. This measure has been a platform pledge, so-called, of the Democratic party in Colorado since 1908, but it has been flagrantly disregarded, the only effort to pass the same having been defeated in a Democratic senate in 1912.

But industrial legislation is not the only legislation needed in Colorado. In no state is the farmer compelled to contend against greater difficulties in the marketing of his products. His fruit, his grain, his beets, his stock must all be marketed through interests which extort from him on the one hand and from the consuming public on the other.

To the end that producer and consumer may be brought into closer touch, we pledge ourselves to the appointment of a commission

283

from the state officers, to serve without pay, which shall work with federal and other authorities and experts toward the working out of a plan by which the waste of the present marketing system may be eliminated. The prices of necessities of life are being raised without justification, and, in support of this fact, we refer to the findings of the district attorneys of Colorado, convened in the last few weeks at Colorado Springs. These same district attorneys proclaim that the present antitrust act passed by a Democratic legislature, contains a "joker" which makes it ineffective, and they recommend all prosecutions to be turned over to the federal grand jury. This same act wiped out the court of appeals decision, gained after years of fighting, giving the attorney general power to prosecute, under the common law, combinations in restraint of trade. Thus we find the sovereign power of the state as helpless to protect the people of the state from extortionate prices in the necessities of life as it has been in the industrial conflicts. We favor the enactment of an effective, stringent, antitrust act which will give the state plenary power to regulate, if necessary, prices of foodstuffs in times of emergency, and to prohibit combinations in restraint of trade.

We favor state farm loans. We believe the school funds, instead of being deposited in banks at a low rate of interest, and by the banks being loaned to farmers at a high rate, should be by the state loaned to farmers directly for the making of necessary improvements, at a rate not to exceed 6 per cent per annum, under adequate safeguards, as to their security and return.

To foster the great dairy interests and to protect the health and welfare of all citizens of the state of Colorado and to do away with graft and discrimination of municipal health boards, we are strongly in favor of a state tubercular inspection law for cattle, absolutely under the control of the state dairy commissioner, and at the expense of the state. To induce the immigration of homeseekers and homebuilders to Colorado, we are strongly in favor of an effective herd law that will protect the settlers' crops from destruction by large herds of cattle, and for this same purpose we favor the sale of state lands to actual homebuilders on long-term payments, at not to exceed 6 per cent interest. We urge emphatically the liberal interpretation and enforcement of the existing land laws of Colorado in the interest of settlers, present and prospective, and the enactment of such additional legislation as will rapidly build up home-owning communities in all of the undeveloped sections of the state.

We believe in protecting and advancing the agricultural and live-stock interests of Colorado, to their utmost capacity and development, realizing these allied industries are the foundation of permanent prosperity. Upon no previous occasion in the history of our country has the finger of opportunity pointed to the necessity of fostering and advancing these industries, in order that we may not only be prosperous at home, but furnish in material quantities meat and food supplies to the nation.

We, therefore, favor a wise and just policy in the administration or disposition of the remaining lands within our borders, whether such lands belong to the state or federal government.

We believe that all lands should be classified and thereafter put to their highest and best use permanently, according to their fitness, in order that the greatest enduring good shall obtain to the greatest number of our citizens.

We believe that the work of the state educational institutions should be extended to the utmost, in order that the people of the state may be given the benefit of the best possible service.

Under both old parties shocking extravagance has reigned at the state house. We pledge ourselves to do away with every expense which may be cut off without impairing the efficiency of the state government.

We pledge ourselves to enact a law to effectually prevent stock swindling and kindred corporate abuses, for the protection of the plain people, the men and women of small savings, from the glittering, false representatives /sic7 of the fraudulent promoter. We remind the people of Colorado that such legislation was vetoed by the present Democratic governor, and that the present Democratic candidate for governor opposed the incorporation in the present state public utilities law of provisions for the regulation of issues of railroad stocks and bonds.

The Democratic party was swept into power in 1912, on the

promise that it would reduce the high cost of living, destroy trust domination, and give the wage earner a larger share in industry. For two years the Democratic party has had its way, and none of these promises have been realized. It secured the passage of exactly the tariff bill it wanted, and the cost of living has gone up, instead of down, while many industries have been badly and needlessly crippled. Trusts dominate business as much as ever and there is no promise in the administration trust measures of any effective regulation or control of big business. Rather the Democratic ideal seems to be to try to restore business conditions outgrown a generation ago. Instead of the wage worker securing a larger share in industry, he gets less, owing to the increasing cost of living, and as a consequence, not in many years have there been as many and as serious strikes and labor disturbances as at the present time. We contend that the remedies advanced by the Democratic party are utterly insufficient for the needs of the times. There must be such a readjustment of present industry as will make it constantly more difficult for a few men to secure control of such a large share of the nation's wealth as they now possess and as will give to the average man a larger share of the wealth he produces.

We favor a tariff which will afford protection to our industries and at the same time insure a reasonable profit to capital and an adequate wage for labor without injustice to the consumer. This end can be attained only by the elimination of the trading and log-rolling methods heretofore employed in the enactment of tariff laws, and we, therefore, reiterate our proposal of a tariff commission for the purpose of securing intelligent and accurate tariff laws free from all illegitimate influence. We emphatically denounce the Democratic program, which demoralizes and destroys home industries by hasty, secret and ignorant legislation without lowering the cost of living, and with equal force we condemn tariff legislation influenced and controlled alone by tariff beneficiaries, as exemplified by the last Republican tariff measure.

As against the Democratic policy of state rights we stand unequivocally for national legislation on all questions of social and industrial justice. We favor national legislation for all those social reforms demanded in the Progressive national platform of 1912: Minimum wages for women, prohibition of child labor, eight-hour day in certain industries, one day's rest in seven, old age, accident and unemployment insurance. Such legislation to be effective and to place the industries of all states on an equal basis must be national, not state.

Since the first railroad was built, Colorado has been charged high freight rates, while freight carried through this state to the Pacific coast has been given very low rates. Colorado has been taxed, in other words, to build up the Pacific coast. We are unalterably opposed to the theory that freight rates should be based on water competition. If elected, we shall use all our power to secure for Colorado freight rates proportioned on the rates charged for through freight. We shall, in season and out of season, demand that Colorado shall be given the advantage of her position, 2,000 miles nearer the eastern markets than the Pacific coast.

The wealth of this nation belongs to all the people, not to a few of the people; therefore, we favor federal conservation and development of all those natural resources still remaining in the people's hands.

Public utilities should conserve, first, the rights of the public, rather than the rights of private corporations. Therefore, we favor such extension of the parcel post as will take over all express and parcel business. We favor government ownership of telegraph and telephone lines.

We favor an amendment to the federal constitution, providing for national woman's suffrage.

We believe that the right to the writ of habeas corpus is one of the most fundamental rights of the people; that its denial by judicial construction in this state is a serious menace to our liberties, and that it should be restored by suitable legislation.

We strongly disapprove of the holding of prisoners charged with crime in connection with labor disturbances or otherwise, incommunicado, and without the privilege of consulting counsel.

We believe that it is vitally essential to the effectiveness of our state militia that its officers and members be fair and impartial in the performance of their duties. The recruiting of the militia from men associated with either side of an industrial struggle should be absolutely prohibited.

We favor the construction and extension of good roads in the state and nation.

We favor a provision for pensions under reasonable regulations for firemen in cities and towns.

We favor the enactment of the initiated constitutional amendment, providing that three-fourths of the jurors may find a verdict in civil cases.

We favor strongly the bill passed by the last legislature and re- ferred to the vote of the people at the coming election, concerning the bonding of commission merchants and the protection of shippers.

We favor the use of public school buildings as centers for social meetings for political and economic discussion, that there may be closer relations between the home and the school.

We favor the consolidation of rural school districts, wherever possible, in order that the children in such districts may have the benefit which comes from close supervision, longer terms of school, and the most efficient teaching. We also favor legislation providing for teachers' tenure of office.

We favor the publication of the initiative and referendum meas- ures in pamphlet form, distributed to all voters along the lines of the Oregon law, thus cheapening the cost of the initiative and referendum, and making the publicity much more effective than by the present means of newspaper publication, which has been disgracefully used for political purposes. We condemn the initiated measure seeking to curb the people's power under the initiative and referendum.

We pledge our candidates to the legislature to use all honorable means at their disposal to secure such amendment to the revenue and tax commission laws of Colorado as will provide that mining property and the output of mining claims shall be assessed equitably with other property in the state of Colorado.

We favor the elimination of the assembly feature of the primary law and we favor presidential preference primaries for the coming presidential election, also a short ballot law.

We respect the request submitted to us by those responsible for the initiation of the statewide prohibition amendment, that the same be not made a partisan matter, but we pledge ourselves to a strict and impartial enforcement of the amendment if carried.

This, the platform of the Progressive party in Colorado, binds every public servant elected under the pledges herein and all appointed officers under them to the unqualified endeavor to bring these pledges into performance.

On these principles and in the recognized desirability of uniting the Progressive forces of the state and nation into an organization which shall unequivocally represent the Progressive spirit and policy, we appeal for the support of all citizens of the state, without regard to previous political affiliation.

*   *   *

In Colorado as in most other parts of the country the Progressives did not make as good a showing in 1914 as in 1912. Mr. Costigan's vote in 1914 was less than half what it had been in 1912, while the Republican candidate of 1914, George Carlson, received nearly twice as many votes as had been cast for C. C. Parks in 1912. In 1912 a Democrat, Elias M. Ammons, had been elected governor; in 1914 the Democratic candidate, Thomas M. Patterson, ran second. In a letter to Amos Pinchot, who had contributed to the expense of the Progressive campaign in Colorado, Mr. Costigan analyzed the reasons for his defeat . . . .

—   —   —

Nov. 11, 1914

Hon. Amos Pinchot
60 Broadway,
New York City, N.Y.

My dear Mr. Pinchot:

You are, of course, entitled to some report on the outcome of our Colorado fight, in which you manifested so deep and appreciated an interest this fall. The informal returns give me something in excess of thirty thousand votes, as against a Democratic vote of approximately eighty-five thousand and a Republican vote of approximately one hundred eighteen thousand. You were, therefore, manifestly right in foreseeing the defeat of the Progressives in Colorado when you offered us the help which proved indispensable for the making of even a respectable showing. I remember very well that you stated to me in New York that the combination of forces against us because we were striving to do a fundamentally worth while thing would be probably overwhelming. It so proved. Perhaps at some near day I may be permitted to tell you by what tricks and strategems the result was achieved. The most important superficial element contributing to the result was the injection of the temperance issue in our fight, and the placing of the dry forces behind the Republican nominee for governor, notwithstanding the fact that the temperance forces conceded that my record in that respect was beyond reproach. The combined interests opposing us managed this feature of the campaign with astonishing adroitness. They did more. On the eve of election day, although the Republican candidate had openly declared for Prohibition, they enlisted in his support great numbers of liquor voters through promises which can be imagined, and about which rumor is busy.

A religious issue was also fraudulently employed throughout the campaign between the Republican and Democratic nominees, and, to complete the outward appeal, the impression was assiduously spread abroad that the Progressives had no chance whatever to win. This is a customary course in political campaigns, as you are doubtless aware, but it was so skillfully used in Colorado as to be effectively "put across." In addition, it will interest you to know that the labor situation was almost unaccountably held inactive. One reason was that the labor leaders, in the face of numerous indictments for murder, growing out of the events following Ludlow last spring, were undoubtedly somewhat intimidated and in fear of prosecuting an open campaign for our cause. They were, moreover, afraid of the prediction that we could under no circumstances win, and, oddly enough, were somewhat apprehensive that unless they passively supported Senator Patterson, the Democratic nominee, in case of his election he would be resentful of their attitude, with consequences more or less serious to them. Our difficulties were added to by the fact that we had no newspaper support, except the Denver <u>Express,</u> a Scripps paper, which loyally and effectively sustained us in its own circle. The <u>News</u> and <u>Times</u>, owned by J. C. Shaffer, owner of the Chicago <u>Post</u> and other so-called Progressive papers, remained entirely neutral, except for the shading of their news columns somewhat in favor of the Republican candidate.

Notwithstanding these impediments, we waged, from a public standpoint, the best political campaign ever made in Colorado, and we have the satisfaction of knowing that we lifted a standard which cannot be forgotten in this state, whatever befalls those who carried it. We made clear that the responsibility for future disaster must rest with the voters. The situation was carefully and fearlessly analyzed and exposed in every section of the state. The Republican nominee was proven to be the Rockefeller candidate. The only definite remedies were proposed by the Progressives, and by them alone were carefully and adequately expounded, and the danger of a military policy of revived Peabodyism or continued Ammonsism in Colorado were contrasted with the peaceful and final solution we offered of arbitration and genuine conservation of natural resources under law and constitutional government.

I think the feeling is wide-spread that we were tricked out of a victory that would have been well worth while, and that the state will regret before many months its failure to accept our program. The praise of our campaign coming to me from disinterested sources, and the genuine grief in many quarters over our defeat are touching and gratifying to an extreme degree. Be assured that your individual share in this work will be remembered to your everlasting credit and good name . . . .

291

TWENTY-FIVE: THE TUNGSTEN BOOM
by Percy Stanley Fritz

*One historian of the Centennial State has suggested that every
generation in Colorado's history has enjoyed its unique mining boom.
From gold and silver to uranium and oil, the rule seems to have held
true. During the years of the first World War, the Boulder County
tungsten mines flourished in true bonanza style, rising — and then
declining — in importance within the compass of a few short years.
This is the story of that short-lived mining boom of a generation ago.**

*   *   *

THE TUNGSTEN BOOM

. . . Tungsten has been familiar to chemists for a long time.
The element was isolated in 1781 by a Swedish chemist, Scheele,
from whose name we get the term "scheelite" to designate one of the
tungsten minerals, the tungstate of calcium. The word consequently
has a Swedish origin, coming from "tung" meaning heavy and "sten"
meaning stone. About 1859 Robert Mushet obtained a British patent
for using it in hardening steel, and near the close of the century
chemists were experimenting with it for high-speed tool steel.

Mineralogists reported the presence of tungsten in some of the
ores of the San Juan region in southwestern Colorado even before the
rich deposits of the Boulder County field were discovered. In one of
the mining journals of 1899 Mr. C. A. Cooper pointed out that the
depletion of certain foreign mines had created a demand for tungsten
which raised the price from $85.00 to $350.00 per ton for seventy
per cent ore, and told the miners of the San Juan how they could recognize this new profit possibility.

------

*from Percy Stanley Fritz, "Tungsten and the Road to War" in *University of
Colorado Studies*, Series C (Studies in the Social Sciences, Vol. 1, No. 2, May,
1941). Used with permission of the University of Colorado Press.

The discovery of tungsten in the Nederland area of Boulder County reminds one of Russell Conwell's "Acres of Diamonds." For years it had hampered the seekers for gold and silver. The miners in the Nederland region called it "that damned black iron." The assayers called it "magnetite." One prospector missed a fortune when he abandoned a claim on which he discovered "a big iron vein" which failed to show worthwhile values when he had it assayed for gold and silver. This later proved to be one of the rich tungsten veins at Stevens Camp (Tungsten). Road commissioners found the ore made excellent road material. Men were literally seeking treasure and did not know that it was beneath their feet.

The first person to "recognize tungsten ore in Boulder County" was John H. Knight, of Ward. The first documentary evidence of the recognition of tungsten in Colorado is a letter of thanks dated April 24, 1899, sent by President Chauvenet of Colorado School of Mines thanking Mr. Knight for the "specimens of Wolframite" (a tungstate of manganese and iron) ore which he had promised them. Mr. Knight's exhibition of these ores at the Paris Universal Exposition in 1900 won a medal and created widespread interest in Europe as well as in America. Steel and ordnance manufactures like Hugo Krupp of Hanover, Germany, personally wrote to Mr. Knight. Such buyers as Ettlinger and Ginsberger of Berlin and Hamburg, Bertrand Hess of Brussels, the "Compagnie des Alliages" of Paris, all were eager for the metal. Several Pennsylvania steel firms sent investigators to Boulder County to look over the ground and make experiments. Mr. Knight discovered and located the Connotton . . . mine on March 21, 1890. It was from this group of mines that Mr. Knight obtained these tungsten ores.

Samuel B. Conger's claim to having been the first to find tungsten in Colorado "during the 90's" is worthy of consideration here although it is somewhat hazy. According to Mr. Conger's own account he was living in Oregon when he learned what tungsten ore was. He remembered an old mine prospect hole which had been sunk back in the 60's "by a man named Towner which was full of the stuff." He returned to Denver to get a lease on the mine, if possible. Here he met Nelson Wannamaker with whom he had mined before. Strangely enough Mr. Wannamaker had just returned from Arizona with the same idea "that the old Towner hole has tungsten in it." They went into partnership and Conger went to the mine, secured some specimens, and returned to Denver. Together they took the specimens to five different assayers in Denver. Three of them pronounced it manganese, just as all /had/ done when Towner first began to take the ore out. Two of them, Victor Blans and John Richards said it was tungsten. "This was enough for us," related Conger. "We got a lease and then began to work the property. It was no time until we had arranged with a European house to ship the ore across the water. We sent a great deal of it away, and made a sufficient success of the enterprise to sell our lease for $5000, Dr. Bell of Canada being the purchaser. The mine has been worked considerably since, but there is still a wide area of unexploited ground; indeed, I believe it to be today the richest and biggest tungsten mine in the United States. Professor Lake named the mine for me, and it is still known as the Conger."

Without casting any discredit upon the sincerity of Mr. Conger, who dictated the above account when he was eighty-nine years old, it needs to be pointed out that memory obscures the relationship of past incidents and creates sometimes a very unintentional distortion. The location certificate for the Conger mine, which is one /of/ the very early surveys . . . and which did prove to be one of the richest of tungsten mines, states that Mr. Conger discovered the mine on May 7, 1873. In this account Mr. Conger confuses the original discovery of the mine with the later discovery of tungsten in the same mine sometime "during the 90's."

By 1900 it was generally known that this black metal was tungsten and had a commercial value. Individuals began to re-examine their properties. Miners began to seek leases on properties they remembered containing the ore. Then companies began to be organized to mine and mill and purchase the ore.

In 1900 the Great Western Exploration and Reduction Company built a concentrating mill west of Sugar Loaf. This company represented the interests of the Primos Chemical Company of Primos, Pennsylvania. In 1906 the Primos people took over this company under the new name of Stein and Boericke Mining and Milling Company, and in 1908 became the Primos Mining and Milling Company which built a huge mill 150 feet by 250 feet at Lakewood. The Primos

Company, under the various titles (a) Primos Mining and Milling Company, (b) Primos Chemical Company, and (c) Primos Exploration Company, owned 1867 acres of mineral land, besides a leasehold on all the Colorado Tungsten Company's property. In 1920 the Vanadium Corporation of America purchased these properties. Not wishing to operate and to avoid losses by vandals they immediately sold the whole town of Lakewood to L. W. Wells, a Boulder mine equipment dealer, who dismantled and removed thirty residences and small buildings and the Primos mill building with all its machinery. In 1938 the Vanadium Corporation built a new modern mill near the Conger mine.

Another important operator is the Wolf Tongue Mining Company. Its history is a long one because it has survived the vicissitudes of the mining industry since 1902. It is a subsidiary of the Firth-Sterling Steel Company of McKeesport, Pennsylvania. This company was experimenting in 1902 on hard tool steel. Mr. William Loach was in their employ as a chemist. At that time there were only carbon steels and self-hardening steels which used a very small percentage of tungsten, never over one or two per cent. One carload of tungsten would then supply the tungsten needs of the whole world for a year. The tungsten used in these self-hardening steels was all supplied by Germany which obtained it from the mines of Cornwall. By the use of tungsten trioxide (WO_3) the chemists of the Firth-Sterling Steel Company were trying to improve a blue chip high-speed tool steel, a steel so hard that it could be operated at such speeds and created so much heat that the chips which flew off would turn blue on cooling. Mr. N. G. McKenna, the chief chemist and metallurgist, was sent to Colorado and Boulder to investigate. He first looked at the Copeland properties on the South Boulder and took back some samples. The outlook was so good that a few officials of the Firth-Sterling Steel Company raised $25,000 and sent Mr. Loach out in 1904 to start operations. The ore was brought to Boulder and put through the Black Swan mill. This first company which was not incorporated, was called the Scrooby Mining Company. It was named after a little town in England where one of the members of the company had lived.

In 1904 the Wolf Tongue Mining Company was incorporated under the laws of the State of Delaware. The name chosen for this new company was, according to Mr. Loach, compounded from the two principal names by which this large family of tungsten ores was commonly known. In the early days all the ore was either called tungsten or wolframite, hence taking the first syllable of each, the name, Wolftung or Wolf Tongue, was invented.

In the summer of 1904 this company purchased seven claims from Robert M. Bell of Nederland and started work on two of them, the Oregon and the Clyde. Then they rented the Black Swan mill and hauled their ore there. In September 1904 they took over the old Caribou mill at Nederland, remodelled it and began operations. As time went on they bought more claims and made many new locations to protect their interests until they . . . /became/ the owner of the largest group of valuable tungsten properties in Boulder County. In 1905 they conceived the idea of buying tungsten ore from miners. They were the first who put into operation this practice. At first they bought the ore as it was shipped to them without making any sample assays. That is, they paid for the ore after it was milled and charged the miners four dollars a ton for milling the ore. This was very unsatisfactory from the point of view of the miners because they must sell the ore without any idea or assurance of what it would bring them. If the returns were unsatisfactory they could not seek another purchaser because their ore had already been milled. It was likewise unsatisfactory for the Wolf Tongue Company. Let us suppose a man had two tons of ore and shipped it in, and that the capacity of the mill was twelve tons an hour. This ore could be put through the mill in ten minutes, but in order to determine what the value of each batch of ore was worth the mill must be thoroughly cleaned both before and after the ore was milled. Two thorough cleanings were necessary because a mill will absorb eight to twelve per cent without a thorough cleansing, i.e., that much would stay hidden in the cracks or adhere to the plates. When the ore shipments were small the Wolf Tongue Company discovered that instead of its costs being four dollars a ton, it was costing them about $8.00 a ton to mill the ore. Additional difficulties resulted from the fact that some ores were good clean free milling ores, while others offered greater difficulties. Some ores would run 60 per cent tungstic acid; others would run 40 per cent.

The Wolf Tongue Company saw that if the mill could be operated continuously without thorough clean-ups after each person's ore was milled, a tremendous saving would result. Therefore, they went over their year's record, drew an average, and then put in a buying schedule based on the assay. Under this arrangement there was no milling charge and only a charge of $3.00 for sampling an assay of small lots of a value less than fifty dollars. For example, under the schedule which became effective February 15, 1927, the Wolf Tongue Mining Company purchased ferberite tungsten crude ores delivered at their mill as follows:

1% tungstic acid	$ 1.00 per ton
10% " "	69.30 " "
20% " "	142.00 " "
30% " "	217.00 " "
40% " "	329.60 " "
50% " "	440.00 " "
60% " "	600.00 " "

The development of the industry was rapid. From 1900 to 1910 Boulder County, Colorado, alone produced almost eighty per cent of the entire output in the United States. With the outbreak of the war in Europe the top prices jumped from $9.00 per short ton unit in 1914, to $53.00 per unit in 1915, and $93.50 per unit in 1916. In less technical phraseology the price of one pound of tungsten rose from 45 cents in 1914, to $2.65 in 1915, and to $4.67 at its highest point in 1916. This war-inflated price caused a veritable boom in the tungsten-producing sections.

The real boom in tungsten was inaugurated by the great demand for high-speed tool steel resulting from the World War. Many far-sighted steel men had been operating and developing tungsten properties for several years before the war broke out. They formed the nucleus. By 1916 when the prospects of five dollars a pound for tungsten was in sight a most feverish activity set in. Capital and labor were rushed to the Boulder tungsten fields to supply the demand for tungsten at these scarcity prices. The gigantic Primos mill at Lakewood was completed and many lessors and contract workers engaged in working their twenty-five hundred acres of property. The Primos Exploration Company shipped from a single mine, the Copeland mine and mill, to the Primos Chemical Company, Primos, Pennsylvania, in 1916 a total of 3949.9 units of tungsten valued at $76,028.97.

297

From May to November of the following year, 1917, they shipped 8922.55 units worth $140,071.90. The Wolf Tongue Company had a tent city of two hundred lessors working on their properties and one hundred twenty-five miners on company account. The Rogers patent was divided into lots called Rogers Patent No. 1 east and Rogers Patent No. 1 west, and so on with some two hundred lessors at work supplying the Clarasdorf mill. The Vanadium Alloy Steel Company (Vasco) was developed to furnish the tungsten in which the seven McKenna brothers were interested. One was president of a steel company at Latrobe, Pa., another was superintendent of metallurgy at Washington Steel and Ordnance Company at Washington, D.C., while three others managed the McKenna Brothers Brass Company at Pittsburgh, Pa. Sixteen sets of lessors were at work. Camp Stevens, named after Eugene Stevens, who was developing the Rogers Patent, was growing rapidly. The Boulder Tungsten Production Company promoted by John G. Clark began a great tunnel to crosscut the properties lying between Nederland and Lakewood. The Black Prince Mining Company had a hundred men working on their properties. The Tungsten Mountain Mines Company was another John C. Clark promotion involving nearly 400 acres and a mill. The Degge and Clark Tungsten Milling and Mining Company was opened on the eastern edge of the tungsten belt about six miles from Boulder. The Western Tungsten Mining Company was being promoted by W. J. Hardy, a Pennsylvania capitalist, who began erecting a large three story building to house his Miner's and Merchant's State Bank of Stevens and provide thirty-six sleeping rooms on the two upper floors.

Nederland was in the heart of this boom. There were about 300 people living in Nederland in 1915 and only a year later there were 3000. An account of the town in that year says:

> It has taken on metropolitan airs with well graded streets, a business street boasting several blocks of handsome and commodious business blocks, hotels, and its beautiful residence section built up with miners' cottages and bungalows of pretty design and construction. Bonds for large extension of the water system were recently voted and a handsome addition to the school building is provided for.

Inside of two years (1916-1917) the capacity of the mills equipped to handle tungsten ores in Boulder County doubled. Capital flowed into the region fairly begging to be put to work. There was, as a result, a corresponding increase in wages and cost of production. In 1913 the miner's minimum wage was $2.00 for eight hours' labor. The cost of board and liability insurance was eighty-four cents additional. In 1917 the minimum wage was $3.00 for eight hours' labor. The cost of board and liability insurance had increased to $1.47. After taking into account the relative efficiency of labor which decreased from 5.29 to 6.87 hours per ton, the cost of production had increased over eighty-seven per cent from 1913 to 1917. Wages still continued to rise. On October 1, 1917, the Primos Mining and Milling Company made a general increase of forty cents per shift. This increased the wage of muckers (who received the minimum wage) to $4.00 per day and for miners $4.60 per day. On September 1, 1918, another voluntary increase raised the minimum wage to $4.40 per eight hour shift. Muckers and trammers were raised from $4.00 to $4.40; miners from $4.60 to $5.00; and others about a ten per cent increase. Everything was going up, and on the surface everything was rosy. Only those well-posted saw on the horizon the specter of cheap Chinese ores.

In the midst of this prosperity the tungsten camps were scourged by the influenza epidemic.

The influenza first appeared in Nederland about October 1st /1918/. Its spread was so rapid by October 18th, the entire district was demoralized. On the 16th and 17th, our mill /Primos/ crew was down to one shift, and on the 18th we shut down the mill and all the mines except the Quaker, as we could not get men enough for even one shift. All other mines in the district were shut down. Out of our mine crew of 75 men, 15 men have died and we lost several leasers. There were, however, no deaths among our mill crew although practically every man contracted the disease.

The Primos Company printed a 6 by 12 inch blue poster headed "Influenza — Grippe" describing the symptoms, methods of prevention and treatment. In large letters the warning appeared "The sick must stay in bed at least 3 days after the temperature becomes normal (98 3/10)." These posters were placarded in conspicuous places in the various camps.

This natural scourge was barely over when on November 11, 1918, the armistice was signed and the wartime demand for tungsten ceased. The boom collapsed, and most of the twenty-two mills operating in the county were closed . . . .

In view of this almost complete collapse of the tungsten industry in Colorado and the United States it is natural to inquire what was the reason for this collapse. A number of factors need to be taken into consideration.

First was the nature of the boom. Every boom must have its inevitable collapse. The war created a very abnormal demand which, of course, was accompanied by a highly inflated war price. The inflation would have been severe if it had been due only to the general inflation of the price structure, but in an article used almost exclusively in the production of steel and ordnance for the prosecution of the war there was no stop to the inflation until after the government fixed the price. When the war ceased, the price inevitably collapsed.

Second was the general depression. When the steel industry was producing at less than twenty-five per cent of capacity it was only logical that there should be a corresponding falling off of all industries subsidiary to the steel industry.

Third was the importation of Chinese ore. China did not begin producing tungsten until 1914, when it produced eighteen tons. Four years later, 1918, it exported 11,659 tons. This competition captured the United States market in spite of a tariff of 45 cents a pound on . . . imported ore imposed September 22, 1922, and on June 18, 1930, raised to 72 cents per pound . . . . In spite of this tariff and in spite of the fact that Boulder County tungsten is freer from impurities, such as tin, arsenic, copper, and sometimes bismuth, than the Chinese ores, yet competition was handicapped. In China the ore occurred in gash veins and blow-outs; coolie labor picked it up from shallow openings. It was a wolframite containing as high as 65 per cent to 70 per cent WO_3. In the Cold Spring mine they were mining at 500 feet, hoisting the ore and pumping the water, for ore running about 60 per cent WO_3, with a small amount of high grade. Instead of coolie labor they paid $4.50 a day for common miners. Besides this, the ocean rate for the Chinese ores was less than the American freight rate from Boulder County to Pittsburgh.

And finally another factor depressing the industry was the development of eastern competition in the milling of the ores. In the early days the ore was refined to a tungsten powder, the W metal, which was added to the tool steel. Now the more common product is ferro-tungsten. Each steel company had been doing this for itself. This was a very wasteful method, for some would recover 80 per cent of the tungsten content and some could recover only 25 per cent. Now the Molybdenum Corporation of America at Little Washington, Pa., and the Electro-Metallurgical Company at Niagara will take any ores sent them and guarantee a 90 per cent recovery of the mineral content. Under these conditions it was far cheaper for the steel mills to purchase the ore in the cheapest market, and have one of these corporations refine the metal for them. Such factors contributed to the postwar depression in the tungsten industry.

TWENTY-SIX: THE DUST BOWL

The decade of the 1930's was a period of depression and difficulty for Coloradans, as for all Americans. Man-made problems in the form of economic decline, unemployment, and the countless other aspects of human difficulties during the "dark decade" were bad enough; to make matters worse, nature herself seemed to conspire against a return to prosperity. Dry weather and winds, and perhaps unfortunate agricultural methods, combined to produce the fantastic dust storms of the middle years of the 'thirties. Something of the nature of those storms is recorded here in two contemporary descriptions by Gene Lindberg and Clyde Byers.*

*   *   *

THE DUST BOWL

WHIRLWIND NEARLY 1, 000 MILES WIDE CASTS PALL OF DUST
OVER COLORADO
GIANT EDDY ENCIRCLES WHOLE WESTERN SKY, WITH STATE
IN CENTER
Showers Fall in Denver and Further Rain Or Snow, Set-
tling Dust, Is Forecast; Lights Go On in Mid-Day Dark-
ness

— — —

(By Gene Lindberg.)

Denver and the entire eastern half of the state Tuesday were in the calm, dust-laden center of a gigantic whirlwind nearly a thousand miles in diameter.

— — — — —

*from *The Denver Post*, April 9, 1935 and April 15, 1935. Used with permission of The Denver Post.

A rain shower in Denver at noon Tuesday cleared the atmosphere temporarily, but moisture in quantity and over a widespread
area will be necessary to eliminate the dust completely.

Never before in the history of the west, according to weather
bureau records here, has such an immense blanket of dust been cast
over this region.

Everyone has seen the tiny spinning whirlwinds that dance in
the street on a summer day, picking up dust and rubbish and carrying it high into the air. When the whirling motion spreads out and
slows down the center of the disturbance becomes calm and the dust
drops to earth.

That, according to J. M. Sherier, chief of the Denver district
weather office, is exactly what is happening now on an enormous
scale. The whirlwind, instead of being a few feet, is hundreds of
miles in diameter. The calm, dusty area at its center extends from
Wyoming to Texas, along the eastern face of the Rocky mountains.

* * *

U.S. ASSIGNS 20,000 MEN TO FIGHT DUST AS YEAR'S WORST
STORM SWEEPS WEST
DRIFTS NINE FEET HIGH PILED UP BY WIND ON ROAD NEAR
DURANGO

— — —

CCC Men to Be Sent to Stricken Region; All Southern Colorado
Enveloped by Haze; No Immediate Relief in Sight

— — —

(By Clyde Byers.)

Another blinding duststorm boiled over parts of five states like
a scourge Monday. It affected all of southern Colorado from the
eastern to the western boundaries, and inflicted heavy damage and

303

real suffering in parts of New Mexico, Kansas, Oklahoma and Texas. Dust drifts nine feet high were blown up near Durango, Colo.

Alarmed by the situation, officials in Washington put the machinery of seven government departments in high gear to alleviate the distress and push programs designed to prevent recurrence of the stifling storms. Twenty thousand civilian conservation corps enrollees are to be sent into the stricken area to work on the latter programs and relief activities are to be broadened.

Monday's storm was a continuation of one that swirled over Colorado and parts of Nebraska, Kansas and Oklahoma Sunday. The storm struck Denver at 2 p.m. Sunday and moved southward about four hours later. It blotted out the sun, blew up sand drifts that stopped trains and automobiles, and grounded airplanes. The gale-like winds tore down wires in Denver and filled homes and stores with a thick film of powdery dust.

Slight Prospects of Relief Seen As Pall Hangs Over Five States.

The storm was the most severe of the series that started March 1 and have recurred with increasing frequency and intensity. In the area affected Monday there were slight prospects of relief, either from strong winds which might blow away the dust clouds or from rain which might settle them.

After it had moved southward the storm Monday covered an area bounded on the north by a line stretching from Durango, thru Pueblo and eastward to the middle of Kansas. The area comprised virtually all of New Mexico, Texas and western Kansas and western Oklahoma.

The dust hung over that area all Sunday night and was stirred Monday forenoon by a strong wind. It was expected the dust would become thicker with the usual increase in the velocity of the wind later in the day. The dust drifts reached their most towering height on the highway between Bernalillo, N.M., and Durango, Colo., where, motorists reported, they were nine feet high.

The development of a low pressure area moving in from the Pacific caused government weather forecasters to predict that the storm would be worse than ever Tuesday . . . .

At Springfield, Colo., county seat of Baca county, visibility dropped to fifty feet at noon. Train service came to a standstill, as did highway traffic. Telegraph service also was stopped by wire trouble, but telephone wires kept the town from being completely isolated.

The Santa Fe railroad rerouted its trains at Newton, Kan., to Amarillo, Texas, instead of thru the La Junta, Colo., short cut. All trains were behind schedule, as were busses. Only the most urgent automobile trips were made where the storm was worst.

For the first time in history, residents of Buena Vista had their view of the Collegiate peaks, Princeton, Harvard and Yale, and of Gold Hill, obscured by dust.

The dust was thick over both the San Luis and Arkansas valleys.

Herds of cattle that have survived the storms in western Kansas were being driven Monday to the lush blue-stem grass pastures in east-central Kansas, which were reported in good condition.

The wires blown down in Denver were power lines of the Public Service Company of Colorado. They were quickly restored.

Residents of eastern New Mexico, from Clayton to Clovis, spent an almost sleepless night. Sweeping down from the north, the dust clouds rolled into Clayton at sundown Sunday, changing day into night almost in an instant.

Clovis, almost 200 miles south, felt the storm at 8 p.m. Traffic stopped. As the evening wore on, the air became so stifling that residents were awakened from their sleep. Drifting westward, the black and sometimes yellowish dust clouds covered Albuquerque Monday forenoon and reached Grant, a community on the continental divide, by noon.

305

Visibility was measured at one-sixteenth of a mile at El Paso, Tex., Monday forenoon and airplane trips were canceled. Other visibility measurements reported were: Las Vegas and Santa Rosa, zero; Albuquerque, one-tenth of a mile; Roswell, one-eighth of a mile, and Santa Fe, one-half mile.

Fiftieth 'Duster' in 104 Days.

Oklahoma residents rushed for storm cellars when Sunday's "duster" appeared on the horizon. Perryton, Tex., was visited by the fiftieth duststorm in 104 days.

Temperatures tumbled quickly throughout the vast area when Sunday's storm struck. The temperature in Denver at noon, according to official recordings of the United States weather bureau, was 71, but in two hours it fell to 49 degrees . . . .

Pueblo-to-Denver Plane Turns Back.

Pilots flying into the Denver municipal airport reported they could not see the administration building from an altitude of 100 feet. A Wyoming Air Service plane, which left Pueblo for Denver during the afternoon was forced to turn back.

The storm generated sufficient static electricity to cripple automobile ignition systems and scores of motorists were temporarily stranded because the static was so intense. When the storm abated, they found they could start their engines again. At the height of the storm, motorists said, they received distinct electrical shocks when they touched door handles and similar attachments on their cars. Motorists made it a practice to drag wires and chains to ground the static and prevent short circuits.

Distinctly different from direct or alternating electrical current, static electricity is produced by friction in the air and differences in temperature.

This static is blamed by agriculturalists and weather experts for helping kill sprouting wheat thruout the drouth and dust area. Fields of wheat sprouts are seared and shriveled from the combined effects of the static electricity and the lack of moisture.

There were reports that jack rabbits have been electrocuted. Many of the pests have perished, but no one has conducted autopsies to determine the cause. They might have eaten too much dust. That has caused the death of livestock in western Kansas.

An interesting contrast to the duststorm was a cold wave in Montana, where the temperature went down to 15 degrees below zero in Glacier national park. One foot of snow fell there.

TWENTY-SEVEN: THE AIR TRANSPORT INDUSTRY IN COLORADO

by Lee Scamehorn

While many examples could be found to illustrate the modern age in Colorado, none seems quite so useful as the story of the development of the air transport industry. The application of the airplane to transportation problems in the region has come closest to solving many of the problems (such as vast distances and rugged terrain) which have existed since the first penetration of the area by white men. As is amply demonstrated in the following selection, this relatively recently-developed industry now forms a major facet of the economy of the state.

* * *

THE AIR TRANSPORT INDUSTRY IN COLORADO

Since the airplane first appeared in Colorado fifty years ago, it has become a vehicle for spanning vast distances in a fraction of the time required by traditional methods of surface transportation. Its application to commercial travel was by no means assured, however, until military demands in the years 1914-1918 transformed the crude models of the earlier period into machines suitable for carrying people, mail, and express.

World War I gave decisive impetus to the growth of commercial aviation. Air power became a major factor in determining the course of conflict in Europe. Vast aerial fleets on both sides reflected a fierce struggle for technological superiority as engineers and production experts turned out a bewildering array of airplanes with improved speed, range, and carrying capacity. Under the stress of combat, advances occurred in four years that would have required at least two decades at the rate of prewar development. At the time of the Armistice, the United States had thousands of trained pilots and aircraft for a peacetime air transport industry.

308

The Post Office Department and the U.S. Army Air Service established the first commercial airline while the nation was still at war. Postal officials opened a 218-mile airmail service between Washington and New York, with an intermediate stop in Philadelphia, on May 15, 1918, using military personnel and equipment. Even before hostilities ended, Second Assistant Postmaster General Otto Preager, director of aerial mail service, outlined plans for a coast-to-coast route with branch lines to Pittsburgh, St. Louis, Kansas City, and Minneapolis-St. Paul.

The transcontinental service was completed within two years after the war. Following a six-month struggle to obtain adequate machines and ground facilities, the Post Office Department opened the first segment to Chicago in July, 1919. Extensions to Omaha and San Francisco were opened in May and September, respectively, of the following year. Branch lines were also opened in 1920, to St. Louis and Minneapolis-St. Paul. All auxiliary lines, including the original Washington-New York service, were quickly discontinued, victims of an economy drive and Congress' refusal to authorize more than the coast-to-coast operation.

From the first, the government venture was temporary, designed to develop airmail on a sound basis, at which point it could be turned over to private enterprise. As early as 1920, Congress authorized the Post Office Department to contract for new routes, providing the cost did not exceed that of surface transportation. Only one of four proposed routes (Miami to Havana) was taken over by a private company. The obvious lack of enthusiasm for such service indicated that businessmen did not consider airmail a field for risk capital. As long as volume remained small, the economic value of airmail was generally unnoticed.

In the next five years, operations expanded at an unprecedented rate. A lighted airway from Chicago to Cheyenne permitted continuous flights on a regular schedule, day and night, across the continent with significant reductions in delivery time for letters and airmail parcels. The extension of lighting equipment to the Chicago-New York airway set the stage for overnight service; letters from either city arrived at the other in time for early morning delivery.

Improved service brought increased volume and revenues which, for the first time in the history of the government-airline, approached costs and indicated profits in the future. The business community, recognizing the change, demanded the transfer of airmail to private contractors in the interest of lower costs and greater efficiency.

In February, 1925, Congress once again gave the Postmaster General authority to turn the airmail over to private enterprise; this time with assurance of profits for contractors. An "act to encourage commercial aviation," sponsored by Representative Clyde Kelly of Pennsylvania, permitted the transportation of mail by aircraft between such points as the Postmaster General should designate, with compensation to carriers "at a rate not to exceed four-fifths of revenues." The Kelly Act laid the foundation on which an air transport industry was organized and expanded in the late 1920's.

The air carriers who appeared in the next few years remained dependent on revenues from airmail. Until that time, commercial aviation's growth had been checked by inadequate finances, weak organization, and obsolete equipment because of inability to overcome public apathy for air travel. The Kelly Act provided adequate revenues from mail as a means of stimulating effective growth in management, ground facilities, and airplanes until the industry could develop reliable service which would attract passengers.

Indirect government aid to fledgling air transport companies aroused little opposition. Such a policy was almost as old as government itself. Furthermore, the Post Office Department had for many years paid railroads and steamship companies for carrying mail. Similar payments to private airlines assured their initial growth, and the American people acquired a vast system of airways linking virtually every large city in the nation.

The Kelly Act encouraged the orderly growth of commercial aviation in Colorado. Two companies responded to the Post Office Department's proposal for Route 12, from Pueblo to the government-operated transcontinental system at Cheyenne, with intermediate stops in Colorado Springs and Denver. When the low bidder announced he could not acquire equipment to begin service within the required thirty days, the contract went to Anthony F. Joseph, president of Colorado

Airways Corporation of Denver.

Celebrations marked the start of airmail from all three Colorado cities. Ten thousand people crowded onto the Colorado Airways Field in east Denver on May 31, to watch the departure of the afternoon mail for Cheyenne. Two Curtiss-Standard J-1 biplanes, war surplus craft, transported 13,000 letters (325 pounds), the first forwarded from Denver by air to cities throughout the United States.

The new airline provided the three major cities of the eastern slope with fast communications by mail. Direct flights to the government route meant savings of up to forty-eight hours to New York, and half that amount to San Francisco. The contractor realized more than $1,600 — eighty per cent of total revenues — from the first day's flights. In 1927, the volume of mail from Denver alone rose to 11,202 pounds, while the yield from all cities on the route exceeded 36,000 pounds. That same year, the Colorado-Wyoming airway ranked second in the nation in ratio of load to population, with 7.7 pounds per one thousand persons.

Air mail opened the way for passenger and freight operations. Inadequate surface transportation in the Rocky Mountain region made air travel especially attractive. Colorado Airways began replacing its original equipment with new monoplanes, enclosed cabins and greater capacity in 1927, in anticipation of extending operations to New Mexico, Texas, and Utah. Plans for new service to Albuquerque and El Paso, and to Salt Lake City, by way of Walsenburg, Monte Vista, Gunnison, Montrose, and Grand Junction, were abandoned later the same year, however, after the Post Office Department gave C.A.M. 12 to another carrier.

Western Air Express, contractor for the lucrative Los Angeles-Salt Lake City airway, won the Colorado territory by under-bidding Boeing Air Transport (predecessor of United Air Lines). Douglas DM-2 biplanes commenced two round trips daily over the route on December 10, but flights immediately were suspended for twelve days when the northbound evening plane crashed in flames shortly after take off from Lowry Field. Boeing, holder of the Chicago-San Francisco contract, provided temporary service from Pueblo to its own base at Cheyenne from early September to December 22.

Western Air Express served Denver and other Colorado cities for almost six years. In that time the company and its subsidiaries linked the state with principal cities in the Middle West and South West. Midcontinent Air Express, organized by Harris Hanshue, Western's president, and Philip Philbin, a Pueblo businessman, opened new routes to New Mexico, Texas, Kansas, Missouri, and Oklahoma. A route to Albuquerque and El Paso was started in September, 1929, followed two months later by similar operations to Kansas City, Missouri, via Garden City, Dodge City, and Wichita. Early the next year, flights began to Dallas-Fort Worth, with intermediate stops in Amarillo, Tulsa, and Oklahoma City.

Colorado's air transport industry expanded rapidly in five short years. Although Colorado Airways Corporation had transported mail and only occasionally a passenger, its successor encountered little difficulty in enlarging its operations for passengers. Charles A. Lindbergh's epic solo flight to Paris in 1927 created widespread enthusiasm for air travel; airlines quickly took advantage of the opportunity to lessen their dependence on airmail.

Inter-city passenger flights became popular as the state's airlines acquired equipment which offered speed and comfort superior to surface facilities. Western Air Express officially opened its mail flights to travelers in May, 1928, using open-cockpit Stearman biplanes. Eight passengers took advantage of the service in the first week alone. The volume of business rose sharply later the same year when six-passenger Fokker monoplanes replaced obsolete equipment. Larger tri-motor craft, adopted in 1930, offered the public the ultimate in accommodations and fast service.

Approximately 3,600 people arrived or departed annually at Denver Municipal Airport (now Stapleton Field) by 1931. Midcontinent Air Express carried one-third of the total; 1,079 on its Denver-Pueblo division, and 116 on its route to Kansas City. Western Air Express confined its operations mainly to airmail, transporting 89,399 pounds and only 365 passengers. United States Airways established a record for passenger traffic as 2,025 travelers made use of its shorter route to Kansas City. The combined air fleets of the three companies flew more than 1,250,000 miles a year.

United States Airways was organized in October, 1928, to provide Denver with direct air connections to Kansas City, Missouri. Passenger flights were inaugurated eight months later, with intermediate stops at Goodland, Hoisington, and Salina. Until 1930, the airline did not have a contract for transporting mail. Although paid the highest rate allowed by the Post Office Department, the company failed to survive the reorganization of routes in 1934 because of inadequate capitalization, plus sparsely settled routes, and competition from Midcontinent Air Express.

Commercial air transport was struck an almost fatal blow on February 9, 1934, when Postmaster General James A. Farley canceled all domestic airmail service. He justified the action on the grounds that all contracts had been obtained from the previous administration through collusion and fraud. Although an investigation failed to support the charge, the U.S. Army Air Corps, by authority of an Executive Order, forwarded all airmail until new arrangements could be worked out with private carriers.

Military airplanes replaced private transports on the domestic airways for a period of more than three months. Except for one week (March 12-19), when flights were suspended for a reorganization of schedules and personnel, Army fliers completed daily trips on which a total of 768,215 pounds of mail traveled 1,707,555 miles. It was a disastrous experiment, however, involving sixty-nine accidents, the loss of twelve lives, and expenses out of proportion to similar service under private enterprise.

The Air Corps, the record reveals, accepted a task for which it lacked personnel, equipment, and experience. Despite assurances by General Douglas A. MacArthur (Chief of Staff) that "there will be no delay, no difficulty and no interruptions," airmail service deteriorated until it was no faster than surface transportation. In early April, two letters sent from the West Coast, one each by air and regular mail, were delivered in New York at precisely the same time nine days later.

Denver experienced slower, greatly curtailed service. Initially, military planes completed a single round trip daily between Pueblo and Cheyenne, replacing Western Air Express' minimum two flights each way. No attempt was made to continue flights over routes served by Midcontinent Air Express and United Airways; all mail to Albuquerque, El Paso, and Kansas City was forwarded by rail.

The Air Corps temporarily suspended all operation on March 12, leaving Denver without airmail for the first time in almost seven years. When flights were resumed a week later, the southern terminal for C.A.M. 12 was shifted to Denver; Pueblo and Colorado Springs were denied service until public criticism prompted the Post Office Department to restore private carriers two months later.

Farley completely reorganized the air transport industry in early May, opening all of the old routes to bids which forced the older companies to compete, often at a disadvantage, with eager newcomers anxious to acquire contracts on which to build passenger operations. The Pueblo-Cheyenne airway, redesignated Contract Route 17, went to Wyoming Air Service, whose offer to carry mail for thirty-four cents a mile was substantially lower than that of Western Air Express, renamed General Air Lines.

Wyoming Air Service was organized in the mid-1920's at Casper, Wyoming, and for several years engaged in various aviation activities. Its handful of pilots, sometimes known as the "Powder River Flyers", offered sight-seeing and charter trips, flight instruction, and exhibitions. Passenger service over a 265-mile airline from Casper to Denver opened in March, 1931, and, the following month, to Sheridan and Billings, Montana. Using single-engine Stinson Detroiter monoplanes, the company maintained regular schedules on the northern division, but, after failing to acquire a mail contract for the southern segment, maintained only irregular service to the Colorado capital for the convenience of through passengers from the north.

When Western Air Express, anticipating the outcome of new bids for the Colorado-Wyoming airway, suspended all passenger flights on May 7, the very day the Air Corps ended mail deliveries, Wyoming Air Service extended its Casper-Billings operations to give the Colorado capital temporary service. A week later, new equipment which conformed to Post Office specifications, restored complete service to Denver and, eighteen days later, to Pueblo. By the end of the month, the new system, two routes joined at Cheyenne, provided combined passenger and mail flights from Pueblo to Billings, Montana.

A second newcomer emerged from the reorganization when, on July 15, 1934, Varney Speed Lines commenced operations over Route 29, from Pueblo to El Paso by way of Albuquerque. Daily passenger-mail flights were inaugurated with four-passenger, single-engine Lockheed Vega monoplanes.

The future of the southern route remained in doubt for several years. Short capital, low load factors from a sparsely settled area, and high operating costs plagued the original company, causing a change in executive personnel within a year, and a new name, Varney Air Transport. Two years later, still another change to Continental Air Lines, after which Robert F. Six took charge of the company, marked the beginning of an era of sound growth and expansion. By purchasing Wyoming Air Service's Pueblo-Denver division of Route 17, the carrier strengthened its system by moving its northern terminal to the natural center of air travel for the Rocky Mountain region.

Colorado's air transport industry was seriously weakened in the mid-1930's by the absence of major east-west airways. The coast-to-coast carriers, serving routes laid out for airmail rather than passengers, avoided Denver, the largest population center in the Rocky Mountain states. As early as 1934, United Air Lines opened negotiations with the Post Office in an effort to gain access to the traffic lying only ninety-nine miles south of its mail line at Cheyenne. In February, 1937, the transcontinental carrier purchased the Cheyenne-Denver segment of Route 17 from Wyoming Air Service; one month later giant Douglas DC-3 "Skylounge" transports began two flights daily from Denver Municipal Airport to San Francisco, Chicago, New York, and other cities across the continent.

The air transport industry survived the fiasco of 1934 and experienced from that date until World War II rapid growth and startling increases in passenger traffic that materially lessened dependence on airmail. Revolutionary improvements in equipment set the stage for the upward trend in business. The fine Boeing 247-D twin-engine, low-wing monoplane, the first of the modern transport planes, replaced tri-motor craft on some of the airlines in 1933, followed within a year by Donald Douglas' revolutionary DC-2. The third model of the famous Douglas Commercial series (DC-3), the "work-horse of the air" introduced in 1935, set new standards with unexcelled accomodations for twenty-one people and three-mile-a-minute speeds. Advances in airport design, improved terminals, new airways and navigation controls, and more effective regulation with the passage of the Civil Aeronautics Authority Act in 1938, lured travelers to the airlines.

Perhaps the most important single cause for the rising popularity of air travel was speed and safety of flight. Nineteen companies carried nearly 2.8 million passengers in 1940; a decade earlier forty-three firms reported 384,506 passengers. Only the larger carriers had used tri-motor planes in 1930, with seats for a maximum of 12 people and speeds up to 120-miles per hour; smaller companies used single engine monoplanes which carried up to six passengers at about the same speed. The elapsed time for transcontinental flights was reduced by half to about fourteen hours by 1940, and similar gains were recorded on all routes where the new transports were adopted.

World War II placed a heavy burden on the air transport industry. Within six months after Pearl Harbor, the armed forces purchased or leased half of the fleet serving the civil airways. Colorado's carriers lost thirty-six of their seventy-two planes, all twin-engine Douglas and Lockheed models. United Airlines, the largest domestic company with nation-wide operations, lost thirty-three, and Continental gave up half of its six Lodestars. Inland Airlines and Braniff Airways, both of whom extended their routes to Denver during the war, made similar sacrifices.

Air transport's rapid wartime expansion removed the last major obstacle to the growth of commercial air travel. Literally over night the American people accepted the airlines as a part of the nation's transportation system. The vast fleets of cargo and personnel-carrying twin-engine and four-engine craft, plus trained crews, assembled by the Air Transport Command and the Naval Air Transport Service formed a pool from which private companies acquired equipment and personnel for expansion of domestic and international service after Japan's surrender.

316

Postwar growth of the industry in Colorado centered about the formation of local service and the expansion of older trunk airlines into complex systems on a regional, national, and international scale. Denver replaced Cheyenne as the focal point of airways in the Rocky Mountain states. Within a decade after the close of hostilities, seven companies maintained regular schedules from the state's capital city to all parts of the United States and to many foreign lands.

So-called "feeder lines" appeared immediately after the war to meet a demand from communities remote from the main airlines for local service. Authorized by temporary certificates from the Civil Aeronautics Board, these small companies combined ingenuity and war surplus aircraft to carry passengers, mail, and express over routes connecting distant areas with cities served by trunk carriers.

The first of fourteen local service companies was Monarch Air Lines, a Denver firm with routes serving twenty-two cities in four states. Major F. W. Bonfils and Ray Wilson, veteran Denver pilots and operators of wartime flight schools for the U.S. Army Air Force, formed the company and inaugurated flights with DC-3 equipment in January, 1947, between Denver, Albuquerque, and Salt Lake City.

A second local carrier, Summit Airways of Laramie, Wyoming, was authorized to serve nineteen communities in four states. Prior to the start of regular flights, the company merged with a Salt Lake City non-scheduled airline and adopted its name, Challenger Airlines. DC-3 service between principal cities in Wyoming, Utah, and Montana commenced in May, 1947.

Operationally, the small airlines were in a class of their own. They spanned regions with inadequate surface transportation and served remote areas of the Rocky Mountain West. Airports on the two route systems averaged more than a mile in altitude; five were in excess of 7,000 feet, and the lowest, at Salt Lake City and Billings, Montana, were above 3,600 feet. Both companies exploited short-haul markets, offering speed and passenger comfort superior to surface facilities.

A merger of Monarch, Challenger, and Arizona Airways into Frontier Airlines, effective June 1, 1950, drastically altered the

317

character of local service in the West. From headquarters in Denver, the new company connected forty-seven cities in seven states. Routes totaling nearly 5,000 miles made it the largest local carrier in the nation, surpassing in size eight of the domestic trunk airlines.

Combining the scattered resources of three companies, one of which was not operative, Frontier Airlines became a regional carrier serving states from Montana to New Mexico. In 1952, the first full year of expanded schedules, its twelve DC-3's carried 127,000 passengers, and more than one-third of the freight transported by all the local service companies. In the next seven years, improvements in routes, equipment, and schedules prepared for a self-sufficient system of the future. New certificates, principally from 1959 decisions in the Seven States Area and Montana Local Service cases, increased unduplicated mileage to 6,819. In the same year, twenty-five DC-3's and five Convair 340's touched down at seventy cities in eleven states, and preparations were being completed for the introduction of propjet Convair 540's in the near future.

Postwar expansion of trunk airlines exceeded the rapid growth of local service. Continental Air Lines, Colorado's oldest carrier in continuous operation, expanded throughout the Southwest, developing new routes to Oklahoma and Texas immediately after VJ Day. Its greatest growth in that area occurred ten years later with the absorption of Pioneer Air Line's 2,000-mile local service system which radiated from Dallas-Fort Worth to cities in Texas and New Mexico.

Continental became a major trunk carrier in 1957, when it inaugurated flights over a new Chicago-Los Angeles route. At that time, the company's operations extended over 6,000 miles to fifty-two major cities in eight states.

Among the larger trunk carriers, United Air Lines' postwar growth had by far the greatest impact on Colorado. Denver became the nerve center of that vast system in 1948, when Operations and Passenger Service were located at Stapleton Field. From a single location the airline monitored all plane movements and allotted seats to passengers over routes extending from New York and Washington to San Francisco and Los Angeles, and to the Hawaiian Islands.

Under the direction of William A. Patterson, president since 1934, three years after several small companies merged to form a single coast-to-coast carrier,. United became a giant in the air transport industry. It was the eighth-ranking transportation firm in 1959, standing for the first time, in terms of operating revenues, ahead of American Airlines and Pan American World Airways. That year United's routes stretched 14,000 miles, serving eighty-two cities within the continental limits of the United States, and in Hawaii.

The Denver Service Case, from which Continental acquired its lucrative long-haul across the western two-thirds of the country, also added two other major routes to the complex network serving Denver. Trans World Airlines, the fourth ranking domestic carrier and major international line fashioned by multi-millionaire Howard Hughes, added the Colorado capital to its transcontinental flights, ending a twenty-year monopoly by United Air Lines on traffic to either coast.

Western Air Lines added service from Denver to San Francisco, by way of Salt Lake City, to its fast growing route system in the West. That company, eliminated from the Colorado scene by the airmail reorganization of 1934, had returned a decade later through purchase of controlling interest in Inland Air Lines. The small carrier was completely absorbed in 1952, at which time it disappeared from the roster of trunk carriers.

Postwar growth has made Western one of the nation's largest regional carriers. Its system serves the principal cities along the Pacific Coast, inland cities as Denver, Minneapolis-St. Paul, and Phoenix, and smaller communities in almost every western state. It proudly boasts of being the "only airline with 35 years of continuous service in the West."

Commercial aviation experienced a dramatic change on October 4, 1958, when a Comet IV of the British Overseas Airways streaked from London to New York in six hours and twelve minutes. Almost three weeks later, Pan American World Airways started daily trans-Atlantic service with Boeing 707's. By the close of the year, the American air traveler had been somewhat abruptly introduced to a new age of subsonic speeds which cut inter-city and transocean flight times in half — or better.

During the first year of pure jet operations, more than sixty giant swept-wing transports appeared on American airways. Two of the so-called "Big Four" domestic carriers — American Airlines and Trans World Airlines — inaugurated Boeing 707 flights in early 1959. United Airlines and Eastern Airlines waited almost another year for the Douglas DC-8 before commencing similar flights. Continental Air Lines was the first to operate the Boeing jet on routes serving Denver, as it had pioneered a year earlier with the propjet Vickers Viscount II.

Favorable public reaction to new transports enabled the airlines to set new records in all categories — passengers, passenger-miles, and load factors — except profits. Domestic carriers operated a total of 1,894 transports in 1959, including eighty-four pure jets and more than two hundred propjets. Those planes carried 43.7 per cent of all inter-city travelers that year, almost twice as many as either railroads or buses.

Local service airlines also contributed to the remarkable expansion of air travel. After gaining permanent certificates in 1955, the small companies enjoyed greater freedom in developing routes and facilities for the benefit of the more than 500 communities partly or wholly dependent on them for air transport. New Convair twin-engine airliners and, by 1959, Fairchild F-27 Friendship and Convair 540 propjet models, replaced obsolete DC-3 equipment. Greater speed and comfort attracted additional customers while the operators reaped the benefits of mounting revenues and lower costs.

Colorado, perhaps more than other states, has become dependent on air travel in the past thirty years. The isolation imposed by vast distances separating it from large population centers in the United States has been eliminated. Travel time to San Francisco or New York, for example, has been reduced to a few hours by air rather than almost a day, or more, by rail and bus. Equally important, mountainous and otherwise remote areas where surface transportation was either lacking or inadequate, have acquired facilities for moving people, mail, and commodities with ease and speed. Airlines have given the state, and the West in general, convenient north-south routes where practically none existed before.

Several thousand people make daily use of the scores of commercial flights which serve twelve airports throughout the state. Short-haul flights intersect trunk operations at Denver, providing connections with cities throughout the United States and many foreign lands. In the Jet Age, Colorado is less than half a day removed from any major American community, and within a day's travel of Europe and parts of Asia.

TWENTY-EIGHT: CORRECTING NATURE'S ERROR: THE COLORADO – BIG THOMPSON PROJECT

by Oliver Knight

Moving water under mountains and reversing the flow of rivers is everyday work for modern engineers, but such contemporary marvels strike the average layman as extraordinary feats. The complexities of a Twentieth Century reclamation project in all its facets — political, fiscal, design and construction — are discussed in this concluding essay.*

*   *   *

CORRECTING NATURE'S ERROR
THE COLORADO – BIG THOMPSON PROJECT

The early nineteen-thirties were bleak years for the prairie farmers of northeastern Colorado. Already caught in a harsh depression, they lost $12,000,000 worth of crops to drought in one year. To make matters worse, their cultivation had outstripped available water, and the nearest surplus was on the yonder side of the Continental Divide. Thus they faced the long recognized anomaly of Colorado: more land than water east of the Divide, more water than land west.

Efforts to redress the balance of land and water had begun in the eighteen-eighties. In 1889, the state legislature authorized an exploration for possible routes to divert western water to the South Platte Basin. Engineers decided a three-mile tunnel was needed, a feature which made the project impractical. During the summers between 1898 and 1905, students from Colorado State College surveyed a route from Grand Lake to the Big Thompson River, involving a twelve-mile tunnel. The new Reclamation Service took cognizance of the project in 1904, deciding more and careful study was needed.

– – – – –

*from Oliver Knight, "Correcting Nature's Error: The Colorado – Big Thompson Project" in *Agricultural History*, volume XXX (October, 1956), pages 157 to 169. Used with permission of *Agricultural History* and the author.

Private interests, in the meantime, tried to best geography. Between 1890 and 1910, three trans-mountain diversion systems linked the Laramie River with the South Platte Basin, and by 1910 four ditches crossed the Divide between the Colorado and South Platte rivers. But the diversions provided only a small amount of additional water. Nevertheless, public leaders recognized that the day might come when it would be possible to divert water from the Colorado to the South Platte on a sizeable scale, and future rights to such diversion were protected by the Colorado River Compact of 1922. Yet the only promise of real relief lay in a large-scale project, and that was merely a dream until 1933.

Then, under the impetus of drought and depression, farmers and stockmen persuaded the Bureau of Reclamation to drill a 13-mile tunnel beneath the Continental Divide, and transfer water from Colorado to the South Platte Basin for supplemental irrigation. The result was the Colorado-Big Thompson Project, which was one of the first large multi-purpose projects undertaken by the federal government. Conceived and initiated when the Central Valley and Missouri Basin projects were mere plans, it was a major departure from precedent in that it sought to provide additional water for land already cultivated. For the Bureau theretofore had confined itself to making waste land fruitful. The project also illustrates the building of a vast government-owned power grid in the West during the Roosevelt-Truman era.

Stretching for 275 miles from the western slope of the Rockies to the Nebraska line, the project originally was to cost $44,000,000, emphasize irrigation, and provide only for mineral power production. By 1953, when it was ninety-eight per cent completed, the cost had risen to $164,000,000, and full power production was more important financially than irrigation. The project had come to include 10 reservoirs, 15 dams, 24 tunnels with a combined length of 35 miles, 11 canals, 3 closed conduits, 21 siphons, 3 pump plants, 6 power plants, 8 penstocks, 821 circuit miles of transmission lines, 43 power substations, and 23,000,000 cubic yards of embankment. It consumed 37,800,000 man-hours of labor.

The irrigation area covers nine prairie counties of north-eastern Colorado--Boulder, Grand, Larimer, Logan, Morgan, Sedgwick, Summit, Washington, and Weld. It is a fertile country, producing sugar beets, potatoes, beans, corn, small grains, fruits, alfalfa, vegetables, dairy products, poultry, eggs, hogs, cattle, and lambs.

The farms have been irrigated by private systems since the eighteen-sixties. Between 1890 and 1910, individuals and irrigation districts built reservoirs and canals. By the nineteen-thirties, the irrigation systems were valued at $34,000,000, and included 124 canals and 60 major reservoirs, serving 6400 farms. The irrigation system was adequate, but there was not enough water. Diversified crops require about 2.5 acre-feet of water per acre annually, but received barely more than one acre-foot in the years 1925-33. The result was an estimated crop loss of $42,355,000. Either more water had to be obtained or farms would have to be abandoned.

Lying in the South Platte basin, the area drew its principal supply from the mountain flow of the Cache la Poudre, Big Thompson, Little Thompson, and St. Vrain rivers, and Boulder Creek. The annual flow of these streams had fluctuated between 420,000 and 1,500,000 acre-feet between 1905 and 1934. Landowners had attempted to get more water from wells, but that had lowered the water table without adding materially to the total available irrigation. Because of the small amount of flood and other excess waters, engineers held that large storage reservoirs would serve no useful purpose. A government report said irrigators had reached their limit by 1933 in obtaining supplemental water through private or cooperative means.

In their hour of crisis, the farmers found opportunity. The federal government happened to be looking for feasible projects on which it could spend money. When the Public Works Administration asked for suggested projects, a group of Greeley men met with Weld County commissioners on August 14, 1933. Under the leadership of Charles Hansen, publisher of the Greeley Daily Tribune, they revived the idea of trans-mountain diversion. The committee determined to find out once and for all whether the project was feasible. Obtaining funds from Weld and Larimer counties, chambers of commerce, and individuals, the Greeley group engaged two engineers--R. J. Tipton, of Denver, and L.L.Stimson, of Greeley--to evaluate the engineering and economic feasibility of diversion. By spring of 1934, the Tipton report was finished. The engineers reported that it would be practical to divert approximately 300,000 acre-feet by tunnel through the Divide and distribute it through existing irrigation systems. They believed that income from irrigation and power would justify the cost of a government project.

Representatives of irrigation organizations were invited to a meeting in Greeley in April, 1934. They heard the Tipton report, and then proceeded to organize the Northern Colorado Water Users Association. The Association had the support of Senators Edward P. Costigan and Alva B. Adams, Congressman Fred Cummings, Assistant Secretary of the Interior Oscar Chapman, a Colorado man, the Union Pacific and Burlington railroads, Great Western Sugar Co., chambers of commerce, State Engineer H.C.Hinderlider, and President Charles A. Lory of Colorado Agricultural and Mechanical College. They also had the support of newspapers, county agents, and civic organizations to an extent that made the promotion of the project a "whole Platte Valley public service."

Moses E. Smith, a state legislator from Ault, went to Washington to arouse government interest in the project. He was received sympathetically by Secretary of the Interior Harold L. Ickes, Commissioner Elwood Mead of the Bureau of Reclamation, and Relief Administrator Harry Hopkins. In January 1935, Ickes authorized a complete survey by the Bureau of Reclamation and provided $150,000 of PWA funds for that purpose. Once assigned to the Bureau, the project came within the purview of Chief Engineer Raymond Fowler Walter who had worked in the northern Colorado irrigation area as a young engineer.

While the Bureau's study was in progress during the next two years, the Northern Colorado Water Users Association improved its organization. With more than 60 irrigation districts holding stock, it was incorporated as a mutual stock company in January 1935, opened offices in Greeley in 1936, and retained J.M.Dille-- a Fort Morgan irrigation superintendent--as general manager.

The directors of the Association provided the leadership for promotion. Besides Hansen, Smith, Lory, and Dille, they were W.E.Letford, president of the First National Bank, Longmont; R.C.Benson, Loveland farmer; C.M.Rolfson, Julesburg attorney; William A. Carlson, chairman of the Weld County Board of Commissioners; Burgis G. Coy, city engineer of Fort Collins; and Robert J. Wright, Sterling, superintendent of the North Sterling Irrigation District. Coy and Wright had been members of the 1898 survey party.

The plan was opposed from the start by farmers west of the Divide who formed the Western Slope Protective Association in 1934. They were championed by Congressman Edward Taylor, chairman of the House Appropriations Committee, who charged the Eastern Slope interests with trying to take water needed in the west. For three years they blocked the project. After several efforts to resolve differences, representatives of the two groups reached an accord at a Washington conference in 1936. The agreement stipulated that a storage reservoir on the Western Slope would protect irrigators there by impounding as much water as was diverted to the Platte Basin.

The agreement was embodied in the final report of the Bureau. Outlining a project that was to be built and operated in conformity with the agreement, engineers planned these features:

On the Colorado River

1. Green Mountain Reservoir on Blue River, near Kremmling, to impound water for the Western Slope.

2. Hydroelectric plant below Green Mountain Dam.

3. Granby Reservoir to collect water on the Colorado River for diversion.

4. Shadow Mountain Lake, to be connected with Grand Lake, to supply the tunnel with water from Granby Reservoir.

5. Pump plant at Granby Reservoir to pump water 179 feet uphill and a distance of 4.5 miles to Shadow Mountain Lake.

6. Outlet channel at east end of Grand Lake to connect with the tunnel and regulate the lakes to a fluctuation range of one foot.

7. A trans-mountain tunnel under the Continental Divide, 13.1 miles long from Grand Lake to Wind River, near Estes Park Village.

On the Eastern Slope

8. A conduit 5.3 miles long from the tunnel to a penstock of a power plant on the Big Thompson River near Estes Park.

9. Waste rock would be terraced and landscaped, and all structures blended into their natural surroundings, to protect Rocky Mountain (Estes) National Park scenery.

10. Power Plant No. 1 below Estes Park Village on the Big Thompson.

11. Four additional power plants in the Big Thompson Canyon.

12. A diversion dam on the Big Thompson 12 miles west of Loveland, diverting water through a nine-mile canal to Carter Lake Storage Reservoir.

13. Carter Lake Reservoir, near Berthoud, to store water brought over during the winter. Canals would take the water to Big Thompson and St. Vrain rivers for irrigation.

14. A siphon across the Big Thompson nine miles west of Loveland, and a canal 10 miles long to convey water from the fourth power plant to Horsetooth Reservoir near Fort Collins.

15. A canal from Horsetooth Reservoir to Cache la Poudre River and to a pumping plant which would lift the water to the North Poudre Canal.

16. Arkins Reservoir, near Buckhorn Creek, to receive water from Big Thompson and balance demands for power and irrigation.

17. Transmission lines connecting the Valmont steam plant of the Public Service Co., with all of the contemplated hydroelectric plants and with various project operations.

The chosen route was designed to deliver water from the reservoirs to farm lands in 60 to 75 days, meeting the demand for supplemental water that usually occurred between late July and late September. Project water would amount to about 40 per cent of the average original supply.

The full report was prepared by Mills E. Bunger under the supervision of Porter J. Preston. Detail estimates were worked out in the Bureau's Denver office by H.R.McBirney for canals, K.B.Keener for reservoirs, L.N.McClellan for power, E.B.Debler for hydraulics, and R.L.Parshall, senior irrigation engineer, Department of Agriculture for economic studies.

After the engineering report was completed, legislative action proceeded in Washington and Denver. In Washington, the Colorado delegation worked as a unit to advance the project rapidly in the summer of 1937. In Denver, the Association sought a new law to hasten the project.

Before Congress were two separate pieces of legislation. One was a Senate amendment to the Interior appropriation bill for 1938, and the other was S. 2681, introduced by Senator Adams, authorizing the project as outlined in Senate Document 80. The Washington delegation was moving too rapidly for Secretary Ickes, who evidenced some displeasure that the Senate had proceeded with an appropriation before departmental action had been completed. He wrote Senator Carl Hayden of Arizona, whose

328

appropriations subcommittee had already conducted hearings, that he had just received the Bureau's report, along with a protest from the National Park Service. Illness had prevented his conducting a hearing to harmonize the conflicting views.

In spite of the Secretary's position, Congress went ahead. Adams' bill passed the Senate, and went to the House. In the House, it was referred to the Committee on Irrigation and Reclamation, which conducted hearings on June 30 and July 2, 1937. At the hearing, both the Bureau of Reclamation and the Colorado delegation battled for the project, against opposition from friends of the national parks.

Commissioner John C. Page of the Bureau of Reclamation testified the project was economically and technically feasible. It would deliver water at $2 per acre-foot, which was less than the going price, and would increase crop production. He also declared that it did not violate the Colorado River Compact, because upper basin states were unable to use their full allotment within the basin. Congressman Lawrence Lewis assured the Committee that the entire delegation favored the project, Taylor having withdrawn his opposition of a year earlier. Even the Western Slope farmers endorsed the project through their attorney, Dan Hughes, of Montrose.

Highly articulate groups opposed the bill. A.E.Demaray, associate director of the National Park Service, feared construction would scar Rocky Mountain National Park. He also believed a different route, which he did not specify, would be better. Similar opposition was voiced by spokesmen for the Wilderness Society, American Planning and Civic Association, Izaak Walton League, American Forestry Association, National Park Association, and the American Nature Association.

The upshot was that the Interior Department appropriation bill for 1938 authorized the Colorado-Big Thompson Project and appropriated $900,000 for it. After conference amendments, final Congressional action was completed on August 9, 1937. President Roosevelt approved a finding of feasibility on December

21, and in May 1938, a PWA allocation provided an additional $1,400,000. The federal government was then ready to go to work.

Meantime, the Association had been creating a legal entity which could contract with the United States, pay for, and operate the irrigation features of the project. Believing that part of the cost should be borne by the general public, which would share in benefits from a large project, they decided a water conservancy district would be the best type of organization. But Colorado law did not provide for such a district.

To draft an enabling act, the directors engaged two Greeley attorneys, Thomas A. Nixon and William R. Kelly. Experienced irrigation lawyers, they drew upon Colorado statutes--namely, the Conservancy Act of 1922, the Moffatt Tunnel Improvement Act of 1922, the Internal Improvement District Act of 1923, the Colorado Irrigation District Act of 1905--and Utah's Metropolitan Water Districts Act, which in turn had been modeled upon a California law. Some sections of those laws were used verbatim. To them they added sections applicable to the case in hand.

The bill was presented to the 1937 session of the General Assembly where it was handled by Smith, who by then was Speaker of the House. As House Bill 714, it was passed without objection in May, and was signed by Governor Teller Ammons on May 13, 1937.

Styled the Colorado Water Conservancy District Act of 1937, the law permitted creation of conservancy districts which could acquire and hold property, levy taxes and assessments, allot water, and contract with the United States government. As a corporation governed by a board of directors, a district was to be formed on decree of a district judge, upon the presentation of a petition. The petition was to be signed by 25 per cent of the owners of non-irrigated land, each of whom must own property and improvements assessed at least as $1,000. The judge was to appoint the directors.

During the summer of 1937, while Congress was enacting the basic legislation, the Association transformed itself into a water conservancy district. The boundaries were drawn along section

330

lines to include 1,481,000 acres and 36 cities and towns. A petition, signed by 1,607 owners of irrigated and 1,388 owners of other property, was presented to Judge C.C.Coffin of the district court for Weld County. He issued a decree establishing the Northern Colorado Water Conservancy District on September 20, 1937. Eight days later, he appointed the first 11 directors... All had been directors of the Association. To make sure of its legal standing, the District instituted a quo warranto proceeding in the Colorado Supreme Court, testing the constitutionality of the law and the legality of the office of the directors. The court upheld the law in a decision of May 2, 1938.

In the meantime, contract negotiations had been opened with the federal government. Since all previous experience had involved reclamation of waste land, a contract for supplemental water presented unprecedented and complex problems. The final solution was for the United States to build the Colorado-Big Thompson project at an estimated cost of $44,000,000. The District was to be liable for one half of the cost, representing the irrigation features, but would not be held for more than $25,000,000. Payment was to be made in 40 annual installments-- the first payment to be made when the project was completed. Certain irrigation features were to be turned over to the District for operation and maintenance, but the United States reserved perpetual title to the power plants which it was to operate and maintain. The District was to obtain revenue for maintaining, operating, and paying for the project from the sale of water at $1.50 per acre-foot and an ad valorem tax that would average out to another 50 cents per acre-foot.

On May 23, 1938, the directs approved the contract. It was ratified in an election on June 28 by a vote of 7,510 to 439. On July 5, the contract was executed by Assistant Secretary of the Interior Oscar Chapman and Hansen.

The Bureau of Reclamation could then proceed with the Big T.--one of the first large multi-purpose projects that reflected a major advance in reclamation. Since the start of reclamation in 1902, the government had built 138 storage and

331

diversion dams, and 20,000 miles of large canals. It had spent $237,000,000 on projects that were in operation in 1938. Only three projects had been undertaken previously in Colorado--the Uncompahgre in 1905, Grand Valley in 1912, and Pine River in 1937. By 1938, the Bureau was engaged in the greatest construction program it had ever undertaken, one that would add 2,500,000 acres of irrigation land in the West.

The new reclamation program envisaged large-scale public power development. The Colorado-Big Thompson contract specified the anticipated power plants, and the Bureau spoke of "two projects" -- one for irrigation and the other for electricity. Commissioner John C. Page saw a "very good" market for power because of an increased demand from the mining industry.

Construction on the Big Thompson project was begun in the fall of 1938. It proceeded in three phases -- the prewar period ending in 1942, the war period ending in 1946, and the postwar period. It encountered many vicissitudes through change of scope, wartime shortages, and postwar inflation. An abiding difficulty was the climate which allowed only about eight months of construction weather a year at the higher altitudes.

Three parts of the project were undertaken in the prewar period. Work was begun first on Green Mountain Dam and power plant, in accordance with the pledge given the Western Slope farmers. Construction commenced November, 30, 1938 on an earth and rockfill dam, which was half finished by 1941. Contractors started drilling the trans-mountain tunnel--which later was named for Senator Adams -- on June 23, 1940. Working from eastern and western portals simultaneously, they drilled a tunnel that passed about 4,000 feet below the crest of the Divide. At that point it is approximately 12,000 feet above sea level. Workmen averaged 40 feet a day in a rarefied atmosphere that affected the efficiency of both men and machines. Eight miles had been drilled by 1942. At the same time, 115-kilowatt transmission lines were strung from Greeley to Fort Morgan, Wiggins, and Brush. Substations were built at those points and Poudre Valley.

The project was affected by a fundamental change that was made in reclamation policy in 1941. Since its inception, reclamation had been self-supporting from a revolving fund that drew proceeds from public land sales, oil royalties, and repayments by irrigation districts. Because the income was much too small to finance multimillion dollar projects, the Interior Department Appropriation Bill of 1942 transferred the Big T. and other large projects to the General Fund of the Treasury. The reassignment made possible large annual appropriations, and removed the earlier limitation. However, the self-liquidating principle of reclamation projects was retained.

By June 1941, the Bureau had spent $7,519,000 in building 13.69 per cent of the Colorado-Big Thompson Project. The estimated cost had risen from $44,000,000 to $54,918,000.

With the start of the war, the reclamation program was linked with the "war effort" -- a handy symbol for the government propagandist -- which enabled the Bureau to multiply and magnify its position in the electric power industry of the West. The Bureau concentrated on war projects, with the expectation that 1942 expenditures would exceed the record of $89,116,114 that had been set in 1940. In 1942, the Bureau allotted more than 90 per cent of its program to hasten power production in inter-mountain and other western areas where strategic industries faced critical shortages. The program was intended to triple the Bureau's capacity of 1,252,000 kilowatts by 1944-45.

The Colorado-Big Thompson Project shared in the public power popularity. For 1943, the Bureau asked $4,830,000 for the project, most of it for power but some for the tunnel and units serving both power and irrigation. Arguing that the development in minerals and other resources would require more electricity in Colorado and Wyoming, the Bureau said the appropriation would place the Green Mountain plant in operation by 1943 -- which it did, production commencing on May 18, 1943. The project's power system was to be interconnected with the North Platte, Kendrick, Riverton, and Shoshone projects in neighboring states.

However, irrigation features were threatened by the emphasis on power. Because the government was eliminating projects that were not essential to war, the Budget Bureau allowed Green Mountain but dropped the Granby Dam because it was intended for irrigation. The adjustment meant the Western Slope unit would be finished while an essential feature of the diversion plan must wait indefinitely.

Consequently, Colorado interests appealed to a Senate committee in 1942 for restitution of the Granby funds. They said it would contribute to power production on the Eastern Slope by 1944, and therefore was essential to war. The witnesses were Clifford H. Stone, director of the Colorado Water Conservancy Board, and Hansen. Hansen also appealed to agricultural necessity, saying the government had asked farmers of the area to plant an additional 96,000 acres to sugar beets. In the end, Congress appropriated $6,249,070 to expedite the project for war food production.

But the War Production Board nullified the appropriation. Trying to save material for combat needs, the WPB halted all reclamation projects on October 16, 1942, except for the Green Mountain and four other power plants on other projects. The stop order halted the Big T. when it was 23.7 per cent completed.

With the WPB stop order,the Interior Department lost 66 per cent of its 1942 appropriation. Immediately, Ickes and his staff began to emphasize food production to justify projects which formerly had been justified by their power potential. Ickes told a House Appropriations Subcommittee on March 17, 1943, that 24 projects had been halted. "Ultimately," he said, "I think this country will decide it cannot run the risk of food shortages by halting these irrigation developments."

Following the new tack, Commissioner Harry W. Bashore presented a modified wartime plan for the Colorado-Big Thompson to a Senate Appropriations Subcommittee in June 1943. The modified plan, costing $3,600,000, called for an improvised dam on the North Fork of the Colorado River to impound water for diversion, completion of the tunnel which was 80 per cent excavated, and a siphon of wooden staves to carry the water from the tunnel to the Big Thompson River. Water would flow by gravity into the tunnel, and existing canals would deliver 100,000 acre-feet of water to 300,000 acres of farmland. Water was expected to reach the fields by the spring of 1945, maybe by August 1944. He said the new plan was "entirely a food proposition," one that would provide the supplemental water the "farmer needs to carry him over the hump" in raising more crops.

The Senators were sympathetic to the plan, antagonistic to the WPB. Several committee members were emphatic in their criticism of the work stoppage, and Senator Hayden, chairman, remarked that the committee had asked for "a complete review of the situation" by the new Food Administrator, Chester Davis.

As a matter of fact, Davis had taken action several weeks earlier. On May 10, 1943, he recommended the WPB rescind the stop order, and issue adequate priorities to renew construction of the Colorado-Big Thompson. He had found that it and three other projects offered a means of increasing the production of beans, peas, potatoes, dairy products, and other foods. Prodded by Davis and the Senate committee, the WPB cleared the modified plan on July 24, 1943, and during the next year permitted construction to be resumed on 24 other reclamation projects.

Construction began again on the Big T. The 13-mile tunnel excavation was completed on June 10, 1944. Although the contractors worked from different sides of the Divide, they came together with a difference of three quarters of an inch in grade and seven sixteenths of an inch in alignment.

With the tunnel drilled through, the Bureau confidently expected to have water ready at least for the 1945 irrigation season. But more trouble lay ahead in Washington. This time it came from the War Manpower Commission, which curtailed operations on the project from January to March 1945.

When the war ended, the Bureau of Reclamation swung into a new record-breaking program, spending $90,000,000 in fiscal

1946 to start a five-year program designed to create 45,000 family farms on 4,000,000 productive acres. The appropriation included $6,550,000 for the Big T., and the Bureau awarded $10,000,000 in construction contracts for the project.

By then the project had been overhauled on the drawing boards. As planning studies continued during construction, Bureau engineers changed the routing on the Eastern Slope, added several short tunnels, designed more power plants, and increased reservoir capacities. However, the planners sometimes were at odds with the people on the ground. This was noted by Dille, secretary-manager for the District, who wrote: "If there is sometimes a gap between the somewhat theoretical approach of the Bureau men and what we think is our more practical slant on a mutual problem, we laboriously and finally work out some agreeable solution."

It was during the postwar period, after 1945, that most of the project was built. The Bureau reckoned the Alva B. Adams Tunnel a completed unit when contractors finished lining it with cement in February 1946. The western portal was 109 feet higher than the eastern, and water could gush through its nine-foot bore at the rate of 550 cubic feet per second. Water was released through it for the first time in June 1947, flowing toward the fields through temporary facilities built by the District.

The short Prospect Mountain and Rams Horn tunnels, on the Eastern Slope, were completed in the 1948 fiscal year, as part of the "highest mark of accomplishment in the history of Reclamation." They were part of the $169,000,000 worth of construction that the Bureau completed in the West that year. The next year, the Bureau again reached an all-time construction record, and 21 contracts were let for the Big T., amounting to $35,000,000. During the year, the Aspen Creek Siphon, Horsetooth Reservoir, and Olympus Dam were completed.

Moving steadily toward completion, the project was subjected to inflation, war delays, unforseen geological conditions, and design changes that boosted 1937 prices 300 per cent in 10 years. As inflationary pressures multiplied in successive years from

1945 to 1948, the total cost of the project advanced to 61, to 96, to 128, and to 150 million dollars. Not until 1949 did construction costs level off.

Increased costs provided an excuse to expand power development. No matter how much the irrigation features might cost, the District was liable for no more than $25,000,000. Therefore, the higher the cost of the project, the greater the government's obligation. The Bureau of Reclamation reasoned that more power plants should be built, because they would produce a revenue that would pay for the balance of the project.

The original plan called for one power plant in the Estes Park area to produce a uniform amount of dump power. Later, the Bureau decided it would be good business to fluctuate output to match demand. The result was the Estes Park Aqueduct and Power System, including two power plants. Where the original prospectus anticipated four possible plants in the foothills, the Bureau built five. Then the Flatiron Reservoir was added, complete with power plant. The electrical system was to be interconnected with the Missouri Basin project, as well as other projects in Colorado and Wyoming. In 1946, the Bureau had hoped to have an installed capacity of 144,900 kilowatts; by 1949 the goal was 175,900.

There was a demand for the electricity, however. The first contract was drawn with Estes Park in 1947, and several other municipal agreements were being negotiated. Another demand was translated into political pressure when the Bureau asked for $500,000 to build a transmission line to Holyoke, where the power would be delivered to a REA district in Nebraska. Assistant Commissioner Kenneth Markwell said 1,400 persons had installed electrical devices on their farms in anticipation of the power. Unless the money was appropriated, they would not receive the power, and their devices would be useless. He held the line to be essential, because none other served the area. The testimony did not indicate why and how Nebraska farmers were willing to obligate themselves for expensive equipment when power was not available and before Congress had been asked to approve the extension. Senator Edwin C. Johnson of Colorado, Senator Hugh Butler of Nebraska, and Rep. Carl T. Curtis of Nebraska urged the Holyoke line be built. The line was built.

The power development has been appraised as a "stair-stepping affair" which, due to cost increases, added plants that will produce twice as much power as originally intended. In contrast, irrigation has been confined within the original limits, although some revisions have been made.

The change in the relative importance of irrigation and power brought the Bureau into conflict with the District. In 1947, Dille testified before a House Appropriations Subcommittee, saying the Bureau planned to use the interest component of commercial power rates to pay for the irrigation features that exceeded the $25,000,000 contract limit. "This does not seem to us to be proper financing or in accord with the present reclamation law as we understand it," he said. As an alternative, he suggested the reclamation law be amended to lower the interest rate on power costs -- there had never been interest changes on irrigation construction -- and permit a 65-year repayment period for repaying the irrigation cost. "Such a plan," he added, "seems eminently fair to us and one which our District can honestly support as the basis for seeking the necessary appropriations to complete the project." The Bureau rejected the revision.

The Colorado-Big Thompson Project was involved in political clashes between Congress and the executive branch. The clashes had been presaged by the contest between Senator Hayden's committee and the WPB over the wartime work stoppage. After the war, the Bureau pursued its program with a singleness of purpose that amounted to an outright disregard for Congress at one time. That came about in 1948 when Congress allotted the Bureau $179,422,239. Within a few weeks, Commissioner Michael Straus--who had once been publicity chief for the Interior Department -- announced a $195,000,000 program for the year. Acknowledging it was greater than the appropriation, he said: "But we have decided to go full steam ahead under our limited appropriation basis." In October, he assured Senator Wherry there was no deficit and that there would be none, but a month later some projects had been halted for lack of money, and by December the Bureau was asking for a "supplemental" appropriation.

338

Straus asked an additional $29, 375, 000 for four large pro-
jects, including $4, 150, 000 for the Colorado-Big Thompson. He
argued the Bureau was short of funds, or had exhausted certain
types of funds that should be available for contracts already awarded. He denied the projects had been "speeded up arbitrarily."

During the hearings, Congressman W. F. Norrell of
Arkansas found the Bureau had awarded contracts for Granby
Dam before money was available for the 1948 fiscal year. This
was explained by A. A. Batson, director of Region VII, Denver,
who said the contracts were for equipment to supply earlier
major contracts, and progress payments had not been anticipated
that early. Assistant Commissioner Markwell said the Bureau
must assume Congress wants it to proceed at the most economical
rate of progress. But Norrell was persistent and aggressive,
noting that the supplemental money would bring the actual appropriation to the amount of the original budget request. "Now," said
Norrell, "I do not think that Congress can ever get in the position
of being in the attitude of having to appropriate money because of
outstanding contracts made by a department of the government.
You operate under laws of Congress. We do not operate under
contracts of the Department of the Interior."

But the Bureau held the whip hand. As an agency of a
Democratic administration, its maneuver forced a Republican
Congress to give it what it wanted. With a presidential election
in the offing, a cutback in the Western program could have brought
political repercussions. Moreover, past expenditures would represent a certain amount of waste if work was interrupted. Consequently, Congress granted the supplemental request of $4, 150, 000 for
the Big T., along with grants for other projects, but it sought to
retain some semblance of control by requiring quarterly reports
showing the status of funds appropriated for construction.

In spite of attack, criticism, and setback, the Bureau continued with the project. During the fiscal year 1954 the Big T.
"was essentially finished to give full service to water and power
users." And in the next year the project met its first test. "A
highlight of the year (fiscal year 1955) was the dramatic service

339

of the Colorado-Big Thompson project to the extensive irrigated areas in northern Colorado which in 1954 experienced the first serious drought in 20 years. The availability of more than 300,000 acre-feet of water from the virtually completed... project prevented total disaster from a withering drought and assured economic and agricultural stability to a farflung area... Project water deliveries which brought a gross repayment to the Government of $770,880, resulted in an increased crop income to the benefited area of not less that $22 million in that one season."

... The significance of the project can be evaluated in dramatic terms. It set a precedent by which the Bureau of Reclamation revolutionized its entire program. Prior to the Big T., the Bureau had concentrated upon making waste land usable, and the Colorado project was the first major undertaking to provide water for land already in use. This change was exploited so rapidly that by 1941 the Interior Department directed reclamation toward preservation of established agricultural communities, instead of providing new settlement opportunities in the West.

The Bureau anticipates the project may transform the life of the region. By overcoming the water shortage, it may remove a limitation on agricultural expansion. By providing additional low-cost electricity, it may encourage the development of agricultural processing, wool, leather, glass, metal, zinc, ferroalloy, and alkali chlorine industries.

In the Bureau's books, it is a paying proposition -- especially through power sales. The first power was sold in the 1948 fiscal year -- 120,729,542 kilowatt-hours for $782,970. Power revenue increased to $1,361,653 in fiscal 1952, and it was estimated that the sale of power alone would yield approximately $150,000,000 during the 40-year repayment period.

The project also was responsible for the Colorado conservancy district law by which a quasi-municipality can be created, cutting across county and city boundaries, for the special purpose of aiding farmers. Through the law, there was created the

340

Northern Colorado Water Conservancy District, which is charged with operation of the actual irrigation features of the project.

As yet, it is difficult to measure the economic benefits of supplemental water in terms of dollars. Delivery of water began with the first tunnel diversion in 1947, continuing in limited quantity in the Big Thompson Valley until 1950. Between 1950 and 1953, water was also delivered to the Cache la Poudre and Little Thompson valleys. District officials noted that the 1953 irrigation season was one of subnormal local water supply, and the effect of the extra water "was forcefully demonstrated in the results obtained from production of irrigated crops in the areas to which such water was available." Operating on both sides of the Continental Divide, the project includes the compensatory storage feature, which protects Western Slope farmers in their prior appropriation rights to Colorado River water.

However, certain criticisms of the project demand attention. The Bureau seems to have been guided by the philosophy of the end justifying the means in pushing the Colorado-Big Thompson Project. As the foregoing material shows, officials once argued for power plants because of war needs. They next argued war food needs when the WPB denied the power argument. And they then again argued for power plants because of project economies. The power plants, of course, increased the cost even more. Clearly, Bureau officials wanted the project at any cost. But then the project was so far along when hit by inflation that the higher expenditures were necessary to complete the project, avoiding the waste of an incompleted undertaking.

Although the twin objectives of increased agricultural and industrial output may be desirable, they raise the question of whether the arid and semiarid West may not paradoxically water itself into a worse problem by superimposing industrial demands upon expanded agricultural demands to a point beyond the utmost physical capacity of streams and reservoirs. A somewhat similar consideration was voiced in an editorial in The Nation, which endorsed the view that the West is being developed on a fragmentary basis without regional fact-finding. The editorial also said the

planning and construction functions should not reside in the same
agency. The plans for such an important project as the Colorado-
Big Thompson "should be fully blue-printed before construction has
started, and the construction agency should not be involved in
lobbying them through Congress." The latter criticism is well-
taken, but it must be acknowledged that the Colorado-Big Thompson
Project broke new ground in the agricultural development of the
western United States.